To walk abroad i
But thoughts, th
Else may the silent feet,
Like logs of wood,
Move up and down, and see no good,
Nor joy nor glory meet.

Ev'n carts and wheels their place do change,
But cannot see, though very strange,
The glory that is by:
Dead puppets may
Move in the bright and glorious day,
Yet not behold the sky.

And are not men than they more blind,
Who having eyes yet never find
The bliss in which they move?
Like statues dead
They up and down are carried,
Yet neither see nor love.

To walk is by a thought to go,
To move in spirit to and fro,
To mind the good we see,
To taste the sweet,
Observing all the things we meet
How choice and rich they be....

Thomas Treherne, Poems of Felicity, 1903 (written c. 1670)

GOLD CUFFLINKS

Tales on my watch as an expatriate
An autobiographical sketch

DERRICK SWAIN

Gold Cufflinks
Derrick William Swain © 2020
www.talesofexpat.co.uk

First Published by Compass-Publishing
ISBN 978-1-913713-04-1

Typeset by The Book Refinery Ltd
www.thebookrefinery.com

Disclaimer
The facts in these tales are true insofar as any memory is ever truthful.
Where the author has disguised the identity of certain characters, to provide
for their anonymity, a footnote has been placed to say so. Every effort has
been
made by the author to ensure the veracity of information.
Printed and bound by CMP Group (UK) Dorset

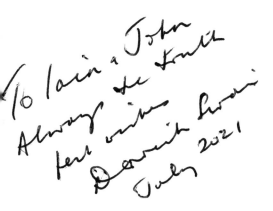

To Iain & John

Always tell the truth

Best wishes from

D........... [signature]

July 2021

Dedication

To Naomi, Max, Jon, and Pauline, who missed the fun.

Contents

Contents cont'

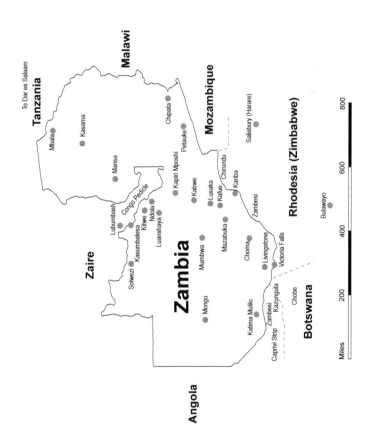

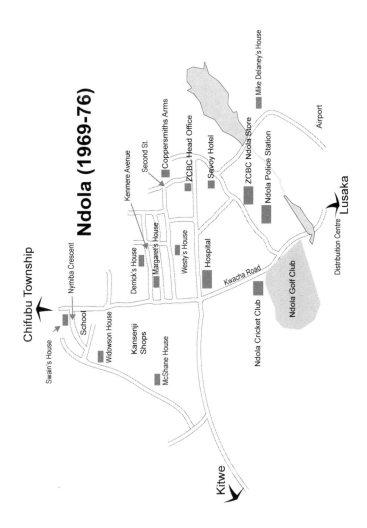

Ndola (1969-76)

Chifubu Township

Swain's House

Nymiba Crescent

School

Widowson House

Kansenji Shops

McShane House

Kenmere Avenue

Second St.

Derrick's House

Margaret's House

Westy's House

Hospital

Coppersmiths Arms

ZCBC Head Office

Savoy Hotel

ZCBC Ndola Store

Mike Delaney's House

Ndola Police Station

Airport

Kwacha Road

Ndola Cricket Club

Ndola Golf Club

Distribution Centre

Lusaka

Kitwe

Kitwe (1969-76)

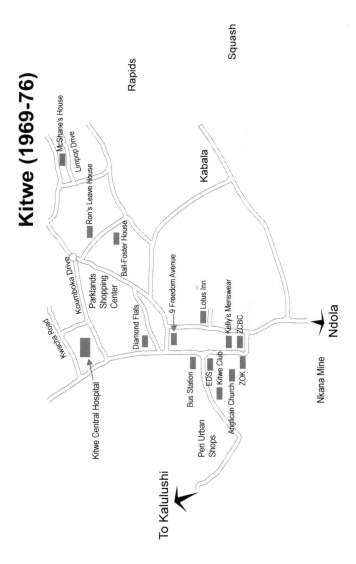

MAP OF ST LUCIA 1976-77

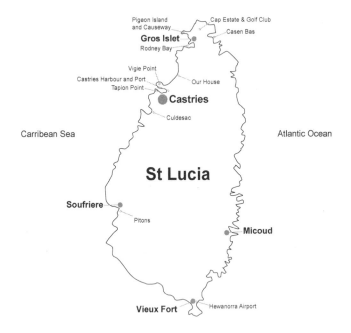

Pigeon Island
and Causeway
Cap Estate & Golf Club
Casen Bas

Gros Islet
Rodney Bay

Vigie Point
Castries Harbour and Port
Tapion Point
Our House

Castries

Culdesac

Carribean Sea

Atlantic Ocean

St Lucia

Soufriere
Pitons

Micoud

Vieux Fort
Hewanorra Airport

Castries (1976-77)

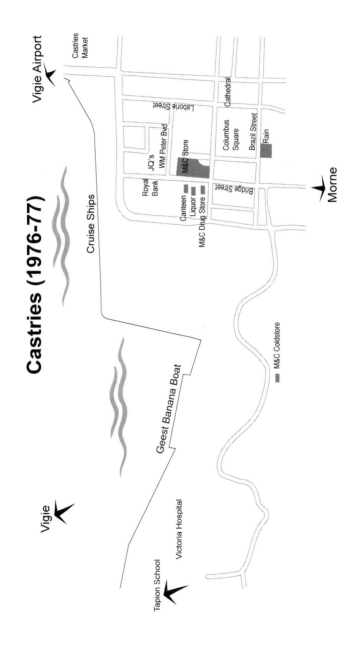

Prologue

I first met David when he was eighty. Kathleen, his companion, had invited friends to celebrate the New Year. My wife and I were staying in Ballina on the Shannon opposite Ireland's ancient capital Killaloe, home to the High King of Ireland Brian Boru. Fiona and Roger had put us up, the latter a friend of mine since childhood, she a poet and he a versatile freelance writer, both members of a literary circle based in Limerick, as were David and all the other guests assembled by Kathleen to bring in 2014. David had worked for *The Irish Times*, reporting from Tiananmen Square, Beijing following a tip-off in early June 1989.

"You should write a book, Derrick, you have many tales to tell" was David's parting line as we shook hands before leaving for home in the aftermath of some strong Irish hospitality and a night of literary fun. Not being a writer of anything other than business reports and correspondence in recent years I did not take David too seriously, but the seed he had planted would surely germinate one day. Before leaving the warmth of Kathleen's house to brave the wind and rain of the early morning, I had traded travel stories with our companions that night, using anecdotes from my times spent in Africa, Asia and the Americas as a way of making my contribution to the evening's fun. I met David again on three subsequent visits to my friends in the West of Ireland, on each occasion he would ask how my book was progressing. So it was that my feeling of guilt at owning only blank sheets of paper gradually transformed itself into a resolve to do something about it (The Book).

I was twenty-six when I left England to work overseas, as it turned out I had a succession of jobs with the same company in two contrasting countries of the Commonwealth, but after returning to a home base I have chalked up visits to eighty-four countries, proper visits, not stop-overs, to justify my pay-slip or for the enjoyment of discovery, eventually gaining the courage to go it in business alone. Life for me has been one of doing commerce internationally one way or another, at first for big public companies and later for my own firm with a trading base in India. By the time I had the confidence to start my own business I was forty-seven, thirteen years after the move back to Blighty. During those thirteen years I had jobs in international marketing with Arthur Guinness Ltd, then commercial fundraising for the *Mary Rose Trust* and finally with Sears Plc, the owners of Selfridges and a host of other retail chains, as a director of international buying.

At Guinness I was Marketing Director of Morisons, their non-brewing operations which manufactured and distributed consumer goods and pharmaceuticals in fourteen countries across Africa and Asia. Componentry and finished goods for our contract manufacturing had to be sourced from all over the world, it was a complex and diverse business which worked by harnessing the separate talents in the Company's Hampshire HQ, and the management and staff of its overseas subsidiaries. We created the largest world markets for *Kiwi* boot polish in Nigeria, *Marmite* in Sri Lanka, *Pyrex* in Malaysia and *Seven O'clock* blades in Bangladesh, just a few examples of the fun and games which would have given me the material for several books, not just one. I left Guinness after the industrial vandalism of Ernest Saunders and his pet consultants, not before I had carried out his bidding to divest the Group of Morisons, sold to Andrew Sadanis who creeps into my later narrative. Not a lot of time went by before Guinness was swallowed up by The Distillers Company who gave birth to the conglomerate we now know as Diageo.

I could write another book describing the contents of the Barber Surgeon's cabin recovered from the wreck of the *Mary Rose*, King Henry VIII's warship sunk off Portsmouth harbour, but others have already done that. The Board of the stamp firm Stanley Gibbons, whose catalogue guided the philatelic collectors of my generation, set me the task of making money to support the enormous cost of paying back the loans taken to cover the skills and equipment needed to raise the wreck and its stray parts from the mud of the sea floor, thereafter to develop an income stream to provide for the future work of the archaeologists who had set up shop in the Old Bond Store in Southsea. The Trust's Patron was HRH Prince Charles, who pioneered the concept of The Court of The Mary Rose, a mix of philanthropists, energetic leaders of industry, and little old me at the time. Eighteen months into the work of making authentic replicas of our mediaeval discoveries, of publishing drawings and texts to disseminate scholarship of the Tudor navy to academia and the creation of souvenirs for the grockle trade, I received a call from my old chum Tony Stapleton, then on the Board of the West End department store Selfridges. Portman Limited, the international arm of the Sears group, were looking for a new managing director. I attended interview and got the job, just as I had been trained to do by Percy Carew, who you will meet on later pages of this book.

At Portman I was *ex officio* the UK director of The Intercontinental Group of Department Stores (IGDS). We ran an export business with customers all over the world, who relied on us as their agents. Famous leading stores like the American giant JC Penney, Au Printemps of Paris, and Takashimaya of Tokyo, who hold the Imperial Japanese Warrant, were a few from our long list of clients. We managed major promotions of British merchandise through our IGDS colleagues, supported by the UK Government, Royalty and Politicians. Both Mrs Thatcher and HRH Princess Anne managed to break into their travel plans to fit in cutting tapes at the opening of our two promotions in Japan. I served on the Japan Trade Advisory Group to the UK Board of Trade under Sir Michael Perry. In the space of six years my colleagues and I had been able to expand Portman's top line ten times. It needs another book to cover the shenanigans of my departure from Portman and its subsequent demise. That was the catalyst I needed to start a new product development enterprise in conjunction with partners Ralph and Naresh in New York and New Delhi, which we called Possibilities, two years after David's shock reporting from Beijing. We later arranged representation in Japan and South Africa.

My book covers the precious time of my life when I lived abroad and met the girl I was to marry, along with a little personal and family background so that you, my dear reader, can know a bit more about me and the times we lived through. My book tells how I came to terms with new surroundings, about friendships made and the surprises and fun of life abroad, rarely considered a worthy subject to write about, but will be appreciated, I hope, by others who have ventured abroad. I write about the hidden contribution expatriates have made to their country's economy.

It is also about some of the birth pains of newly independent Commonwealth nations and the punctuation marks that contemporary history has printed in their stories. "They'll never believe us" goes the song from *"Oh what a lovely war"*. The squaddies went on to sing *"There was a front, and we were there"*. Those soldiers felt that only those who had served with them would understand. I hope this book will shed some light on the expatriate experience and encourage young people to get out there and take on life dancing. It has been my joy to make lifelong friends, they stem from times of shared stress, be it under the authority of a boarding school steeped in Victorian tradition and discipline, or in another country finding shared solutions to difficult problems and circumstances, or as parents, untrained in the art of mastering the foibles of children, where mutual support can help overcome those fears and problems, all the way to the passing of teenage, indeed it does not stop then.

Only by travelling can you appreciate your own country. I have bucket loads of love for the UK and will never take for granted all the good things it has to offer. Those who expect no favours are never disappointed.

1

Landings

(September 1969)

I grew up in a world of aunts and uncles, siblings and cousins and the greats of the previous generation still actively part of my life, at least those on my mother's side. Not each one of those aunts and uncles were family but good friends all, hardly any of whom seemed to have children of their own, whilst the cousins of my generation came and went at family gatherings. Cousins seldom keep in active contact once launched into adult life, not in the way most siblings do, not like we are led to believe it was like in past ages of social immobility. Mind you, in my later life I have made many efforts to renew contact with my surviving wider family, those first, second or twice removed relationships, for example, and have found joy in kinship rediscovered. Nonetheless, it is a certainty that the friends we make in life are the ones who provide most of the excitement and stimulation we nurture. The closeness of friendship and the gifts from human contact are life's treasures. Let me tell you something about my life beyond my childhood, of travel and of friendships, most kept and few lost.

When this tale begins, I was twenty-six years old. I had just been made an offer of work in Zambia for one of those formidable British trading companies which prospered throughout Asia, Africa, and the Americas. There had been no serious thoughts of marriage and I was rather enjoying life as a bachelor, so I was still single, ambitious, immortal and appalled by the government of the day which naïvely held that inflation could be controlled by freezing wages. Not for me, said I to myself, I am off, with really no idea what life would be like in central Africa. My imagination threw up pictures of nights teeming with rain, viewed from a wicker seat on a veranda, the sounds of trilling cicadas and clinking highball glasses ice-laced and filled to the brim with gin and tonic to quench the thirst and keep the mozzies at bay. How little I knew, but how willing I was to take it all on in the pursuit of adventure.

A hundred days after the Americans first landed on the moon, my flight at a more modest altitude, in a Zambia Airways Dakota, arrived at Ndola airport. The trip north from Lusaka to my new home on the Copperbelt was the final leg of a long journey from England. The earlier flight from London had been my first in an intercontinental airliner. The McDonnell Douglas DC8 seemed so huge at the time; it would be a few years later that the Boeing Company launched its first Jumbo Jet. The long journey was never boring, for whilst sleep had come in short naps I had met an elderly flight companion called Sam Kelly, a kindly faced businessman from Kitwe who regaled me with tales and facts about the land I was to live in for at least the next three years.

Kelly was not his real name, but one adopted to fit into the British colony of Northern Rhodesia, for Sam was a refugee from Poland via Palestine. He had escaped from Warsaw ahead of the German and Russian invaders. In Palestine, the British authorities provided safe passage for Miriam, his wife, and Sam himself to join other escapees in central and southern Africa. Sam had taken ownership of a menswear store now bearing his name where he had first found employment. He had inherited the business from the previous owner's estate, explaining that his erstwhile employer had joined the Rhodesia Airforce in early 1940, leaving him in charge, only to get shot down over Kent in a dog fight with one of Goering's elite a year later. Suffice to say it was not the last time I was to see Mr Kelly, but I bade him farewell for the time being as I emerged from the Nissen hut that served as a terminal building.

Ndola was, and still is the Copperbelt's administrative centre and provincial capital, its airport boasting Africa's longest runway, 5,500 feet above sea level on the central African plain. The neighbouring urban sprawl of Kitwe was the largest of the six copper mining towns some forty miles away through the bush by road. After collecting my two green suitcases from a smiling porter, I looked around for the Company man I was assured would be there to meet me. Sure enough, up came a friendly pipe smoking Scotsman showing a flagrant disregard for the No Smoking notices on the wall behind him. Roy "the pipe" Ritson was one of those softly spoken Highlanders you would find all over the former Empire, part of the Scottish diaspora, clad in baggy cream shorts, long socks, and a loose khaki bush jacket. He presented the figure of a benign colonial to this newcomer.

Roy drove us in his white Peugot 404 saloon, a model of car I came to know as "the camel of Africa", to his Company bungalow at Kansenji, a tree lined suburb of Ndola. A first and hugely welcome icy beer was swiftly followed by a deliciously cold shower. Zambia is hot in September; it was now the time for the last few weeks of the dry season before the November rains. The musty scent of the blue jacaranda trees, in their seasonal bloom, matched the less fragrant red blooms of the flame trees otherwise called flamboyant, and the yellow acacias which lined the avenues of the inner residential suburban sprawl.

Clean shaven and freshly changed, a chance brushing of shoulders and welcoming hug from Roy's wife Joey still on my mind, I was introduced to Mike Delaney, who was to be my new boss in the Booker McConnell managed and newly nationalised stores business called ZCBC[1]. Mike was to become a close friend, but for now it was a cautious and courteous encounter, me wanting so much information about everything I was likely to confront in the coming days and Mike fishing for information about me, my experience, my suitability to his world of work and my knowledge of local history. By luck I had done my homework before leaving England, reading Sir Roy Welensky's book about the Central African Federation which had collapsed only six years earlier, and studying the reams of reading matter handed to me by Bookers' David Taylor who had first interviewed me in London. Mike seemed sufficiently satisfied by the snippets of my recently found knowledge but left my questions unanswered for the following day. I spent my first night at The Savoy Hotel, Ndola's premier digs, a poor relation to its namesake in London, but clean nonetheless and friendly enough to its new guest.

In those early post-colonial days Zambia played host to over 140,000 expatriates of European origin, white men and women, some locally born or who had come up from South

---

1. ZCBC: Consumer Buying Corporation of Zambia. When the Company of Campbell, Booker, Carter Ltd., incorporated in Zambia and was part nationalised (51% State ownership) in 1968, its abbreviated trading name CBC was synonymous with its established goodwill which the new set up wished to retain, hence the contrived business name was designed to fit the letters, just adding a "Z".

Africa, many more still from the UK and other parts of the Commonwealth, as well as significant numbers of Greeks and Portuguese and others from various parts of Europe. There were a lot of Malawian Africans who found work more readily in Zambia, their neighbouring country to the west, than they could find at home. To the south lay Rhodesia, where there were over a quarter of a million whites, mainly of British or Afrikaans Dutch origin. Both countries had seen a big intake from servicemen and women of the allied forces after demobilisation in 1945 and 1946. They had come to settle and make their homes in new surroundings with the offer of good jobs on the land or down the mines. They did not anticipate the *"winds of change"* that were to sweep across the continent less than 20 years into the future, by which time a following generation was growing up.

In Northern Rhodesia independence from Britain came in October 1964. A new member State of the Commonwealth, the Republic of Zambia, was born and mostly all the expatriates who had stayed on were given permits of residence. Those who came later were to be issued with work permits. Like me, they were employed under formal contracts which allowed for the legal remittance of money abroad. In other words, provision was made for suitable people with proven qualifications and expertise to be brought in to hasten the development of the new nation whilst training and education caught up with the needs to equip locals, and to replace the many whites who decided to decamp, largely to go south, when majority rule replaced the colonial government - at least, that was the theory.

Land-locked and dependent upon the transit of goods through its neighbours, whether by rail or by road, the new nation of Zambia was bordered by friends and turmoil. From where I had arrived in the Copperbelt, the war-torn Congolese province of Katanga, rich in copper and other precious metal ores, was only eight miles to the north. Still struggling in the aftermath of a civil war in which it had been led by the self-styled businessman and supremo Moise Tshombe, the rich province had declared its secession from the former Belgian territory. The Congo was ruled from Leopoldville, later to be renamed Kinshasa, by the neo-communist Patrice Lumumba, whose life was cut short by assassination. Tshombe, a well-educated capitalist, with world-wide connections through mining, had met the then General Secretary of the United Nations, Dag Hammarskjold in a bid for peace in 1961. The mission had failed, and worse, Mr Hammarskold's 'plane crashed on its return trip to Ndola only a few miles from its destination, killing all on board. The circumstances surrounding that disaster remain a mystery to this day.

The northern provinces of Zambia could be reached from the capital city of Lusaka by travel along the Great North Road, a stretch of many hundreds of miles of the Cape to Cairo route established by Cecil Rhodes. From the Copperbelt the route to the north crossed through Congolese territory known in Zambia as The Congo Pedicle, some fifty miles of red laterite road which passed over swamps before reaching Zambian territory once more at the Chembe Ferry on the Luapula River. It was a drive I was to take many times in the years ahead, always watchful for armed gangs from the newly re-named Zaire, which was awash with all kinds of weapons following the civil war. Tschombe died in 1969, shortly before the beginning of my time in Africa, by when General Mobutu Sese Seko, with whom Tshombe had collaborated in the death of Lumumba, was well in charge of the vast Zairean territory using force of arms whenever required. It is worth noting that the UN had sent in troops to quell the rebellion in Katanga, their efforts were foiled for a long while by mercenary forces. These forces were funded allegedly by the French, who had serious designs on benefitting from Katanga's metal ores under secret arrangements known only to them and to the ambitious Moise.

The northern boundary of Zambia is formed by the southern shore of Lake Tanganyika and by a land border with Tanzania to the east of the great Rift Valley lake. Zambia's Great North Road crosses the border with Tanzania. Continuing north eastwards over the most difficult terrain, the road provides the principal truck route to the Indian Ocean port of Dar-es-Salaam. Trucks owned by ZamTan Road Services trundled along the 1,500 miles route, bringing supplies into Zambia and copper exports to the world, their journeys to or from the coastal port taking a week if lucky, more often a month. The passage of cargo was almost always delayed by mechanical breakdown or accidents, not so much the cause of bad driving as from poor maintenance, and the constant erosion of the road and its foundations by the heavy tropical rains.

A railway had been considered, but thus far had failed to get off the planners' drawing boards, for the very reason that rains and termites would undermine the tracks quite literally. In the years that followed the Peoples' Republic of China signed a trade deal with Zambia to build a railway, the Uhuru Railway, so called after the Swahili word for "freedom", an event which had its repercussions for our business in the next few years. Tanzania is a federation comprising Tanganyika, formerly German East Africa, and the Sultanate of Zanzibar, the latter being a one-time British protectorate and former centre of Arab slave trading on Africa's east coast. The German armed forces which had invaded Northern Rhodesia in the Great War had carried on their hostilities for a week beyond the armistice of November 1918, before receiving orders from Berlin, which had taken a week to reach them, then laying down their arms at a river bridge near Kasama, which they had captured.

The highlands in the east formed the border with Malawi. Formerly the Crown Colony of Nyasaland, Malawi was renamed by its charismatic first president, Dr Hastings Banda, at the time of its independence at much the same time as Zambia became a new name on the map. Although a much smaller land mass than its neighbour, Malawi's population was much the same as that of Zambia, about five million. A fertile country with a mighty lake, the most southerly of the African Rift Valley, it enjoyed a big fishing industry and was well placed to feed its people and indeed export food. Nyanja, the language of Zambia's Eastern Province was also spoken widely in Malawi, so there lay the foundation of cultural collaboration poorly exploited. Malawi was otherwise largely surrounded by the Portuguese territory of Mozambique whose capital city Lorenzo Marques lay on the Indian Ocean. LM was a favoured destination for colonial R & R, with Beira as its main port. Zambia shared its south eastern border with the Portuguese colony, where Samora Machel led a long running rebellion against the Lisbon dictatorship of Antonio Salazar, controlling FRELIMO[2], one of several rebel groups rampaging through the huge territory. Like other strong men at the time in Rhodesia and Angola, Machel, an artful politician, preferred that the world should see him as a liberating freedom fighter. In a sense this was true but at the cost of many lives lost before

---

2. FRELIMO: Frente de Libertação de Moçambique" or Front for the Liberation of Mozambique, the ultimate winners in the rivalry stakes between the different freedom fighter groups.

independence finally arrived, after the eventual collapse of Salazar's successor, Marcelo Caetano, in the Portuguese "Carnation Revolution" of 1974-75.

In 1964, Southern Rhodesia became plain Rhodesia, a self-governing British colony ruled by Ian Smith and the Rhodesia Front Party; it shared a border along the Zambesi river to Zambia's south. There were three main crossing points between the territories, one a road bridge at Chirundu, on the main road between Lusaka and Salisbury, the second being the road over the Kariba Dam near Siavonga in Zambia's Southern Province, the other at the Victoria Falls near the town of Livingstone, once the capital of Northern Rhodesia, where there was also a rail crossing. The *"line of rail"* ran from Benguela in Angola in an easterly direction through Katanga, then along Zambia's Copperbelt before swinging south at Ndola towards Lusaka and Livingstone, where the line crossed the Zambesi River on its way to Bulawayo and Wankie in Rhodesia. At the capital city of Salisbury[3], the railway joined the line to the Cape. The track made its onward way to the South African Gold Reef in Johannesburg, reaching Durban on the Natal coast, then calling at the other Indian Ocean ports of East London and Port Elizabeth, before finally reaching Cape Town. The railway line was then, and still is a vital supply route.

The civil war in Rhodesia had not reached its zenith of the late 1970s when I arrived on the scene, but the Zambian President Kenneth Kaunda (KK) already had a close relationship with Joshua Nkomo, head of ZANU[4], whose camps and combat training centres were hidden in the bush

---

3. Salisbury was re-named Harare in 1979

4. ZANU: Zimbabwe African National Union. Predominantly staffed by fighters of Matabeleland (Ndebele) descent.

along the northern (Zambian) banks of the Zambesi from where raids and other disruptive sorties were made across the river. At the point where Rhodesia bordered Botswana on the south side of the great river, and the Chobe River ran north to join the Zambesi at Kazungula, there is a ferry crossing. At the central point of the ferry route there is a spot where a fourth country, Namibia (formally German South West Africa), touched the other three. West of that point, Zambia shares a river border with the Caprivi Strip, a salient which runs eastwards from the Okavango Swamp, named after Chancellor Leo von Caprivi, who negotiated the land transfer with the British in 1890. The salient is now better known as the Okavango Strip, but von Caprivi's legacy lasts to this day. About 90 miles further west, passing by the settlement at Katima Malilo, the land border swings north all the way to the Congo, where we started this geographical tour, on the other side of which lay the huge Portuguese colony of Angola, whose western limit is the Atlantic Ocean.

When I arrived in Zambia, Angola's troubles were just starting. The three main rival groups, UNITA[5], MPLA[6] and FNLA[7], all acronyms for various freedom slogans, were at odds with each other as much as they were fighting the Portuguese regime in Luanda. The Western Province of Zambia was sparsely populated with even fewer people living in that part of eastern Angola on the other side of the national boundary. Nonetheless Kaunda seemed to back Jonas Savimbi and his MPLA, eventual losers in the power struggle to follow, just as he had made the same misjudgement in backing Nkomo, who

---

5. UNITA: União Nacional pela Independência Total de Angola or Union for the Total Independence of Angola

6. MPLA: Movimento Popular de Libertação de Angola or Popular Movement for the Liberation of Angola

7. FNLA: Frente Nacional de Libertação de Angola or National Front for the Libération of Angola

was later to become victim to a vengeful Robert Mugabe in Zimbabwe.

My first night at The Savoy passed in oblivion, I was done good and proper after more welcoming beers at the Ritson's and needed a good sleep. True to his word, Mike Delaney collected me at 7.30 am the next day and drove me to his office. "Trust you slept well, Derrick" was his opening and rather formal greeting, and whilst that was certainly the case, I failed to point out that my boiled egg at breakfast contained a chicken foetus. The replacement I ordered to be scrambled. By the time we got to the office a few minutes away, the sun was high in the heavens and I felt good.

2

The Eskimo Hut

(September 1969)

Courtaulds had employed me in England for three years before I jumped continents to start a new life. This was the age when Concorde, the supersonic airliner, was being test flown in the skies over Swindon where I lived during the week. At weekends I would go visiting friends or travel home to be with my parents and whichever of my three brothers happened to be home at the same time. In summer I played a lot of club cricket in the Thames Valley. My teammates' sisters were a good source of female company at post-match parties invariably held in vacant parents' houses. My split-screen Morris Minor had given way to a new Ford Corsair which was eventually traded in for a gleaming black Sunbeam Tiger.

The hierarchy at the Company's HQ in Coventry gave me extra work on top of my day job in distribution so to dream up solutions to the problems the Group would face with the impending metrication of Sterling, due in 1971. That suddenly got me involved in the plans they had for computers throughout the distributive side of their empire, wholesaling was a big business still in those days of independent retail shops. I guessed I could turn my hand to most things, but early days' computers hardly inspired me. Maybe the thought of endless reams of printouts decided me to look anew at life's opportunities for adventure. I had reached that fork in the road moment so I sought inspiration and hope, a life beyond that of my dull employer, a life that made full use of the training years I had spent with Lewis's and in Germany before that. It is so easy to drift along in life, waiting for someone else to take a decision for you to follow. We all do it, but subsequent life has taught me that the British expatriate does it less.

It was the age of the miniskirt and panty hose, Carnaby Street, Sandy Shaw and Francoise Hardy, The Supremes and Motown. The leaders of fashion were Mary Quant (she with the jet-black fringe) and Jeff Banks. I was discovering what life held for me as a trainee adult, without seriously breaking the social conventions of the age. A few of my friends rushed into early marriage but most embraced the world of work, jobs being plentiful. I wonder where those lovely people ended up and how their lives made out? My erstwhile companions of the opposite sex were doubtless swallowed up in marriages to blokes I was never to hear about, starting families somewhere without leaving me a forwarding address.

By some good fortune I had been accepted by Lewis's, the Liverpool based retailer, as a graduate trainee in 1962 following a tough interview in London. I had just returned from West Germany where I had spent my nineteenth year and a few extra months besides in training with a textile business, working in Frankfurt and Munich. Lewis's sent me to their huge store in Birmingham. The avuncular Mr Berry who had held the meeting at Selfridges store in London, which Lewis's owned, had told me, rather unoriginally that *"In our business never,*

ever, forget that the customers always have a point however wrong they might be, so never argue and remember that to give good service is a joy". That evergreen mantra remained with me all my working life and beyond. The bit about good service being a joy stuck. I think the company must have felt, as I did, that the times I had spent in Germany after leaving school was enough to qualify my entry to their programme, although I had not been to university. The fluency in German I had acquired was rarely helpful in England's second city but had its uses later. The work ethic I learned was a greater help.

What I did glean from those early years away from my mother's home cooking and comfort was, progressively and in stages, a knowledge of how to survive on little money and a big appetite, expanding on the skill of handling a tin opener learnt at school, to snipping open packs of dried peas, chow mein noodles, curries and rice or even mashed potato powder, then to be poured into boiling water fired by a gas ring (saving silver shilling coins for the meters). My learning curve took a giant upward movement when I came to share a flat In Moseley with my great chum John Allsopp (*"two ells and two pees, dear boy"*) who I had first met some months earlier at digs I shared with him and others in Sutton Coldfield.

John was from Birkenhead, the son of a police officer, who modelled himself on Frankie Vaughn, then a big star who was, I thought, a handsome cross between Fred Astaire and Dean Martin. Frankie would have loved John's boiled brisket, although it was likely he would have passed on the pork chops. I made efforts to learn Welsh as John took a language course delivered from a long-playing record, he, not I, was intent upon impressing a sweet girl from North Wales with a barely pronounceable name. We both worked long hours, John as a sales rep for an engineering firm from Nottingham, and me in retail, but the fun we had flinging parties, living on a shoestring, treating hitch hiking as a sport, climbing in the Welsh mountains and occasionally renewing our Christian allegiance at the local parish church in Moseley, made for a full life. It all came to an end not long after the Kennedy assassination when, simultaneously, Lewis's sent me to London after two years in store management, on a transfer to central buying, and John got married to Jacky, a girl he had met at a nurses' ball and had fallen for overnight, *comme ca*, just like that.

Leaving the Midlands for London gave me the chance to move back home with my parents and commute to town by rail. My job in the Buying Office took me away, travelling by train first class (for the first time in my life) and getting an expense allowance of five guineas a night from which I generally came back with change. Lewis's Board would not let their buyers be ticketed in lesser carriages else they might encounter suppliers with whom it was infra-dig to develop cosy friendships. I was under the tutelage of Geoff Gallimore, a Brasenose scholar with a lovely French wife called Nicole. Geoff was my boss and my mentor. Like John, he was from Merseyside. We remained friends despite the eleven years difference in age, our paths were to cross more than once in the years ahead.

I had turned twenty-one that year. The launch of Stanley Matthew's biography a month after the master dribbler's knighthood was one of the highlights of the book business I was put in charge of, buying for the lending libraries we had in the department stores. "It's all right, lad, just call me Stan" the great man declared when I attempted to address my hero with the respectful *"Sir"*. The immediate sequel to the twelve months with Geoff buying stationery and books in London was my transfer to Bristol in 1965 and back into stores management.

Bristol was far from being a backwoods provincial city, I loved it. George's Brewery owned most of the pubs whose cheapest tipple was rough cider or *scrumpy*, as it was affectionately known. Two pints cost half a crown and rendered most men legless. The city's many older buildings were built from cream coloured sandstone, which brightly reflected the sunlight and showed little signs of pollution. The city enjoyed the invigorating fresh sea air blown in from the Atlantic Ocean. Bristol's importance as a major port in the days of sail, competing as it did with Liverpool for dominance of the Atlantic trade was never lost on you if you were able to take the time to interest yourself in its history. Road names such as Black Boy Hill and Whiteladies Road hinted at the nature of a chunk of the trade which had taken place in the eighteenth century, vividly exposed in Marguerite Steen's novel, *"The sun is my undoing"*, thousands of copies of which I sold, following its launch in paperback that year, from the shelves of one of the departments I managed on Lewis's ground floor in Broadmead.

I moved my few possessions from the small hotel I had been billeted in by the Company into a bedsitter in Redlands Road up on the Downs, not far from Brunel's bridge over the Avon gorge. I discovered to my joy that my childhood friend David Taylor lived in a squat close by. David was on a post-graduate course at Bristol University, as were most of the other students living with him in a large and dilapidated Georgian town house we dubbed *"the pit"*. I felt sorry for my old pal, whose tidy room contrasted uncomfortably with the chaos of his slovenly neighbours. How he stood for it I never discovered, perhaps it was the weekly rent of only twenty shillings, or perhaps he just enjoyed the company of the hippies or the music of Sonny and Cher, Bob Dylan and The Beach Boys which drifted unrestrained through the walls between rooms.

I teamed up with Peter Brawley, who had arrived from our Glasgow store. We made the best of our free time, various sports and *chercher la femme* a couple of evenings each week at the Grand Spa's ballroom. Over thirties night was more popularly known as *"grab a granny night"*, not that there were many grannies to grab. Another friend was Tony Stapleton, who ran the top floor of our store in Broadmead, and his gorgeous wife Deana, a buyer at Peter Robinson's. The couple were coming to the end of their lease of *Musthay*, a Napoleonic cottage on the village green at Tockington, about 5 miles north of the city.

Although she was reluctant to take on young bachelors as tenants, the combination of Tony's words of praise and our own sweet talk seemed to persuade the Canadian landlady to let Peter and I have the keys. After only a brief spell in bedsitter land, we took on the dwelling, which had internal plumbing only recently installed, but no heating other than a single coal fire in the front room. We loved the cosy cottage with its steep stairs and three tiny bedrooms. Imagine, dear reader, the house vibrating as we danced a twenty person conga up and down the steep narrow stairs to the sounds of a young Shirley Bassey thumping out *"La Bamba."*.

Not far from the tiny village with stone dwelling houses surrounding the green was the construction site of the new Severn suspension bridge at Aust. A good number of workers and engineers employed on the project stayed at or drank in the bar of *The Swan* pub, where Peter and I worked as barmen three nights a week, on the opposite side of the green to our *Musthay*. The extra money helped me. Peter learned to get his ears tuned to the broad Gloucestershire accents which sounded off loudly around the scrumpy tap we kept out of arms' reach behind the bar.

John and Dilly MacEwan, the landlords and one-time Ceylon tea planters put us on the receiving end of much kindness. I think it was Dilly who first got me thinking that a life abroad was not a bad idea. The Stapletons met us most evenings for a pint, and to help our domestic survival we willingly joined Deana's easy cooking course; dishes such as roast chicken, plaice and mushroom casserole or meat balls became regular fair at *Musthay*. The food got washed down with ale or scrumpy carried over from *The Swan* in jugs to the sounds of von Karajan's *Berlin Philharmonic*, oozing rustic joy from a scratchy LP of Beethoven's wonderful Pastoral symphony. A chap I had known in Birmingham called John Lurie arrived on our doorstep one Sunday, announcing his transfer to Bristol. Peter quickly signed him up to take on our top spare bedroom. His arrival eased our share of the rent, a fair trade off for having to accept John's non-stop verbal onslaught. There is always one joker in the pack.

At the end of a memorable year in Bristol I had sensed the bloodletting which was to befall management as an inevitable outcome of the takeover of Lewis's by Charlie Clore's British Shoe Corporation, later re-named Sears plc. My ambition to earn three thousand pounds a year by thirty appeared to be at severe risk, so I handed in my resignation and started a new job with Courtaulds. That took me to Swindon, where I had a room in the company flat which was set within the business compound.

A few of us who stayed there would watch the football at to the County Ground, where Swindon Town might be playing a mid-week fixture. In the spring of '69 I joined a charabanc full of fans to see the "Town" play in the League Cup Final, completing a famous giant killing episode by beating the Arsenal at Wembley Stadium, a story to dine out on for years to come. We always love to witness David disposing of Goliath, don't we?

It was in the same year that John and Jacky Allsopp, by then living near Coventry, and Tony and Deana Stapleton, who had moved from Bristol to Ormskirk, honoured me with two fine godsons. Friends from different chapters of my life, they never met each other.

All this and more about my former life Mike was able to get me to admit to as we chatted firstly in the Company headquarters building and later when on the road to Kitwe where I learned I was to be stationed. The new Company formalities were completed efficiently and in double quick time, thus by mid-morning I had opened an account at the Standard Bank and signed all that I was required to do. Mike used lunchtime to drive me eastwards along the Copperbelt highway, in those days carrying only single lane traffic each way, bordered by deep storm ditches.

Just past the city limits there was a sign on the right advertising *"Phyllis's Pleasure Resort"*. Spotting my inquisitive expression, Mike commented: "I'm not sure you should go there, Derrick". A one-time family destination for days out in colonial times, the resort had later become a night spot of dubious notoriety under the tutelage of local courtesan Mercy Lubinga. Beyond the entrance to Phyllis's we had made a short diversion to see the memorial to Dag Hamarskjold at the 'plane crash site. There was just a modest sized stone pillar on which an engraved plaque recorded the great man's name and date of death. The small well-kept clearing contained a number of stone benches for visitors to contemplate the memorial.

Back on the road the bright blue sky was stacked with banks of puffy white clouds. I asked Mike to explain the strange tree covered mounds I spotted either side of the highway. "We call them anthills, but they are really termite mounds, they pepper the landscape throughout the bush in this part of central Africa. Some are as high as twenty feet" he eagerly explained in his precise and matter of fact way, adding "the earth secreted by the termites is rich in minerals and supports the growth of trees and other plants which make them useful hiding grounds for wildlife". Mike certainly knew his natural history.

Where the road to Luanshya turned off the main Copperbelt highway to the left I saw a new plantation of evergreens, the trees were saplings less than three feet high. It was the start of a new timber project. The forest nursery stretched several miles along the north side of the route. Luanshya is just one of the six main mining towns which make up the present day Copperbelt Province, in fact the first to be established in the territory, as it was there that agents sent to reconnoitre the land by Cecil Rhodes had shot a roan antelope in the 1890's and spotted a seem of copper ore body on the surface rock where the animal had fallen, or so the story goes. The abundance of copper ore gave rise to the Copperbelt, one of the world's most prolific areas for lightening, the explosive powers of nature gorged themselves on the attraction of shallow veins of minerals. The fallen antelope gave its name to the Roan Selection Trust, then Zambia's largest industrial undertaking which, Mike had explained, was recently nationalised.

As our conversation reverted to the job in hand, we passed large trucks belching thick black smoke, which I guessed meant that the air filters in their diesel engines were blocked or not cleaned. We saw young boys selling wire bicycles (I still have one) cleverly made from coat hangers and bicycle tyre tubes. A coach bearing the acronym CARS came towards us in the opposing lane, crablike, with its chassis bent from some previous accident. "That stands for Central African Road Service, the name has not changed since Welenski's Federation, like a lot of other institutions here. The dirty trucks belong to the ZamTan Road Services Company, they haul freight from Dar-es-Salaam", said Mike, as he avoided an upright cyclist dressed only in hessian with a loaded bundle of charcoal measuring twice his size tied to the seat.

I was to stay for one week at the Company's expense in the Edinburgh Hotel (the *"Eds"*), just a short walk from the department store (where I would be the assistant manager), before moving into unfurnished company accommodation. In my formal title I was to be known as *Manager Sales & Training* to satisfy the work permit authorities. I would need to buy a car. The small townhouse allocated to me was being decorated but nonetheless I would need to find furnishings, although a cooker and fridge were provided. I had just about enough money transferred from England to cover those costs but little more besides. A busy week lay ahead, I could plainly see.

Dropping my bags at the *"Eds"* reception desk, we left immediately for the store, driving down the wide service alleyway which ran behind my new place of work, entering the premises through the loading bay. Mike was greeted by a host of Zambians whose strange names I struggled to take in but with whom I soon became familiar. The men wore blue shirt jackets above black trousers, the women modest royal blue A-line dresses, the supervisors and sales staff were clad in black trousers and white shirts with a smart bow tie. I was impressed.

The store kept trading at the same time as it was being rebuilt, converting three adjoining stores into one much larger one. The way I found customers and staff negotiating their passage over the rubble and cast aside equipment would have caused a fit in a Health & Safety Manager today, but those were the days when practicality took precedence over procedure. How I miss them now in these days of political correctness and the "nanny state", and accident chasing lawyers!

There were 450 people working in the store whose combined sales area would measure over forty thousand square feet, including a modern supermarket, once the conversion work was complete. I learned later from a Macey's man from New York that this remote retailer in central Africa achieved a higher sales intensity than the Mark & Spencer's store at London's Marble Arch, which hitherto had held the world record for highest sales per square area of any department or chain store. I thought that was some claim to fame.

Above the supermarket was a mezzanine floor which housed the management offices, accessed from the ground level by a wide staircase. To the right I spotted a bank of two dozen checkout points, each manned by a till operator and more than one packer on hand to get the customers through the paying stage quickly and to be ready to carry the good to cars if needed. At the top I encountered a man of my own age waving a clipboard, sporting steel grey hair with bright ginger sideburns, who wore shorts with long socks and a bright red shirt "Meet Brendan McShane, my special projects manager" said Mike "I see you have matching shirt and eyes today, Brendan...." as he greeted the Liverpudlian, "....does the theatre club bar need stock replenishment?" he continued, not missing a trick.

I was led past a service desk to encounter a narrow office area whose windows overlooked the sales floors. Good for spotting the local talent was my idle thought. I was introduced to some of the other European managers. First off was Alex Riddle, formerly of Hong Kong, who ran the supermarket, a gnarled and wrinkly Scot whose Chinese wife Jenny was just taking her leave with a little boy I presumed to be her son. A tall fresh-faced fellow called Richard Harper then appeared from the far end, turning out to be the general manager.

At his metal desk sat Dean Wright, a man with a swarthy complexion and jet-black hair who was born in the Botswana bush, I later learned, and whose job I was about to take on. Dean, I was told, was much more comfortable with a set of architects' drawings and a tool kit than he was with a sales floor full of stock and had been horribly miscast in the job. He was leaving that afternoon on transfer back to Ndola to head up a new Projects Division, maintaining and updating the fabric of the Company's properties. There would be no time for a handover, if indeed that were possible, but he passed me a bunch of keys along with a big smile. The place was hot, I was sweating and longed for a cold beer or anything else which was wet.

There was no air conditioning in the store at a time in the year when humidity was rising ahead of the annual rains which were due to deliver their first deluge at 5pm on 4th November, so the locals assured me. That was only five weeks away. "Every year, the same, like clockwork", I was assured as Richard ordered tea, "and by the way, this is Alice our secretary, Alice, this is Mr Swain who you'll be looking after", he went on as the said Miss Sakuwaha shimmied into the room making the best of her full figure and wide eyes. I thought at the time that Mike was itching to get on, but tea-time is a ritual wherever you are on pink atlas territory, only here there were no cucumber sandwiches, just a quick slurp of Typhoo and on with the programme. There followed a whistle-stop tour of the store. Off we went, stepping over the teams of African workers moving stock struggling to do Brendan's bidding as he laid out plans with the architect. It all seemed rather chaotic.

As the day ended so Mike left me with Richard and Brendan, Alex went home to his wife and young son, with Dean following Mike back to Ndola. "Beers at the Eds on Swain" proposed Richard as we strolled across President Avenue in the direction of my hotel. I kept my counsel being the new boy on the block. Out of the corner of my eye I spotted a shop front across the road with *KELLY* posted in large letters above the entrance. I had soon found my talkative companion who had occupied the adjoining seat from London, only yesterday, and made a mental note to pay my respects as soon as I could.

The binary choice at the bar was Lion or Castle lager, served in bottles, bitterly cold. Both were brewed in Ndola under licence from SA Breweries. Zambia's beers regularly won Gold Medals awarded by trade bodies in Africa and further afield, due to the famed near perfect water source and the skills of the Austrian master-brewers who worked at the Northern Brewery. Dehydrated from my first full day in Africa, I downed four bottles quickly before the chaps departed with the promise of joining me for dinner. I now knew on whose hotel bill the meal was to be tabbed, but it was good to have company. I needed a shower and change of clothes, so found my room with its single bed and went out on to the balcony to watch a crowd of young Africans milling around the ice cream stand called "The Eskimo Hut" which stood beside a bus station. I delayed my shower long enough to nip out of the hotel to buy a small tub of smooth vanilla from the "Eskimo Hut" with the small change in my pocket from the Savoy, as I did so I caught a whiff of dagga (cannabis). The young man behind the counter seemed to me to be from the Mediterranean rather than The Arctic, he was called Marius. He clearly had devised a lucrative second income stream with no shortage of customers.

3

Lobster Thermidor

(September – October 1969)

The ice cream was the sort of little treat I needed. I made short work of it before shedding my clothes, they were damp from perspiration, and I did not bother with the shower's hot water tap, the cold water met my needs entirely. I must have dozed off because knocks on my room door confirmed that the party had returned to join me for dinner. We met in the main bar of the hotel overlooking the restaurant and dance floor, where earlier I had met Gilbert, the Head Waiter, to make the table booking. Gilbert knew his craft, I soon discovered, having worked in one of the big coastal hotels of Lorenzo Marques, the capital of Mozambique. The affable and dapper Zambian had learned the art of dealing with South Africans taking a break from apartheid. There were no *immorality laws* in the Portuguese colony, unlike the *apartheid* State of South Africa at that time, so contacts between the races were unrestricted there

Kitwe's *Edinburgh* was by far the best hotel on the Copperbelt and whilst the people staying were generally businessmen and professionals, the restaurant was a favourite meeting place for the many expatriates living locally, such as ourselves, and prominent local citizens. I have no recollection of the meal we had that evening, but I do recall Marie, Richard's wife, explaining her love of art in a broad Irish brogue, and that she spent most days painting to escape the boredom she felt at home in the large company house which the couple occupied on Freedom Avenue. Wives could not have a paid job without a work permit.

I was at the store the following morning to start my new job. I opened the drawer of the desk with the keys bequeathed to me by Dean the previous afternoon to discover a handgun and box of live ammunition instead of the expected stationery supplies I was looking for. The thought crossed my mind that I'd better re-lock the drawer and ask questions later. Work started in earnest as I explored the nooks and crannies of the four buildings, discovering how to get from one to the other whilst all the building work was taking place and at the same time maintaining a service to the heavy stream of customers. Cast-out fixtures and fittings lay everywhere amidst the piles of bricks, stacks of timber and hardboard, pots of paint, reels of wire and so much more under the many dust sheets covering swathes of fixtures in the stockrooms and on the sales floors.

In one stockroom at the back of what had been the Standard Trading store, owned by a Sidney Diamond and his family, I was shown a rack of a dozen mink coats. Apparently, when the mines paid out their twice-yearly bonus, the furry garments were put on display for expatriate miners' wives to buy and wear overseas on leave, not to keep warm, it was alleged, but as tokens of prestige. There were fur stoles and chunky gold jewellery lying in another display cabinet. Along with a stock of dinner jackets, those expensive items formed part of the kit worn when having a night out at the *bioscope*, the Rhokana Cinema on the Nkana mine compound, where evening dress was *de rigeur* for some who wished to show off when having dinner before the film show at a famed local eatery called Ernie's Mine Mess.

As I did the rounds of the apparent labyrinth of stairs, passageways, stockrooms, and sales floors I made notes of names and the jobs of the staff I was meeting for the first time. The tailoring section I found on the horseshoe shaped mezzanine floor above menswear. It was busy making alterations for goods sold from the department below. Wellman Zulu, the stout supervisor, undertook patching pockets on all my wonderful cotton shirts from London by taking fabric from the shirt tails and filling the gaps with curtain lining, which no-one saw when tucked into my trousers. Shirts without breast pockets are quite useless in the tropics, where else do you put you pen and notepads?

Cigarette brands such as Rothmans and *"Peter"*, as the Stuyvesant mark was known, were sold in packs of thirty, the backs of those packs left unprinted, blank white for taking notes and fitting neatly into the shirt pocket. When the packet was finished a smoker would carefully transfer all his notes to the back panel of a fresh pack before casting the old one away. I made a mental note to write to Allkit in London where my shirts had been purchased. Surely, they should know about the tropical smoker. I confess that the local pure Virginia leaf tobacco was not only cheap by comparison, but much superior to the saltpetre laced blends peddled by Players and WD & HO Wills at home.

One of my first tasks was to organise the Company's contingent for the Independence Day march on 24th October, less than four weeks ahead. We were to get at least two hundred volunteers from our staff to join the ranks of marchers, so I set about getting a small team of supervisors and work out how to persuade the "volunteers" to come in to town on their day off. Would they give up the chance to drink *chibuku*, the local maize brew, with their mates and so celebrate five years of independence in the township shebeens, or join our marchers? There were the banners to be carried, but first we had to make them, a job for the display team. We needed transport and food as a special reward, and drinks for the post parade party I planned as a morale booster or arm twister for attendance. Everyone was to be in their best clean store uniform, as we were to parade in a paired phalanx in front of the District Governor and other UNIP bigwigs.

Kenneth Kaunda's United National Independence Party was by then the ruling political force, so well organised it was said to have more representatives and party hacks on the ground per head of population than the National Socialists had in Germany at the height of the Third Reich. Kaunda managed to claw his way to become vice-president of the pre-independence Africa National Congress Party led by its president and prime ministerial hopeful Harry Nkumbula. However, in 1962 Simon Kapepwe, another V-P, along with Kaunda and other rebels, broke away to form UNIP, and fought Nkumbula at the elections for an interim government in the year leading up to full independence after the colonial regime stood down. Kaunda (KK) won the election, whether by fair means or foul depending on differing points of view.

Despite compulsory education to Form Three level under the British or Federation rule, there was nonetheless widespread illiteracy, so voting forms carried symbols to indicate the parties, UNIP sporting the regal lion whilst the ANC had the Hyena allocated to them by some strange quirk in the Electoral Commission, allegedly run by a covert UNIP supporter. As KK consolidated his power, his erstwhile partner Kapepwe, who was a ChiBemba speaker from the Copperbelt, broke ranks to form another breakaway Party, the Progressive Peoples' Party (PPP) which then opposed UNIP.

KK's native tongue was Nyanja, a language of Malawi and of the Ngoni people in the eastern part of Zambia, and, for good measure for my readers the said Harry Nkumbula spoke Lozi, the language of the western tribes and clans in what had been Barotseland. The fiery Kapepwe was never able to release the UNIP stranglehold and eventually gave up. I digress with purpose, since the prominence of UNIP in the lives of Zambians was in practice a demand for their acquiescence, so when the District Governor announced his parade no effort was to be spared in making it a success, and in any event, it behoved the expatriate management of ZCBC to be seen to be taking the Party line. After all, the Zambian government by then owned 51% of the Company through part nationalisation with its shares held through the newly formed Industrial Development Corporation (INDECO). *INDECO's* top executive was a Greek called Andrew Sadanis who had made his number with Kaunda by secretly joining the ANC during the six years of Welenski's Central African Federation, by now a fading memory, then following KK into UNIP.

In life there is a first time for everything, the "March" being no exception, but it all went well on the day. "I don't know why you were so worried" the laid-back Richard Harper had chipped in as we were about to enjoy a *braaivleis* (barbie to Aussies) outside in the garden of his house at number 9,

Freedom Avenue (formerly Fleming Way, as in the great scourge of bacteria). In truth I was more worried right then at avoiding the Harpers' feisty dog Sammy, a Rhodesian Ridgeback crossed with a German Shepherd, whose ferocious barking seemed to threaten the impending removal of parts, if not the whole of my legs and lower regions. I decided to stare him down and somehow achieved a truce, which was just as well, for when the Harpers finally left Zambia in early December, I took Sammy on as my own guardian and companion. Little did I know that by then I would be living in Ndola, with a new job.

I had moved into Diamond Flats next to Brendan a few days before, managing to get hold of a bed and a chest of drawers, but precious little other household effects of good use. My kitchen needed equipping, in fact the whole place needed to be filled so that I could make a home for myself and I needed help; I did not want to take too much advantage of the proffered hospitality of The Special Projects Manager next door. I had found a small Japanese car for myself, paid for out of the funds I had brought in with me from the UK. At home, Japanese cars were a rarity but Toyota and Datsun had a strong foothold in the market in this part of the world. A week or so after my initiation into the Kitwe store I found time to drop in to see Mr Kelly. It was a joy to meet him again. I not only met Miriam, his wife, but also Ruth, his daughter up from university at Witwatersrand near Johannesburg. We made a dinner date for the next day at their flat above the shop.

When I went to dinner at the Kelly's home the following evening, Miriam gave me some telephone numbers to call. A few of her friends had furniture and furnishings to offload, so my problems were quickly solved. Ruth was happy to lend me her company for a date the next week, although I had no clue where to take her. She fascinated me. Her wistful distant gaze, her dark hair and delicate features showed me what her mother must have looked like when she was fleeing Poland. In the end we settled for a meal at the *Lotus Inn*, Kitwe's only Chinese restaurant, whose stocks of chopsticks had been long depleted, but I was reassured by Ruth who announced that "the scoff was *lecker*[8]", so all was well.

Time went by and a daily routine developed, I found I was enjoying the work. I met another one of Mike's 'special managers', Malcolm Westmore (aka *Westy*), whose wide powers of expression were always augmented with flaying arms and finger tapping as if to give greater emphasis to his speech. I gathered Westy was involved in developing new systems. He visited Kitwe often, and joined us nightly at the Theatre Club, where I had become a drinking member, a title attributed to non-thespians. It seemed important that the empty upper bookshelf which surrounded the club's busy bar, a horseshoe shape about forty feet from end to end, must, by some long-standing tradition, be filled by a single continuous line of empty beer bottles before anyone was "allowed" to leave. The process took about 50 minutes and was not particularly challenging since most of the drinkers arrived parched and gasping for beer after a long day in the heat. You might think this was all a bit laddish, which it was, but understand there were many young male expatriates on contract with the mines and the service industries which supported them, just like me, and the camaraderie of the daily club rendezvous was a useful release from pressure. I was usually well into my fourth bottle before I passed water, having not done so since before breakfast earlier the same day.

---

8. Lecker, low German or Dutch meaning delicious

I had once brought Ruth to the club, but decided against it when she suggested another visit, and when we did go back, I neatly avoided my drinking chums by taking a tour of the auditorium whilst a rehearsal was in progress. She gave me cause to believe she was unimpressed that I had not secured a role in any production. She saw through my weak claim of the pressures of work. Our short friendship came to an abrupt close when she returned to her studies, leaving me sad. She was, after all, a clever and decent person who would one day meet some high flying academic or scientist and feed her intellect in a marriage made in the lecture hall, which is what happened, sooner than I predicted, in Pretoria the following year.

One evening we learned that the *Eds* had lobster on the menu, my new pal Gilbert had managed to secure a shipment to come in overnight by air from LM. I think it was Brendan who paired up Westy with a leggy blonde of few words called Cathy and whilst I cannot recall my own partner that evening, I am sure McShane was with yet another bottle blonde South African called Yvonne. There were six of us at the table, we were happy to share a couple of large lobsters served cold with trimmings, but it was the vacant Cathy who insisted she order Lobster Thermidor as it was by far the most expensive item on the menu. Our gesticulating chum, who had been holding forth on some subject of apparent importance, was made to dig deep for his Kwachas (local currency) that night, a worthwhile investment he must have believed, since he ended up marrying Cathy four years later.

On another occasion Brendan and I hosted a candlelit dinner, or at least that was the plan. He had arranged for Yvonne to bring a friend as my blind date to make up the party. Yvonne was a married woman whose husband, it transpired, was serving a murder rap in a Lusaka gaol. It was my turn to be the chef, so I produced one of Deana's cottage pies topped with creamy mashed potato. Yvonne arrived with her friend, a plump Afrikaner akin to a young Bessy Braddock, the MP for Liverpool Exchange not known for entering beauty contests, whose husband it turned out was a cell mate of the murderer and up for something similar. Conferring with each other as we made drinks in the kitchen, out of earshot from our challenging guests, I made it clear I was not amused by Brendan's matchmaking prowess. I returned to the living area with an overarching sense of impending doom. I served up the scoff as fast as possible, with the Bessy lookalike tucking in with speed and great intent, so much so it transpired that when she looked up to answer one of my questions about her loved one's sentence her face was covered with mash. "You might need this" I said to my would- be amorous dinner partner, handing her a paper roll and a finger bowl full of water. The predicted night of doom had arrived early. Both B and I collapsed in uncontrollable laughter.

Chaps like Brendan and I were contract employees, others like Dean and Westy had been employed on local contracts with the company. After the business was nationalised our management team was under some pressure to "Zambianise" many of the jobs presently carried out by local whites. We had over fifty such people in the Kitwe store and were overstaffed with Zambians as well, the legacy of a paternalistic approach to employment by the likes of Sidney Diamond and his neighbour Mr Lev Collengberg, previous owners of parts of the new combined store. Something had to be done to turn the store to profit, but as it happened I was not to get deeply involved because in November I was called over to meet Jim

Lafferty, who had just then succeeded a man I never got to know but had met briefly on the day of my arrival called Jim Garrard. Mr Lafferty was now the Chief Executive of our Company. He reported to Wally Lewis, a well-liked Chairman of Bookers in Zambia. Whilst Bookers was now the minority shareholder in the ZCBC Group, the firm was still responsible for its management under a long-term contract signed in London. As a contract employee I had been hired by Bookers but was on the local payroll.

The Group comprised three retail divisions, namely Department Stores, Rural and Peri-urban Shops. Mike Delaney, who you have already met in these pages was Stores' Divisional Manager. He controlled five good sized stores with two more planned, all located in the main centres of population along the line of rail. Mr Lafferty had a number two, a long serving Zambian by the name of White Chilambo, who had been given direct responsibility for running the two shops divisions. In turn, Mr Chilambo had two men under him to run the Rural Shops, Joseph Chishimba covering shops in the north and Daniel Margaden Bwalya for the southern areas. A chap called Fidelis Kangwa looked after the Peri-urban outlets, situated as they were in the commercial sectors of the inner suburbs of the main mining towns and the capital city of Lusaka. In all we had close to one hundred and twenty outlets. ZCBC was the dominant national retailer.

We had a Sales Agency business and, importantly, a Wholesale Division which had been foisted onto the Bookers' management contract by *INDECO*. The Zambia National Wholesale Corporation (ZNWC) had been freshly established at Independence by the UNIP Government only five years earlier, which by now had nine branches across the country. ZNWC had, nonetheless, a major political purpose to supply goods to local Zambian traders, offering credit lines as finance so that indigenous Africans could get into competition with the Asian traders who had dominated the retail market during the earlier Colonial and Federal days. In Zambia, and indeed in Rhodesia, there were lots of descendants of people who had migrated from the sub-continent to work in the wattle plantations of Natal, who worked hard and saved enough money to start a business elsewhere in Britain's African Raj, far from South Africa's Nationalist government. Such were the opportunities of Empire.

Some of the "Indians" had taken Zambian nationality at independence, but most retained their British nationality as a hedge against the future. Some had both, others had managed to acquire Pakistani or Indian nationality as well during the melee following the British withdrawal from India in 1947 and the subsequent chaos of partition. There was already unrest brewing for the South Asians, not so much in Zambia, but certainly in Uganda and the other East Africa nations. The scourge of Idi Amin, former soldier, and newly appointed dictator in Kampala, was about to be unleashed.

Supporting the Group's operations were the accounting and distributive divisions, the latter being re-organised to include a new central buying office based at our Head Office in Ndola's Second Street. The OK Bazaars and Mwaiseni Stores were our main competitors, along with specialist stores such as Kingsway who were stationers and booksellers, and a host of independents. The ZCBC group had just about one third of all the retail action in the country at that time, but it was also vital that we made some success out of ZNWC, since it was part of a Government strategy to localise business ownership by overcoming the main problems of finance and expertise deficiency.

ZNWC was already up to its neck on its balance sheet with trade debtors outstripping assets. The wholesale business finances were kept in running order through Bookers' good standing with their commercial bankers, specifically Standard Bank, Barclays DCO and Grindlay's, and by Bookers having very recently agreed to incorporate ZNWC's accounting within the Group as a whole. All that had followed some serious arm twisting by the Minister of Trade and Industry in the halls of power in the country's capital city. The eyes of the UNIP Government were upon us, indicating the fragility of the Bookers management contract. It was our essential task to get earnings out of the Group's enterprises now under majority State ownership, so that Bookers could get at least some payment for their shares in the goodness of time. "Some hope!", do I hear you say?

Poor old Bookers, lovely Fabians that they were. The same problem was soon to hit them in Guyana, where the Government of the leftist firebrand Forbes Burnham was about to feast itself on the Company's sugar estates along the Demerara river. Booker McConnell's share price looked good in London until someone twigged that the debt assets on the balance sheet were hopelessly optimistic given the ability of the debtors to cough up. They never did. Mind you, the profits from food distribution in the UK kept the group afloat for many years until they were eventually gobbled up by Iceland and eventually Tesco. Lord Colin Campbell was chairman when I joined Bookers, a war time pal of Ian Fleming of 007 fame. Campbell bought the copyright of Fleming's books from the author's widow, thus securing her financial security from his Company's resources. Bookers were now in the book business, as it were, and set about establishing their annual prize for fiction writers.

Meeting Mr Lafferty for the first time, I was impressed. He bore his large frame with an aura of confidence and without any sign of aggression or malice sometimes found in lesser men. He was wearing an old gold coloured bush suit and a pair of light bronze horn-rimmed spectacles which revealed his extreme myopia. I learned that although missing active combat service in WWII, he had been, like the Tory Leader Ted Heath, a Colonel in Army Intelligence by the time he was 25 years old. After a polite greeting we got straight to the purpose of my visit. It was the Board's decision to appoint me, immediately, as Acting Divisional Manager of ZNWC since the incumbent Jim Whelan had suffered a heart attack and was yesterday flown home for surgery in Scotland. Jim had left Ndola with his wife Caroline, and their baby daughter, vacating his house and car, which I was to take over, as soon as I had completed a handover from his deputy, Dennis Slattery. Dennis was an old hand from the United Africa Company (UAC owned by Unilever), a *"Coaster"* who was about to retire in five days. An exclamation mark immediately registered in my brain.

"Why me, after all I have just arrived less than two months ago?" I was bold enough to ask, getting the answer that I was the only new manager in the Group with experience in wholesaling (three years with Courtaulds, one of which spent on the road as a commercial traveller). "It's a case of must" added the great man, "It's sink or swim, so show me your buoyancy". At which point I was introduced to Mr Wally Lewis who had entered the room quietly, my first meeting with the Chairman. Like Mike Delaney who joined us a few moments later, Wally was dressed in a starched white long-sleeved shirt and tie, with gold cufflinks. The two men appeared to me like a team of half-dressed undertakers about to tend to my funeral.

Silently I reflected on the enormity of the task in hand and my likely demise from a job failed. Heavens above, I thought, I am supposed to manage a business in places called Solwezi and Chipata, let alone Mansa, Kasama, Mongu and Choma, place names I was hearing for the first time. "Holy MOJ, is there no escape route?" I cried inwardly. Clearly not. I came to my senses as soon as I realised that I was being instructed to take details of my transfer and domestic arrangements. The smell of St Bruno tobacco alerted me to the presence of Roy Ritson, who took my arm as we made our way to his office for further briefing.

Brendan, late of Marks and Spencer and UAC in Ghana, was to remain in Kitwe and absorb my role in addition to his "special one". Maurice Widdowson, formerly with Littlewoods and already two years into his time in Zambia was being brought in from a training function in the bush (Rural Stores Division) to take over from Harper. I was to leave my newly acquired possessions at Diamond Flats until they found me a place to live in Ndola, meanwhile to move into the Whelan house with the elderly Mr Slattery with whom I would spend the latter part of the day to make an early start on my two day handover. "Aye, aye, sir" was the only possible retort I could make if asked, which I was not. There comes a time when the hand of God is on the rudder, so I might as well sail in whatever direction the winds took. "Swim, I would show 'em" thought I, wondering how I would describe the events when next I wrote home to my father.

4

Crystal Springs

(Late 1969)

I set off back to Kitwe after sundown, which took only thirty minutes to arrive from broad daylight. Night driving over those forty miles was hazardous. It often happened that the trucks ahead could be seen only in silhouette from the oncoming headlamps, the tail and brake lights of the 40-ton ZamTan monsters were almost always coated with exhaust black if indeed the lights worked at all. Thankfully, most locals wore brightly coloured clothing. Folk walking along the roadside would be otherwise tricky to spot against the oncoming traffic.

There were still two weeks before the Harpers returned to Britain, so I called in to the house on Freedom Avenue to bid farewell and make some arrangements for the dog. Sammy was barking loudly as usual, this time at their visitor Maurice, just arrived from the north by pick-up. It seemed that we were both embarking on crash courses for our new jobs. Maurice had given a lift to a couple of schoolteachers who were proving themselves further sport for Sammy, the air seemed thick with profanities from the man, with Maurice offering somewhat disproportionate protection for the distressed pretty schoolmistress until the disobedient hound calmed down.

Whilst Maurice Widdowson brought his Littlewoods training to the field management of the rural shops throughout all nine Zambian provinces, I learned that he had been licenced to trade in beeswax and ivory, then lucrative and legal exports of a business started by the African Lakes Company, Bookers' first investment in Northern Rhodesia. Beeswax was collected by villagers, who rendered down the empty honeycombs in enamel bowls which they heated above a charcoal fire, standing the bowls in pans of boiling water and slowly melting the wax as if it was in a *bain marie*. The blocks of wax produced were in the half-moon shapes of the bowls. The wax "cakes" were delivered to a special warehouse section at Ndola run by a former RSM in Lord Campbell's regiment, Martin Halliday-Brown. It was Maurice's task to authorise the trades with reliable village headmen and set a market price. It was Martin's job to ship the wax back to England. Beeswax is still a major and valuable component of lipstick.

I bade them all a swift goodbye and left to spend my final night at Diamond Flats nearby on the other side of the fenced-in swampy parkland opposite the Harpers' house. By sunrise at six the next morning I was on the road with my green suitcases in the boot, passing mineworkers on bicycles and on foot at the start of their day. Many lived in the mine compounds, but lower ranked workers came from the large townships outside the city, preferring their own transport to the cost of riding in overcrowded buses.

It was said that in Zambia there were seventy-one different tongues apart from English, which was the one official language. There was certainly considerable distrust between the main population groupings, the Bemba people on the Copperbelt being the most numerous, followed by the Ngoni, eastern Nyanja speakers, the less numerous southern Tonga and the western Lozi or Barotse traditionalists (close relatives of the South African Zulu), with yet smaller groups in the north, across the Congo Pedicle, and the northwest beyond Solwezi; the good thing was that unlike its neighbours, Zambia had no dominant population grouping, and because of the mines and urbanisation in general, people were learning to live amongst each other.

Employees were all paid monthly but received "ration money" weekly by law, thus ensuring there were adequate funds for the family food (a forty pounds bag of maize flour cost half one week's ration money and could provide enough meal for the family for two weeks) even if the monthly salary pot had been binged away on beer in the shebeens or on an expensive pair of new shoes. Lots of workers formed themselves into trusting teams whereby one received all the monthly pay of the whole team in turn and were thus able to make some large purchases at least once every few months when it was your turn to have the collective pay. To afford to buy good quality fancy clothes and footwear was an important consideration for the younger men, whilst the older men might buy something to bring peace to their household.

As a white man I never felt threatened on account of my skin, although it cannot be denied there was a lot of non-violent crime such as thieving. It got worse as time went by. Most Zambians blamed the Congolese and it was certainly true that bad elements with firearms crossed over from Katanga and disappeared through the bush before they could be caught. There was hardly anyone I knew who had not had a burglary, despite the prolific presence of ornate but strong window bars and night security patrols. Then there were the pole thieves who would stick a long rod through the window, on its end a hook protected by razor blades and grease, causing horrible injuries to those bold enough to grab the intrusive implement without wearing gloves.

In our stores we were always on the lookout for theft by servant or collusion between staff and outside third parties, indeed those who had jobs were put under pressure to provide for the extended family, often an impossible demand to fulfil out of simple earnings. Shoplifting was an art form practiced by a sizeable cross section whether they were black, brown, or white in colour. In our Kitwe store I had relied closely on the security team in their smart grey uniforms, led by Telephone Mvula, the boss and ex-police sergeant, and his formidable assistant Snake Lungu, also a past officer of the law. I had once sat in on one of the Snake interviews with a male shoplifter caught pocketing a bottle of gin, and decided against interference, preferring the role of the army officer telling his NCO to "carry on". The bald, bullet headed Mr Lungu was never seen without his black rubber truncheon, a man hardened by years of police service but always firm and fair. I was glad he was on my side.

I drove straight to the Whelan house in Ndola to collect Dennis and arrived at Second Street just over an hour after leaving my neighbour Brendan asleep next door in Kitwe. By mid-morning I had mastered the daily branch contact routine, met Bert Craig, the Chief Buyer and his staff, and toured the Ndola depot on the far side of the street from my new office, which also housed a distribution warehouse. Dennis had ordered a nationwide stock taking which I felt was an excellent idea, bearing in mind we were changing top management.

Nobody had a clue how long Whelan would be away or indeed if he were ever to come back. It turned out that he did recover and returned within a year, but probably wished he had not done so after experiencing the tragic event which was to unfold in his personal life not long after resuming his job.

Dennis left for home in Wales where a faithful wife awaited him no doubt, and I moved into a small detached bungalow which stood back from the road behind a low wire fence. The little brick bungalow with a corrugated iron roof had been built in the middle of a plot of one acre in Kenmere Avenue, a quiet road not far from the shops at Kansenji. The road was, like many others in the inner suburbs, an avenue lined with the ubiquitous jacaranda trees and the red-flowering flamboyant, only a short drive of four minutes to my new office in Second Street.

I hired a wonderful cook-cum-housekeeper from Mumbwa in Central Province called Jonas Mackay Kapolasa, and took on two young lads, Andrew, and his cousin Friday, to look after the plot and tend to the garden. It was not long before I had a mealie plantation (white maize which grew to eight or nine feet), inter-planted with fat yellow pumpkins. Each plant bore two corns on maturity, edible but not so sweet as their yellow cousins in Europe or The States. My social life remained in Kitwe, where I spent most weekends, and from where I had collected Sammy to stand sentry for me.

Most pet dogs seem to show bias towards people of the same colour as their masters, so all hell used to break loose when darker complexioned folk came onto the plot, with the one exception of Jonas. In Jonas's eyes Sammy could do no wrong after he had dug up a scrumptious brown mole in the garden and delivered the delicacy to him at the kitchen door. Sammy was kept inside when the gardeners were on site but escaped once and disappeared for over two weeks. When he did return, to the expressions of great joy on Jonas's face, he looked as if he had been shot by a machine gun, so many were the holes all over his body. I took him immediately to the vet. It transpired the dog had joined some other sex-mad canines to chase down a bitch on heat and had come off the worst. Canine teeth certainly deliver a horrible outcome, dog on dog. Tail between his legs, he had spent the time of absence without food and had only rainwater to drink. My dog's further troubles had been inflicted by the much-impregnated target of his absence, it cost me dearly in vet's fees to treat him for canine VD.

Maurice had put me in touch with Margaret Lumsden who worked as a buyer manager in the Ndola department store. A German by birth, she had been previously married to a British army officer and had three boys before meeting Douglas "Jock" Lumsden, a sergeant serving in the Palestinian Police. When the British decamped from the Holy Land he joined the Northern Rhodesia Regiment, was promoted to RSM before being offered a commission with the Zambian Army, later formed from the Regiment at Independence in 1964. Jock and his bride Margaret had two daughters, Marlene and Trudi, the latter born in 1960 six years or so after her big sister. I was invited to dinner and was more than glad I went, Margaret's cooking was as good as my Mother's, and so I had found a home from home.

Not long after that first meal with the family in Jock's army house, he left the Service to join the big mining company RST in logistics, moving to a new company house he had been allocated in Kenmere Avenue, of all places, just a few doors from me. It was after a Sunday lunch and afternoon spent happily around the Lumsden's pool at their new house when my bungalow got burgled and I lost just about everything, certainly all my clothes apart from one black shoe and a bow tie. Sammy had been fed drugged meat, and Jonas had been with his wife asleep in his house at the bottom of the garden. When the police arrived, I suggested they look for unsavoury characters wearing cotton shirts with curtain lining patched into the tails. I contacted Harry Healey of Old Mutual, the insurers, who paid me up in full. Harry was another non-acting member of Kitwe Theatre Club.

As luck would have it, I had to drive to Kitwe the next day to buy a new tyre and have a puncture repaired, so I called into Kelly's menswear to spend most of Harry's promised insurance pay-out. I replaced the stolen shirts and trousers with cotton bush suits, long and short trousers and long socks, so taking on the outward appearance of a local. I had been given a 35mm Mamiya camera by my widowed grandmother as a leaving present. I thought about her, living as she did on her own in Burnham. My father had found her a cosy flat just over a mile from our family home where my mother could keep a good eye on her. I resolved to send her some photographs showing me in my new surroundings along with a long letter I managed to finish a couple of days later.

In those days we used the post prolifically, relishing the arrival of the red, white, and blue rimmed airmail envelopes, immediately identifying the senders by a familiarity with handwriting. Mail was sent to the Company PO Box, then distributed soon after its arrival by the messengers who ran all sorts of errands if asked and who also made tea and coffee. I came to find composing letters a more difficult task as I became more familiar with the new world around me and a routine settled into my life, but in those early days everything was worth describing in vivid detail. I had a great desire to share my discoveries in Zambia with old friends and close family at home, assuming rather optimistically that my words would hold their interest.

A new person entered my life when Captain Denis Sakalla knocked on my office door a week or so after the other Dennis had returned to England. I was expecting him. In his early forties but still slimly built he presented a smart figure. I took an immediate liking to him. He smoked a pipe, which was unusual for a Zambian, perhaps a habit adopted from some of his fellow officers, I thought. The scent of Erinmore, his favourite brand of tobacco, accompanied his entrance. it was not so long since he had taken leave of his army commission and found his way to our Company through various contacts in the Government, and had subsequently been hired by Jim Lafferty to join me at ZNWC in training as my deputy, In the days and months ahead, Denis was to prove his worth to me as a very competent interlocutor with our Zambian staff, who numbered over five hundred spread within the national warehouse network in all the distinctly different Provinces. Jock Lumsden had known Denis in the Regiment and spoke well of him.

As the weeks went by my social life took some turns for the better. Mike introduced me into the Ndola Cricket Club, which fielded teams on Saturdays and Sundays in separate leagues comprised of the ten other clubs along the Copperbelt. Not long after that I joined the Golf Club. I made friends with other people through the business and found that whereas we Europeans worked harmoniously together with our African and Indian colleagues, even played sports together, when it came to social contact folk seemed to keep to their own kind;

that was not because of any racial prejudice, it was just that we relaxed in our own cultures more comfortably. It was, perhaps, and would remain forever thus despite the shrill demands of social engineering, just as young people prefer the company of their own age groups or farming folk find urban tribes difficult to come to terms with.

If I was to take full control of the Division then I had to make a tour of all the Branches and set about a programme that I could complete within two weeks, driving the white Peugot 404 left behind by Jim Whelan, a car whose suspension, I found, was brilliantly suited to the corrugations of dirt roads. The distances were great, but Denis and I resolved to cover most of the ground by car, hiring a small Piper Cherokee single engine aircraft to take us on round trips over two days and 1,800 miles to Choma and Mongu, then to Mansa and Kasama after an overnight stay in Barotseland.

We were able to drive to Solwezi in the northwest and back in one day, and we had two days away on the long return trip to Chipata in the east, close to the border with Malawi, calling in at Broken Hill (now called Kabwe) and Lusaka on the journey. I was able to meet the staff in all those branch operations and was impressed favourably with the calibre of the Branch Managers I met, although I detected problems in both Solwezi and Choma. The Boma (seat of administration) town of Choma was the capital of Southern Province bordering the Zambesi, lying on the long road from Lusaka to Livingstone. I resolved that the matter of staff changes needed addressing quickly. It was accomplished by moving the Kasama manager to Choma, replacing him with the deputy head of the Mansa branch, and sending the assistant sales manager of our main operation in Ndola up to Solwezi as a temporary assignment.

All those moves were made simpler because the Company owned management houses.

Solwezi was, I learned, a hot bed of traditional tribal superstitions, with self-styled witch doctors at large holding sway within the surrounding villages from where we drew some of our staff. The replaced manager had been thus affected and believed himself accursed, poor fellow, so I fired him and paid for his return to the East where he had come from originally. It seemed to me at the time that in Solwezi they did not like "foreigners" in the form of people from outside their part of the land. In Chipata, formerly Fort Jameson, the manager was a delightful character called Brave Ndlovu, who courageously invited Denis and I to his home. His charming wife had been a schoolteacher, as had been Brave. Both had worked with Anglican missionaries before starting a family. Their twin sons were called Heathcoat and Amory after the said British politician Derick who was a Chancellor of the Exchequer and had, allegedly, visited the town where Brave had lived in Northern Rhodesia before the twins' birth. Oddly, I was to meet the ex-Chancellor's nephew David years later in Nigeria.

After a good meal and a wide ranging but very informative conversation following dinner at the Ndhlovu's, who I had found to be refreshingly direct and delightfully unphased by their visitors from Head Office, Denis and I took our leave, retiring to the Crystal Springs rest house. Our overnight digs were situated on the west side of the Boma township, where we shared the only available twin room and where each bed had its own mosquito net draped from a hook on the ceiling, the smell of recent insecticide spray heavy in the air. Like the good soldier he had been, Denis retrieved his field kit containing a bottle of Johnny Walker and we took a few fingers each in tooth mugs onto the veranda, contained as it was within open window spaces covered in mesh to keep out the creepy crawlies. The bush beyond was pitch black, with the sound of cicadas and croaking frogs providing a night-time tropical symphony almost as I had imagined it would be before leaving Blighty.

In our cups that night the two of us compared lives from contrasting backgrounds. Denis, it transpired, was one of twelve children to his father who had worked his way from a farmhand to being boss man on a ranch owned by people called Malan. It was Mr Malan, a South African who had settled in the north who had eventually paid for Denis to go to boarding school in Bulawayo, where he had shown greater prowess at football and acting on stage than in passing exams. It was his choice to join the armed forces under the colonial Government.

He had lost contact with his surviving three brothers and one sister after the death of both his parents but had been thrilled to find that two of them, both older than he, were alive with their families living outside Lusaka. Having said that, he confessed that now he was out of the Forces and in a relatively well rewarded job, he had to figure out how to avoid the financial demands of an extended family, as was the tradition. So far so good, but you never knew, he opined. I asked him about his duties along the border with Rhodesia, he replied that the Zambian Army was a defence force, not an aggressor and he saw no likelihood of open warfare with the Smith regime, rather a proxy conflict carried out by freedom groups. There would likely be a border closure at some time, he thought, so the country needed to get its economic act together; he was glad to be working now in that direction rather than carrying arms.

By the time it was my turn, the tide in the bottle was some way on the ebb. I revealed a little of my school days at Aldenham and about the friendships I had established there. Denis suggested the sort of Victorian discipline I had experienced was on a par with the Rhodesian boarding school system he had been subjected to. I rambled on, telling him about my family and something of my work experience, so much as was relevant to the business in hand. I described my three brothers; John, who was older than me and my younger siblings Adrian and Andrew, the former about to take up a university place in Kentucky, the latter at the London School of Economics, I explained. John was a qualified surveyor with a young family in the making.

We will pick the boys up later in this narrative, suffice to say that regardless of the three or four years spacing between us, we remained a close family. Alan Swain, my father, was in the process of retiring from the one textile firm he had worked for all his life which supplied women's and children's fashion, notwithstanding the seven years' of "wavy navy" war service. He had volunteered in the RNVR before the war and was a ready trained navigation officer when hostilities began. My birth in 1943 was the result of an extended shore break while the corvette under my father's command underwent a refit in a Belfast shipyard, allowing my mother, the former Mary Nicholls, to join him in Ulster. Dad had received his sailing orders three weeks before my birth. Before embarking on *convoy* duty to Reykjavik and the run to Murmansk he took the family back by boat and train via Holyhead to London, where they moved in with my grandparents.

Luckily for the unborn me, Dad was able to sweet talk the Matron at Queen Charlotte's hospital who made space for my mother and was gone back to the war before I made my entrance on the planet. Three years passed by before he rejoined the family, newly demobbed following VJ Day, as I have previously explained, when there was no longer a need for our naval forces to fight in Asia. He came to collect us from a farm in the tiny village of Foxcote, a few miles from Cheltenham, where we had spent two years following evacuation. "War, even when necessary and justified, is terrible" said Denis "Let us pray we are all spared conflict here" to which hope we both drank before moving inside to sleep soundly through until the morning.

I do not recommend a hangover in the humid rainy season, and particularly not before embarking on four hundred miles of potholes, more so with only two bottles of body-heat *Fanta* to combat thirst, in an age long before bottled drinking water was widely available.

Sharing that time with my new friend and colleague heightened my respect for the man who in time succeeded Jim Whelan as head of the nation's largest wholesale organisation, and I wished him well. I had begun to make my contribution to the process of "Zambianisation", which was really the reason why we expats were hired in the first place and given work permits and set term contracts. That is not to say that Bookers, the minority partner in the large state owned business, would not hope that those they had recruited, like me, would be able to protect their assets in Zambia, and thus the balance sheet of their publicly quoted firm in London.

5

Gedi

(Year turn 1969/70)

Maurice quickly established himself as master of the house on Freedom Avenue and threw open his five bedroomed home to host a bachelor house party over Christmas, organising a whole pig to be slow cooked on a spit over a bed of charcoal in his open-fronted carport, with the help of his guests, me included. It was delicious but took until nightfall to be ready. There is a first time for everything, I mused once again and not for the first time in Zambia, but big-hearted Maurice had given Christmas Day off to his house servant and cook. We were poor substitutes, exposed wanting in the skills of the grills.

The two days off work spent in Kitwe gave birth to a poker school which lasted twenty subsequent years in three continents. The original members made good use of a bag of plastic gambling chips which I stored in a bag emblazoned with the brand of a now long defunct chain of high street British chemists called Timothy Whites and Taylors. I became the official guardian of the chips. House rules emerged over the years, always dealer's choice, games such as five card draw, seven card high-low, Dr Pepper, Betty Hutton and even pontoon were freely chosen, the dealer having to fund a pot, which he retained if the pot was still in funds on completion of the round. Thursdays became the regular poker night, venues at home taking turns to host, even travelling between Ndola and Kitwe. House sayings were coined, our chief bard, the gesticulating Westy, whose "pay, pay, don't delay" kept us from wasting time. Impatience at the new dealer's preparation or choice of game was met with the mantra "dealer gets thirty days", a term borrowed from commercial invoices. Any reserve or shyness quickly disappeared as our group became close friends at ease with each other, capable of throwing insults and praise in equal measure.

Work contracts in our firm lasted three years, and if renewed, further spells of two years. Paid "long" leave at the end of a contract could last two months, but we also enjoyed two weeks of local leave each year, local being defined as within Africa, and whilst it was paid time, we forked out to cover our own travel costs. Long leave was typically taken back home in Europe or wherever one came from, the Company paying the air fares as it was contracted to do.

The rainy season was already well into its fourth month, the torrential downpours, orchestrated with dramatic thunder and lightning, came mostly at night-time. Work had been good, and my circle of friends had widened, largely through Company connections, but also the result of having joined the Theatre Club in Ndola, and the Lions. As Mike Delaney was no longer my boss it was probably easier for Mike and his wife Lorraine to offer me home cooking and good conversation, and I continued to enjoy Margaret's table at the Lumsden's.

Brendan had moved into a much bigger and better house in Kitwe's Riverside district, so I called in on my way back from a trip to Solwezi in time to join one of our card evenings. Between hands I suggested to that we take a week's local leave and go to Mombasa, 1,400 miles or so away on the Indian Ocean coast of Kenya. We needed a break.

It was difficult to think that it was only seventy years since the roan antelope was shot outside Luanshya. In the time since then vast mines had developed, deep open pits some a mile long and half a mile wide, man-made holes in the Earth deep enough and with the space to turn round a light aircraft. There were yet other deep shaft mines reaching below sea level a mile or more below the surface. I was in awe of the achievements of those who had come before. The advent of colonial settlement had brought much technical advancement to the territory but led to a shift in social structure from the disciplines and traditions of life under village chiefs and age-old customs.

There had been no written records, so history had been passed through the generations by word of mouth, just as it had been with the Scandinavian s and their sagas. Zambians soaked up knowledge in their schooling and job training and had a thirst for self-improvement. Being able to go to school, for example, was a privilege, something to be greatly proud of, how different that was from the sense of resentful compulsion I had displayed as a boy. The schoolchildren wore simple uniforms which were compulsory but inexpensive, yet still, for some, a heavy financial burden often paid for by those in work under the extended family code.

At ZNWC we supplied huge quantities of gingham or plain blue, green or grey fabrics for home sewn pinafore dresses worn by the schoolgirls, or coloured cotton short-sleeved shirts, some in plain khaki to match the boys' shorts, others navy, white or grey. We also sold large numbers of metal lunch boxes which contained small water bottles which the children carried to school each day. Few schools were able to provide meals, and few had more than one or two permanent buildings. Lessons were therefore taken under the shade of trees within the school compounds. Children would often have to walk a long way from their homes to get to school on time. I met one family who lived eight miles away, the children setting out from home at five o'clock to get to their destination in time for assembly before first lessons at half past seven every morning. They seemed a joyfully happy lot. Jonas's children did not live with him, rather they were with other family people in his home near Mumbwa, 250 miles away. I know he missed them, but that was the way of life and the price to pay to get decent paid work. It was much the same for the thousands of men who worked on the mines.

The road infrastructure inherited from the Federation provided metalled surface roads linking Livingstone and the Victoria Falls with Lusaka, which in turn was linked by a similar road to cover the 200 miles to the Copperbelt via Broken Hill and Kapiri Mposhi, where the Great North Road turned off to Dar es Salaam in Tanzania. That was also a largely metalled two-track highway which needed constant repair due to rain damage and the wear and tear of heavy vehicles.

The road to Chipata along which I had driven with Denis had tar surfaces, at least in part and had some impressive river bridges along the route. All the roads outside the towns, other than those linking the various mining settlements were made from laterite, a kind of red dirt, very dusty in the dry, whose construction was raised above the surrounding ground level of the surrounding bush. Storm ditches at least three feet deep ran each side of the road, just as I had observed on my first journey to Kitwe with Mike. These main dirt roads were maintained by government graders, powerful vehicles fitted below with sharp heavy blades to scrape and level the surface, set at an angle so that the resultant loose aggregate was pushed to the sides.

There were no dual carriageways outside the large conurbations, traffic passed in single file each way, which made overtaking a precarious gamble on occasions, given that dust and exhaust smoke limited one's field of vision. Road accidents were common occurrences. We passed wrecked cars and buses at the roadsides on every journey. It was vital to take great care behind the wheel. Indeed, we had lost two trucks in the north during February with one of our drivers and his mate losing their lives. I had travelled to Kasama to console the families and our local staff and to offer them a small amount of money, as much as I was permitted under standing orders.

I was glad not to have imported my beloved Sunbeam Tiger from home, its four inches of road clearance would have proven quite inadequate in Africa. My thoughts drifted back to the time news arrived from my father that he had sold the V8 powered speed machine to the lead singer of a pop group called "The Nashville Teens", at a considerable loss to the £800 I had paid for it a year ago. Nothing to be done and it was hardly fair that I left the old man the responsibility for my car which had taken up space whilst remaining in his driveway.

It was only in the July of the previous year when the letter arrived at home telling me that my work permit for Zambia had at last arrived. Booker's David Taylor had written to me at my parent's address in Burnham to deliver the confirmation I had been waiting for since January. I picked the letter up at home after driving the Sunbeam from Swindon. I had called in to get what I needed for the holiday I had already planned with my brother Adrian when I saw the letter. I resolved there and then not to respond to Bookers until after my return two weeks later, despite feeling cock-a-hoop that at last my exit was assured. In short order I packed and drove to London, where I spent the night at an awful basement squat in Kensington where Adrian lived, glad to leave at five in the morning for the drive to Glasgow.

Peter Brawley of Mustay Cottage fame had arranged our overnight stay in Motherwell at his father's high-rise flat overlooking the route of the Orangeman's parade through the town the next day. From the balcony seven stories above, Adrian and I watched the marchers below in the early morning, later reflecting on the irony of being in a household of Roman Catholics who treated the Presbyterian pipe bands celebrating King William's victory at the Boyne as a circus act to be cheered and enjoyed. I can now recall that years later I sat next to the Reverend Ian Paisley on a Sabena flight from Brussels some time before the Ulster *troubles* of the nineties. Mr Paisley was quite a charmer in private. The parade below us was long gone when we left for the drive to Mallaig, where we were to meet our parents for lunch.

We were not the first people to take the wrong turning north of Glasgow. As a result of that lapse in map-reading we paid the penalty by arriving two hours beyond our given ETA, much to my Father's chagrin. The moment was saved by my Mother, whose warm welcome overrode her husband's disappointment. We could stay in Mallaig with them for only two hours, long enough for me to announce the news of my work permit before we caught the ferry boat across to Skye to stay a night in the Cuilllins, the island's southern mountain range.

The roof cover came off in the morning sun and to let him try his hand at the wheel I passed the keys to Adrian. We were unable to travel at more than 30 mph on the rough roads which took us to the Macbrayne's Transport ferry boat terminal at Uig. By the time we arrived at the small harbour settlement of Lochmaddy on North Uist we needed a drink.

The gloomy building alongside the jetty housed a long solitary bar in a single room with a few tables and chairs on which sat a group of five or six locals, probably fishermen at rest or out of work. Our eyes were drawn to the century of plain glass whisky bottles whose liquid contents revealed many shades of gold, some light straw and others intense bronze depending upon the age of the spirit they contained. They were lined up on the shelf behind the bar, like a regiment awaiting inspection. The locals quickly identified us as ignorant foreigners or worse.

We spent a couple of carefree days on the Uist islands, North and South, which were connected by a causeway through the middle island Benbecula, finding a room in Lochboisdale where we enjoyed the best cup of tea I have ever tasted. The shallow soil on those islands can only support heather and brush, there are no trees. All locally sourced wood used to build the crofters' homes in past centuries was tropical driftwood from the Caribbean, carried by the Gulf Stream until landfall on the white sandy beaches of the west Hebridean coast. On the east side of the islands we found sea and rainwater lochs, alive with fish and sea mammals, and precious few humans. The outline of Skye loomed into view across the calm water to the east, indistinct and grey, the raucous screeching of gulls appeared to declare their ownership of the enormous sky above.

My shiny black Tiger took us further on our journey through the Kyle of Lochalsh by a different ferry route, then up the west coast to Ullapool before crossing to the Black Isle on the Moray Firth north of Inverness, where my friends John and Dilly, late of the Swan at Tockington, welcomed the two of us to the house they shared with their cousins in Fortrose. The MacEwan clan were great hosts, generously taking us salmon fishing on one of the inland Highland rivers, where, to my utter delight, I landed my first catch. Better still, the not so large fish was cut into steaks only moments after its demise at my hands, then placed in a pan of butter atop a wood fire with a squeeze of lemon and a sprig of parsley to be washed down by whisky and water from the fast-moving peaty river. Such a delicious meal consumed in a Highland idyll could never be forgotten. It was the last occasion I would see John and his wife, who both died within two years. Dilly, who had admitted to herself and to me that she was a victim of alcoholism, had taken the pledge all too late in her otherwise adventurous life. I learned about Dilly's death in a letter from her husband which had arrived on the morning Brendan and I flew to Mombasa.

The flight had called in at Zanzibar and Dar es Salaam, where I first felt the impact of the hot humid air of the Indian Ocean. Our shirts were wringing wet before we stepped off the bottom rung of the portable stairs which had been shoved alongside our *Fokker Friendship* aircraft, its distinctive overhead wings cast a welcome shade. We had booked the *Nyali Beach Hotel* on the north shore, easily the best hotel I had ever stayed in my limited travels to that date. The whitewashed walls of the main building as well as those surrounding the adjacent swimming pool and bedroom blocks were covered in purple bougainvillea. The gardens leading down to the beach were laid to lawn and the deep flowerbeds stocked with plants of intensely bright colours. I did not appreciate the festival of colour until the next morning, since the sun had disappeared by the time we had checked in to our twin-bedded room and the hot tropical night had taken over.

Desperate to get a dip in the ocean, we raced into the sea, diving headlong into water which was over one hundred degrees Fahrenheit (38C). Ignorant of what lay below the surface inside the coral reef I kicked into a spikey sea urchin and was rewarded with a fragile crumbly black shaft of pain under the nail of my big toe and in the sole of my other foot. Ouch and ouch again! Hobbling back to the hotel a guest took me aside and suggested a squeeze of lemon juice would dissolve the stony substances injected into my feet. I learned later that urine was an even better solution, but on this occasion, I took the lemon from two long gins and tonic water at the pool bar.

We had not eaten since buying bananas from a stall vendor in the transit hall in Zanzibar, so we both relished the buffet dinner offered to us in the hotel dining room. I piled the cold food to my plate, digging into the attractive bowls of different salads and seafood. Little did I realise that the tiny shredded green peppers were only distant relatives to the anaemic capsicum of my mother's kitchen garden and after taking an injudicious mouthful I lurched for the water jug, but there was no relief from the gasping heat which consumed my whole being. I could only run to the sanctuary of our room and a ready toilet, laughter from my companion receding as I fled. A good hour elapsed before I could re-join my unsympathetic chum who, by the time I found him again was in conservational cups with two middle aged fellow guests.

Ken and John were from Leeds in Yorkshire, Ken a brewer and John a chartered accountant, they were taking a sabbatical from their wives as they did for one week every year without fail, so they said. Revenge was not long delayed. Brendan had helped himself to a ladle full of beef and oyster goulash, unwittingly ignoring his allergy for the fruit of the ocean, my favourite shellfish. It was not long after we turned in that I was awakened by the clamour of my roommate throwing up in his attempt to redecorate the bathroom. When he had finished, a major mopping up exercise ensued completed by deodorising and masking the smell of colourful vomit by sprinkling his *Tabac* brand talc and aftershave into all corners. I am for ever reminded of that night by any whiff of a smell resembling *Tabac* but could not resist the temptation to present my chum with a further supply the following Christmas as a means of jogging his memory.

In later conversation we learned that John Fullerton had been at one time the youngest ever Chartered Accountant in England due to spending the year in study at Mount Lavinia whilst a patient at Lord Mountbatten's hospital in Ceylon. It had been set up for troops surviving the Japanese camps in Southeast Asia. John had been sent to Burma on his seventeenth birthday and had been captured three weeks after joining his unit along the coast south of Rangoon, before rescue came seven further months later, by when he weighed just over four stones. The Attlee Government did not want the British public to see the emaciated bodies of the survivors, some would say understandably, so hospital camps were set up in the sub-continent to nurse the men back to a semblance of their former selves. On his release he took articles with a firm in Huddersfield, his hometown, making a success of his career thereafter. He reckoned WWII had a silver lining for him, and I took to his positive take on life, so much so that the four of us agreed to share a car to drive up the coast to Malindi, a centre for big game fishing.

One day later in the week before our trip north, we had been on the beach, this time wearing plimsoles (simple trainers) and had waded over to a dug-out single sail boat whose owner, a local fisherman, beckoned us join him and the two pretty blonde German girls he had already ensnared into his custom. We needed little persuasion and took the bait, glad we did because it was a thrill to sail over the reef at high tide, taking care to keep to channels between the sharp coral growth. We were still in high spirits when we returned to Nyali Beach and stood drinks for the girls at the pool bar. Now it happened that a Royal Navy warship was visiting the UK base in Mombasa, and a bunch of ratings out of uniform on short shore leave came to spend an afternoon of fun in the hotel pool, trying their luck with anything young and female, including our lovely new friends from Hamburg. When they approached their prey I donned my best officer's stance, adopted from experience at Pirbright when on an Army Cadet Corps camp a decade earlier, and ordered the sailors to back off; at which point, and to the eternal delight of McShane sitting at the bar beside me, a rating declared "c'mon lads, no point in competing with these rich smoothies". Well, rich no, but smooth for sure, and so the soubriquet was adopted for ever and a day by the pair of us.

That evening we experienced the rigours of an east coast shebeen, perhaps it was the *Sunshine Day and Night Club.* I could not swear that was the time when we visited a night spot of that name in Africa, but it is of little account what the name of the place was, only that it had another purpose and we Westerners, with plenty of East African Shilling notes in our pockets, were fair game. Thank goodness Ken pulled us out before amorous hostilities commenced, suggesting a safer spot to drink might be the hotel bar.

If you visit Mombasa you can never forget the giant elephant tusks spanning the main drag past Fort Jesus along the Mombasa River, not too far from the New Nyali Bridge which separated the Old Town from the tourist residences, and which closed at night. To those who ask whether the tusks, height about 30 feet, are real I must put on a doleful expression to explain they are in fact made from plate metal. Bang them hard to get a hollow clang to become yet another fool in the eyes of all the vendors around you, selling their trinkets and masks as well as strange goods crafted by local Kenyan artisans of more reliable provenance.

The car journey up the coast took over three hours although it was only 80 miles, taking us through dense forest and thick undergrowth, lined by palm trees and decked with creepers and other parasitic vegetation. We were only some seven miles short of our intended destination when we spied a wooden signpost to Gedi, barely visible and part hidden by a leafy creeper. Here were the ruins of a fifteenth century Portuguese settlement which had been unearthed from a hiding place beneath the jungle growth. British archaeologists had been excited to find reminders of the voyages of discovery and evidence of trade by the ships and men from Lisbon, along with the massive fortifications they had taken so much trouble to build. Those are found all along the coast, Mombasa's Fort Jesus being one we had seen for ourselves. That the Portuguese should build a permanent town suggested to me that there must have been important business to be watched over. What, I wondered, were they buying or selling? There were no nearby sources of precious metals nor was there evidence of any crops or other natural resources worth building a base for, so I came to my own conclusion that Gedi (now Gede) was another staging post in the huge east African and Arab slave trade in the fifteenth century.

6

Quatre-Quatre

(Late 1970)

After a week crammed with events on the coast of Kenya, I threw myself back into a life of hard work and hard play on the Copperbelt. I began learning to play bridge under the tutelage of Jim Crawford and his wife Nan. Jim was a slightly built chap who had first ventured out to Africa after being demobbed from the Forces. I first found him strutting around one of the Company's warehouses blinking rapidly as he glanced left and right, with his reading glasses hung by a cord around his neck. Jim and Nan had represented their adopted country at Bridge competitions around the Commonwealth. Jim was razor sharp at cards, if not in his office, where he grappled with the legacy of change.

The Coppersmiths Arms was the most favoured drinking hole after work, located not far away at the end of dusty Second Street. The pub was reached inside through an arbour and a courtyard, its bar service conducted by waiters dressed in white jackets worn with a broad crimson sash and toggle and a dark red fez as headgear. It had bench seating outside and along one side of the area was a covered restaurant, rarely patronised.

Measured in terms of time in the territory and not seniority in the office, I was a new boy having to earn my spurs in the eyes of the old timer soaks such as Norrie Gregg, a rotund bald headed former Scottish naval rating who had broken the unwritten social order through his marriage to a pretty African lady. He was usually found in the company of Chick Beveridge, also a buyer and a fellow Scot with firm and sometimes loud opinions on just about everything. Chick missed his forte in life, he should have been head of the TUC. I have met many barrack-room lawyers in my life, but none measured up to Chick when it came to raw verbal aggression.

John Mwanakatwe was the Minister of Finance in Kaunda's Cabinet and the only Zambian at the time of Independence who had a university degree from Witwatersrand. One of his distant relatives had come to us from college in Lusaka, we shall call him Gerry, to be trained by our team at ZNWC. Gerry was a very quick leaner and a likeable fellow and unmarried. When I had to make further changes to the management at Solwezi, I sent Gerry there for three months to hold the fort as a reliable and safe pair of hands.

The domestic postal service in Zambia was good, so it was only at times of urgency that we used the telephone to connect with branches other than the scheduled morning call to receive the trading figures. When the telephone rang on my desk, I recognised Gerry's voice and asked him to explain why he was calling me; the young man's normal calm voice spluttered incoherently until I managed to calm him down and get his story. He was convinced that he was under a spell and had to come back to Ndola. Indeed, he begged me. I refused him with admonishment, suggesting the power of witch doctors or whatever was old fashioned tribal poppycock and he had better get a hold on himself. To my eternal sadness and shame, the next I heard from the branch was that Gerry had been found dead.

The subsequent police investigation revealed no sign of violence, and the coroner's report suggested there was nothing amiss with Gerry's health. Make of it what you may, I found it spooky, let alone tragic, and felt wholly responsible at the time. Luckily over the next few weeks Denis Sakalla persuaded me to drop any self-blame expounding his pet theory that if a man believed in bad *ju-ju* he would be a willing victim. I never did understand how a man with a background and family like Gerry's could succumb to a belief in hostile spells, I only knew that I had sent a man into an area where outsiders were not welcome. I did learn at the time I got the police report that Gerry had fired a locally recruited salesman who could not explain a cash shortage.

One Sunday I went riding at stables not far out of Ndola with three friends, including Brendan who stayed over from Kitwe. I am not an experienced horseman but was assured by the stable's owner that I would be saddled with a gentle nag. As it turned out, not a bit of it. I was allocated *Blackjack*, a skittish stallion recovering from a foreleg injury, but all went well as our little posse was led by the stable boys to the gate at the edge of the compound to start our trek through the bush.

Just as we approached the gate my man handed me a switch of short tree cuttings neatly tied together like a witch's broom. He passed the handy weapon up to me in front of the horse's line of sight. My *Blackjack*, who was sadly not blind, reared up, did a quick full about twist and headed back to the stable block at a full gallop, with me clinging on for dear life. I stayed aboard until the hack put on the brakes, at which point I continued in the direction of the stable door with the horse behind me, achieving a double somersault in the process before landing on my coccyx. You got it, "ouch and ouch again" I cried or words to that effect. Then nothing, I had no feeling from the waist down.

"Get me to the hospital fast", or something like that I moaned to the other chaps who had abandoned the ride, showing some rare concern for me. On the way to the hospital we made a pit stop at the Coppersmiths, believing me to be thirsty, and in any event a cold *Castle* lager had anaesthetic properties, so one in our party alleged. It was the strangest thing that having been carried into the arbour, when it came to move on for medical attention I simply got up and walked to the car. The heavenly intervention I had cried for at the point of my landing was evidently forthcoming, it seemed I had experienced a miraculous recovery.

There was a Salvation Army captain called Bill Gold, who together with David Elliott, the Anglican Dean at Ndola's Holy Nativity Cathedral, and the Catholic Monseigneur Benedict, was a main player at the Ndola Theatre Club which I had joined as a liquid supporter in my quest to widen my social outreach. Bill was a short red faced and energetic sort with a fine tenor voice, as I recall, in contrast to the tall Dean and the popish figure of Father Benedict. That year those three ecclesiastical thespians put on their version of "My fair lady", the musical.

All agreed the show was a hit and a catalyst to many long-lasting friendships established among the cast, many of whom were from David's congregation and choir at Holy Nativity.

Before ordination David had played piano in more than one Soho jazz band. The man had a colourful earlier life. He was certainly an encouragement to me to become more involved in the congregation at Holy Trinity. I began to focus on my faith once more.

The Copperbelt towns are situated about twelve degrees south of the Equator. The seven months of dry season began in April, which heralded the start of the cricket season. Ndola boasted two clubs, Ndola CC, to which I belonged and the Orientals CC, largely if not wholly made up of Asian players. Every one of the Copperbelt towns had at least one club. The season started with a twenty overs league, the matches required each player from opposing teams, other than the wicket keepers, to bowl two eight-ball overs. The fixtures were played after work between 4.00 pm and sundown at 6.15pm, and were a warm-up for the season proper, when the clubs entered teams to compete in the separate Saturday and Sunday Leagues. Being single I often played on both days.

Having dabbled at Minor Counties level in England I came to respect the high standard of play achieved in the Copperbelt leagues. The high veld altitude enabled the batsman to see the ball very clearly, even when wearing spectacles, as I always did. I could pick out the seam on delivery in the bowler's hand. The games revealed some fine characters. One I remember well, a South African named Basil Karg. Basil had a mutton chop moustache and had suffered from polio as a child, whereby he played with one foot confined in a solid high heeled boot. He was a demon spinner, leg breaks and china-men, and a formidable slogger with the bat. He and I shared century partnerships on two occasions, I never contributed more than twenty to the total. The problem was, of course, that Basil, who used a runner, was never worn out running between wickets.

The cricket ground bordered the main Kwacha Road which ran from the airport to the intersection with the Copperbelt Highway on the west side of the city. The surrounding trees were yellow flowering acacias, themselves covered with climbing bougainvillaea whose varied shades of white, orange, pink and purple provided a backdrop of vivid colour when viewed from the cricket square or the pavilion opposite.

We had fun with club and representative matches against touring sides from abroad, ready to offer hospitality to visitors needing a bed and dig into the back pocket at the bar. Some evenings I would play tennis, teaming up at mixed doubles with Bunny Mackintosh, who ran a local travel agency. Bunny shared my love of the *zigeuner* violin as exploited by Mendelssohn and Bruch, for example, and had a fine collection of long play records, something I had not bothered with since arriving in Africa. It was through one of Bunny's tennis pals that I joined the squash club.

Work continued to be interesting and frantic. The recruitment of staff and training became my main preoccupation, although we had to prepare for an upcoming buying trip to Red China which would be undertaken by Bert Craig. The Peking (now Beijing) Government provided Zambia and Tanzania with credit to buy goods in China worth many millions of US Dollars each year, which would then be offset against the local costs incurred by the Chinese engineers and workers who were starting to build the new Uhuru Railway (the one the British rightly said would cave in because of rains and termites).

The Chinese set up camps along the route, where local villagers had their first glimpse of the oriental workers. There was a strict control over the workers' movements, exercised by Communist Party team representatives who were themselves supported by government appointed translators, the latter were always alongside any group moving away from the designated work areas. From time to time I would bump into groups of four Chinese on their purchasing missions to our branches in Mansa and Kasama.

There was always a purchasing officer who doubled as the money man carrying wads of local Kwacha notes, his three companions always a Party Commissar, a translator, and the pick-up driver. The branch staff found them pleasant enough and honest with money, but there was to be no official fraternisation with the locals. In any event, there was only one man, the interpreter, with whom they could talk English.

Chairman Mao's Little Red Books notwithstanding, boys will be boys, presumably the inscrutable Orientals being no exception to the general rule that boys need girls, and the only ones available were those in the Zambian villages. Inevitably, in the language of the day, the outcome of illicit inter-continental couplings became known as Chinese *kusakaniza*, although that was all mischievous hearsay as I had no first-hand evidence to go on.

On my return to Ndola from a trip to the bush I was called in to see Mr Lafferty who gave me the news that Jim Whelan was on the mend from major heart surgery and likely to be well enough to resume duties later in the year. Whilst I feigned my delight at such an outcome, I felt more than a little cheesed off, believing that the progress I had achieved as a stand-in would have impressed the Board to the extent that I would take over from Jim permanently. Now the man who I had never met, but who I felt I knew intimately, was to come back and reap the reward of my labours. Well, what the heck, I thought, recalling my Father's assertions that life is never fair.

I had little appetite for returning to my job in Kitwe, despite liking that town and indeed the staff. As it happened, we had a poker school that evening, the usual gang with a new arrival called Peter MacManus. Peter was one of about eight consultants sent out by city accountancy firms such as Coopers and Lybrand, Price Waterhouse, and others to help sort out the prevailing mess in the central warehousing and distribution systems supporting the retail divisions.

I had volunteered to take Peter in as a paying guest, finding the monthly rent a handy contribution to my housekeeping cash pool, and invited him into the card school after some heavy vetting by Steve Smith, Westy, Maurice and Brendan, the latter licking his lips at the prospect of a fall guy at the card table. But Peter, having first found his feet from some losing hands proved otherwise. We gladly welcomed him as a more permanent member of the school. Before we cashed up our chips, three of us agreed to cash in our outstanding local leave on a holiday in Mauritius, which I was charged to arrange through Bunny.

Not long after Peter's first card evening with us I found myself winning a big hand of brag (about one hundred Kwacha) against Steve, who had not long moved to Ndola from the smaller mining community of Mufulira, along with his then pregnant wife Rita. It was a pretty well known fact that in the Smith household the lovely Rita wore the trousers, so when I agreed to exchange Steve's IOU for a six feet long counter bar he had in his house, arrangements had to be made for the collection to take place at a time when Rita was not at home. I never did find out how Steve explained away the absence of a prized piece of furniture, worse still was the legacy it left, namely that Rita could never be invited to any event I held at the house in Kenmere Avenue lest she might spot her bar in the corner of my living room.

With Jim Whelan returning to reclaim his job I made speedy arrangements for our local break, flying out to Mauritius with Westy and Brendan on the Zambia Airways BAC1-11 service from Lusaka via Madagascar. We were quickly settled into the Morne Brabant Hotel beside an idyllic tropical shore, with a full two weeks to discover the island and have fun.

In later life I have often been asked to name my most favourite place on God's Earth. One of the strongest candidates must be the enclosed sea lagoon near the mouth of La Riviere Noire on the island's west coast. There you can walk out for a couple of hundred yards or more on the white sand devoid of pebbles, spotting colourful fish darting between your legs as you move through crystal clear warm waters. Inland and behind you can see the distant dark mountains which make up the central massif, on whose slopes grow sugar cane or at higher levels, tea.

Along the coast the fresh water, which is used to irrigate the plantations, trickled down through the cane fields until it gathered in pools formed under the raised level of the coastal road, and there you found giant fresh water prawns, a local speciality, they could be cooked in chilies. They have a distinct sweetness taken from the sugar cane. Absolutely delicious!

Another delight of the table was the freshly poached tuna prepared for us and the other guests by the hotel's chef, to whom we had gifted a metre-long specimen caught that morning on a game fishing trip. We had set to sea, passing through the coral reef in a boat loaded with fishing gismos, hoping to find sailfish and blue marlin in the open ocean beyond. Meeting the swell head on, the symptoms of *mal de mer* on a hangover took total charge of me and my body. I spent a large part of the eight hours at sea feeling sorry for myself, to the amusement of my fellow fishermen who were occupied opening beer cans when not tending their rods. Coming to, and ultimately refreshed on my very newly found sea legs, I spotted dorsal fins following us. We were being trailed by sharks who were unashamedly feasting on our bait, far too canny to bight. The tuna was our sole catch, but at least there was something to show for the travails undergone.

There were plenty of events in our African social life which provided the opportunity to don evening dress, indeed demanded that such attire be worn. I had bought a sky-blue tuxedo in Kitwe when my dear friend Sam Kelly hosted a preview to his closing down sale. I had the appropriate dress on hand for a night with the boys at the casino in Curepipe. Arriving mid evening in our hire car we were fully unprepared for the sight inside the casino which we beheld with delight. There were no croupiers, only croupettes, an array of the most beautiful young women from all continents who worked on the gambling tables. The three of us looked at each other, eyebrows raised, the faintest of smiles reflecting fun to come.

Taking our dry Martinis, unstirred, to the blackjack and roulette tables we proceeded to offload our stakes, although I do recall Westy enjoying a big win on a roulette number. What brought us away from the seductive smiles of those gorgeous chip grabbers was the commotion coming from one corner of the main gaming hall, where a door provided entry to another, smaller space, in which a large crowd of ethnic Chinese men were clapping hands, shouting, and banging their fists on the gambling table they surrounded.

Now Mauritius was home to many races of folk who had followed the French and British colonisers, so the population was a mix of peoples stemming from China and India, who had worked originally in the tea and sugar plantations, Europeans and Africans and every combination of all of the above. Whilst some of their pretty daughters worked at the casino, the Chinese, who could never resist a good gamble, occupied the noisy forum in which the mysterious game of *quatre-quatre* was being played.

The game involved four four-sided lozenge shaped dice, each face bearing an ace, a king, a queen or a knave, the punters being paid out for successfully backing the landing face after the dice had been flung onto the high-sided green baize table, for example a ten rupees chip on the king would pay out forty "rupes" if there were three kings, returning the original stake plus winnings. I have never seen what was most surely the loudest of betting games anywhere else on my travels, nor have I been able to buy the dice, so I assume it to be an exclusive Mauritian pastime. It was, as it happened, the one game our trio of would be James Bonds made a profit on, to the chagrin of our new-found oriental companions.

There were a couple of German chaps staying at our hotel, so I was able to speak in their tongue and challenge them to a game of *skat*[9] which I had learned to play on my many visits to Lo Siegert's family in Geisenhem in my Frankfurt days. The contest was played out on the beach with cards borrowed from one of the hotel waiters. In the audience were Brendan and Westy, my companions, and a guy called Pete from Durban, who we had met on our first day when we spotted him riding

---

9. Skat is the national card game of Germany for three players taking tricks from a reduced pack from aces down to sevens.

a giant tortoise three or four times his age. I won the *skat* and could not resist writing a post card to Lo's mother Lieselotte, thanking her for all her training, which must have amused her greatly as she never failed to mention it every time we spoke on the telephone in later life.

My winning streak did not, however, follow me on the golf course at the Morne, where I was taken to the cleaners by my companions. Whilst recounting his exploits on the ninth green to our German friends during dinner on the final night of our stay, Westy became so absorbed in his story that he failed to notice the bottle of ketchup he was vigorously shaking had lost its lid. I sat silently spellbound opposite him, watching a rainstorm of bright red goo land on the diners behind him occupying the four window tables, trying desperately to contain myself lest the entertainment should stop before the sauce bottle was empty. I think we were still laughing about it when we finally arrived back in Zambia.

7

Versailles

(1970 – 71)

My second tropical Christmas was spent in Lusaka as a guest of John and Mary Carver and their daughter Jane at their company house in Ridgeway. The Carvers were close friends of Diana and Wilfred Homer, our neighbours at home in Burnham. Mary and Diana had been school friends. John managed the *Steel Company of Zambia*, producers of corrugated roofing widely used in local house building.

I had been working with Bert Craig, our buyer, at John's office in Lusaka on a new project to distribute the corrugated sheeting through our warehouse network at ZNWC. Some quite big sums of money would be involved in any such deal, so Bert was keen to have my support. John discovered that we had mutual friends and later, as we were leaving, invited me to join the family for Christmas.

It transpired that the Carvers had been stationed in India for the past fifteen years where John had been in engineering. Mary had years of experience in the craft of expatriate hospitality and had organised a traditional Christmas, much of the essential kit had been brought out by Jane from London, where she lived and studied at one of the secretarial colleges in Kensington. She had a boyfriend, she said, in London, so put the dampeners on any moves from me. I resolved to ignore her defences and have some fun. When it came to say goodbye, I found my hands held tight and we both looked at each other through tears. It was during my stay that I learned to play a vicious form of whist they called *"oh hell"*, a card game which was to travel with me and be enjoyed for fun and wager.

We had been cocooned inside a sprawling bungalow safe from the incessant rains which thrashed down on us relentlessly for two days, adequately stocked up with all we needed, quite a change from last year's slow cooked pig.

Beyond the spacious plots and residences of the Ridgeway district lay a series of townships, none as big as they were on the Copperbelt, but spread over a large conurbation of some 250,000 people making up the city of Lusaka. The main drag is called Cairo Road, which runs from the Freedom Memorial on the roundabout on the southern edge of the city in a direct northerly direction, effectively bisecting the Capital City. As the road leaves the central area it passes a large trading estate on its way to the Copperbelt. Several tens of thousands of workers are employed on the estate, which is probably the largest light industrial centre of its kind in Zambia.

The road is so named in line with Cecil Rhodes' dream of building a route from the Mediterranean to the Cape. Cairo Road is an avenue of two lanes each way, divided from each other by a central tree-lined reservation, where vendors of all kinds gather to hawk their wares, be they tourist items of Africana such as masks and carved bowls, or more essential goods competing with the larger stores and specialty shops. Our wholesale warehouse was in a road running parallel to Cairo Road to the west, and the ZCBC department store stood in the prime spot midway between the commercial limits of the city.

On several occasions when I visited the Capital I stayed overnight with Alan and Pat Marples, who lived not far from the newly built Intercontinental Hotel, pride of Lusaka, which was handy for the twenty minute drive out of the city to the airport, although I would typically make the 200 miles journey by car, as I had done that Christmas.

Alan had worked previously with Lewis's, my old firm, and came from Manchester. His boss was an ex Marks and Spencer manager called Ray Broad, a pleasant enough fellow, but generally acknowledged to be poorly suited to his job as store General Manager. Mike Delaney must have sensed the same thing, as Ray was eventually moved to a senior position in retail buying at head office, a position I was eventually to take over, but much had to take place over the next four years before that happened.

Having missed the Christmas services at the cathedral, I resolved to attend the morning communion that Sunday, where I now had a few acquaintances, not least Chris Chapman, who worked for the Company as its buying manager, and his wife Denise, both ten years older than me although dear Chris, looking every bit an Alfred Hitchcock doppelganger, gave the impression he was close to retirement. He was soon moved by Wally Lewis to manage the menswear factory Bookers owned in Kitwe.

The expatriate community was still quite large, I estimated that the cathedral congregation probably comprised equal numbers of British and Zambian worshippers. The cathedral was really the only place of worship used by Anglicans (there were separate Roman Catholic and Methodist churches) and many chapels, churches and religious meeting places spread around the townships. I believe there was a mosque in Lusaka, and certainly one in Chipata, close to Malawi which hosted a minority of Muslims in an otherwise population of Christians and animists.

After the Sunday service I met Maurice Renwick who worked for Barclays Bank. Maurice was a softly spoken Scot in his mid-forties; he invited me to join the Lions, a service club like Rotary and Round Table. I attended the Club's next meeting as a guest not many days later and became a Member. I bought two tickets for the forthcoming annual Lions' Burns Night dinner at great expense, knowing I had a lady in mind to be my partner.

Those dinners were quite something, black-tie and ball gowns, usually held at one of the sports clubs where the Lions met at least once a month. The *Burns Suppers* were sponsored in part by British Caledonian Airways, who flew out copious quantities of haggis with the traditional accompaniment of 'neaps and tatties, not forgetting the Arbroath smokies for starters, and better still, the airline gifted a couple of gallons of Scotch whisky with bags of rolled oats and jars of honey so that the boys in the Lions could make Athol Brose, one of life's great pleasures. The *"Brose"* made the task of celebrating the great Ayrshire farmer thoroughly worthwhile. The local *"B-Cal"* station manager was also a Lion, as indeed were many of the leading commercial and professional men around our area who became my new friends.

Maria, a pretty dark-haired girl from a Greek family who I

had met in the showroom where she worked when buying two new trucks from Northern Motors, had agreed to partner me to the dinner and proved a big hit with the boys despite the killer looks from their ladies. I stood little chance with Maria if I valued my life, as I did, and realised I had to act quickly if I wanted another date before Tony, her Greek boyfriend, returned from Athens

The following Sunday Jonas packed my car with a hamper of food and cold beer. I set off to collect the lovely Maria for a bush picnic at a quiet secluded spot I had found alongside a dambo not far from the Dag Hammarskjold memorial. A dambo is a large shallow pool of collected rainwater, sometimes the dambos grew into lakes. All went well with a successful meal after which I managed a couple of sweet kisses before urging us both to strip for a swim. Maria sensibly declined, but muggins me donned trunks and took a running dive, leaping into the dark placid water, a big mistake. The water was only six inches deep. Bedraggled and humiliated, I emerged, covered in black mud from top to toe, and worse still, not only did I look the fool I was, but the mud had penetrated my ears and I could hardly hear. Suffice to say, the homeward journey was largely silent, and Tony the Greek was never aware he had a rival. It took at least four years before cotton buds could no longer fish out specks of mud from the inner passages of my head handles.

Excursions into the bush for picnics or camping became a regular part of life, on occasions we would go out to somewhere along the banks of the Kafue river, which bypassed Kitwe rising or falling as much as twenty feet in a day during the rains. I liked it best in the dry season, there was generally enough of a flow of water to avoid still water pools. Those placid backwaters could provide breeding grounds for a type of freshwater snail which spawned a parasitic worm. If that worm got into the body, which it did, it caused schistosomiasis, better known as bilharzia, which is not nice. The river made an exciting swim or more particularly the opportunity to body surf over the smooth rocky rapids but making certain where the escape routes lay to avoid any watery denizens waiting in the wings.

In addition to weekend cricket I sometimes played squash at a court built by a farmer on the banks of the river, a short drive from Kitwe. The court building had to be accessed, with difficulty, by a wire-rope bridge stretching a hundred and fifty feet over the water. The "bridge" comprised one strand of rope for the feet, and two higher ones as handrails. Below, curious hippos looked up from their mud baths at people crossing, so it was a bad idea to miss your footing whilst carrying squash rackets and gear, including the obligatory white soled tackies (plimsoles). The reward for making the journey was a well-stocked bar with an honesty box, taking care to remember that there was a return trip over the perilous "bridge" to follow any refreshments before getting back into the parked car.

In early February 1971 I received the exciting news that my parents would be visiting me for a stay of three weeks or more in March. Before that I had to make a second trip to Livingstone, where I stayed overnight in the new Intercontinental *Hotel Mosi-o-tunya*, Chitonga words for the Victoria Falls, aptly describing them as "the smoke that thunders". It was there that I met two couples from the USA, who, it transpired, came from the state of Kentucky where my younger brother Adrian lived. He had stayed on in The States after studying at the University of Kentucky in Lexington. Fresh in my mind was a recent letter from my brother in which he gave me his new address in a town called Versailles, which I related to my newfound

American friends whose first responses were querulous blank faces. "Oh!", declared one "You must mean Ver-sales". It was a lesson well learned that to communicate you really need to adapt your speech to the ear of the listener, such is diversity in the Anglosphere.

That trip I met some Canadian schoolteachers who had been seconded to a secondary school in Livingstone. I learned that the Canadian Government, very sensibly in my view, recognised that they could not provide foreign aid to all corners of the globe, rather they supported and funded education and civil projects in the Commonwealth countries of central and east Africa, and throughout the Caribbean islands. That was not to exclude emergencies wherever they occurred, one of the older men assured me. He went on to say that their Government covered their local living costs and continued to pay their salaries at the rate they would be earning at home. It gave teachers of all ages and experience a great opportunity to broaden their outlooks. How very sensible, I could not help thinking, we should be doing the same, on a larger scale but concentrating our resources and manpower on the Commonwealth.

On my return I learned that Jim and Caroline Whelan were on their way back, and that I was to be assigned to the Group's retail distribution division to support Jimmy Crawford, my erstwhile Bridge teacher, with the specific task of commissioning a new central warehouse of some 100,000 sq. ft. already under construction, the largest of its kind then in Africa north of the Limpopo.

First off, I spent three weeks helping Peter McManus and his fellow consultants to sort out the unmitigated mess caused by huge volumes of freight and stock spread around at least seven temporary buildings and goods sheds mainly undocumented, the legacy of times before ZCBC was incorporated in 1968. The construction of the new distribution centre, or DC as it became known, was within the brand new *Copperbelt Showgrounds*, not far beyond the city limits of Ndola.

At that time the Showgrounds, a centre for trade fairs and for staging all sorts of events and sports, had been officially opened by Julius Nyerere, President of Tanzania, a State Occasion which several of us attended and were presented to the famous man. The building was well advanced and so I set up an office on site to start one of the most rewarding phases of my working life. My job was to liaise with the architect, set up systems, procure all the fixtures and fittings, set about staff recruitment and training and much more besides, including arranging a railway siding, the latter task requiring me to negotiate with the Central African Railways Authority, a left over from the days of Federation, which was based at Bulawayo in Matabeleland, Rhodesia. The Rhodesians, I soon discovered, showed little love for those of us living north of the Zambesi in Zambia.

The war in Rhodesia had become intense, the forces of Ian Smith's rebel regime were fully engaged fighting three "freedom movements" simultaneously, namely the Zimbabwe African People's Union (ZAPU), led by Kaunda's close friend, the Ndebele speaking Joshua Nkomo. Nkomo was a huge man from Matabeleland. The other movements were the Zimbabwe African National Union (ZANU) led by the Shona speaking Ndabaningi Sithole who was later deposed by Robert Mugabe and The Patriotic Front (PF), led by Bishop Canaan Banana. The latter brokered a deal between the rivals to combine, becoming ZANU-PF (Patriotic Front). They did not know it at the time, but it was to be another eight years before one of them took over the new country, and only after a certain Margaret Hilda Thatcher intervened in 1979. Suffice to say, I had to deal with the officers of Smith's Rhodesia Front government in my quest for tracks and permits to link up our yet to be built siding within the national rail network.

Jim Crawford and I had supported the firm's offer to Peter McManus for him to stay on at the end of the consultancy period, effectively to be seconded from Price Waterhouse to ZCBC. Peter did the hard work of proposing systems for the control of goods passing through the DC. We had decided to use electric fork-lift trucks from the UK to service the high level Dexion pallet storage, Peter devising a random placement system for our more than 4,000 pallet bays above the ground level picking shelves, which was so clever I thought he should copyright it. Everything we achieved in the set up and the commissioning of that warehouse operation broke new ground in Africa at the time.

By now Peter had moved into a flat provided by the Company, which was just as well, as my parents were about to arrive from Britain. At home I think Jonas was getting worried about having to be tested in his rule over my kitchen, given the impending arrival of an *umfasi*[10] in the form of my mother, and was relieved to know that I wanted her to have a complete holiday from anything domestic, so he was to stay in charge and not let me down. As it turned out he did a wonderful job, and for a lot of the time on their visit we were travelling away or on the receiving end of generous hospitality from the many people who had become my friends and colleagues.

---

10. Umfasi, meaning a woman

When the big day arrived, I flew down to Lusaka to meet them at the main International Airport. I cannot describe how thrilled I was to see them both, Dad now in his mid-sixties, Mother ten years younger and not a grey hair on top. She never once used colouring. I was proud of my Dad. He had been a fine athlete. On leaving school he had taken up an apprenticeship with a city textile firm he worked for all his life, wartime service in the Royal Navy apart, becoming Managing Director and eventually seeing to its floatation on the London Stock Exchange.

His own father had chosen to walk away from his family when he was just twenty-one, leaving his mother destitute as the country was hit by the Great Depression. It fell to Alan to support the family. Mira his mother and my grandmother, took in laundry and worked as a part time physiotherapist, barely making ends meet. Mira died, broken in heart and body in 1935. My paternal grandfather made no further connection with Dad, who sarcastically commented that he was a "nice chap", a coded epithet he was to award anyone who did not match that description. Dad never spoke to us of his father, who died in 1945, rather he directed his paternal admiration to his Uncle Harry, who had migrated to Brisbane and had later fought with distinction at Gallipoli and in France with the ANZAC forces in the Great War.

When I was nine the family left our London home for a brand-new house near Burnham Beeches, built to our parents' order. It was a wrench for John and me to leave our school in Ealing, the very excellent Durston House, John to go boarding in Hertfordshire and me to Farnham Common near Slough.

Behind the big oak tree at the bottom of our garden, the place where the fairies frolic, was an adjoining property owned by Walter Robins who had been cricket captain of Middlesex and England. He and his son Charles encouraged many of us local boys to learn the finer points of the great game. It was Mr Robins who proposed that I join the MCC at Lord's Cricket Ground. Our garden provided ample play space for the family of four boys which now included my two younger brothers. At weekends and during school holidays we took turns to help Harry, our ageing gardener, with his various chores and cutting the grass. It was a fair trade off for having the gift of space to run wild in and play games, the work experience taught me much about caring for my own properties in later life.

The family had not been at South Ley for a year when on the first of June, 1953 our Grandpa arrived unannounced with the gift of a flagpole which he put up on the front of our new house in readiness for the young Queen's coronation the following day. A month later we got news of his death from a heart attack, he was only 64. He was returning by bus with his wife from an event in Newbury, to where they had moved a couple of years earlier. The story goes that Grandma took a break in her one-way conversation expecting her husband to respond, but when there was no reply, she turned to see her husband sitting serenely still, smiling and quite dead. The bus had stopped right outside the General Hospital, too late to be of any help.

After years of growth Dad's firm became a takeover target for Courtaulds. He fought and lost, but at least got a better price for the shareholders. As is the nature of such things, he later paid the price of taking on Courtaulds chairman Sir Frank Kearton. Having seen the business digest its change of ownership, Dad took early retirement at 64, tired and frustrated by colleagues he felt had let him down, but at least he was now free to undertake a trip to Africa. Before standing down he had been succeeded by the cricketer Colin Cowdrey in his role as president of The General Porters Benevolent Fund. Those who are familiar with the textile industry would identify the charity by its present name, *The Cottage Homes*, which cares for the wellbeing and, through their several managed homes, residential care of several hundred pensioners from the distributive and textile trades.

If you, my dear reader, have ever been an expatriate in some far flung corner of the globe, or have lived for a time a long way from home, you will know how exciting it is to receive visitors and how much you want to conduct their stay to make it happy and memorable. It was just so exciting for me when, for the first time in my life I was host to my parents. I was fortunate to have the support of my friends and colleagues in planning and executing a programme for my visitors.

On the second night of their stay I held a party for them at my small home on Kenmere Avenue. Jonas press-ganged a couple of his Mumbwa relatives from nearby to help him out. Unwittingly he committed me to hand out generous tips, but I was rewarded by some generous smiles at close of play. Invitations were showered on my parents which solved the problem of what to do with them on days I had to work, although I had plans to fill most of the evenings and weekends ahead and local leave set aside for some travel.

I had finished work at the temporary office site early on the day after the party and had driven home to pick up Dad, the two of us taking the short trip to the Coppersmith's Arms on Second Street. There we had shared a few beers with Norrie Grieg and others who had appeared for sundowners. Dad hit it off with Norrie, who had served as a gunner in the

Royal Navy: by the time we reached home we were in high spirits, joining Mother, but just as we sat down to a supper prepared by Jonas the telephone rang. I answered the call, immediately recognising my Uncle David's Lancastrian voice on the crackling line from northeast England where he was a parish priest. Grandma had died that day whilst in their care at the vicarage in Jesmond. She was eighty-one. David wanted to know if he should defer the funeral date.

I called back after dinner and spoke to David's wife Barbara, my mother's sister, suggesting that the funeral should go ahead and be at David's church. There was little my parents could usefully accomplish by cutting short their stay. The programme I had planned rolled out.

Steve Smith, who by now had got over the inconvenience of having no bar in his house, had his grandparents from Yorkshire to stay at the same time as my parents were in Zambia. Through Steve's contacts with the mines in Mufulira we arranged a trip for the four visitors to see an open pit copper mine together, and later to go down the underground Mindola deep shaft at Kitwe. I think we were all deeply impressed by those massive industrial undertakings. Now it was time for me to impress the wonders of the African bush, I had plans for us to fly up to Kasaba Bay on the southern tip of Lake Tanganyika for three nights at a game camp before which we would make a trip in the opposite direction to Livingstone and the Falls. We were well set for some great adventures.

8

A Nurse

(April 1971)

The architects were managing the construction of the warehouse project. They were due to hand over the entire development to my team in less than a fortnight. It was still rainy season, but the heaviest storms had abated by mid-March. I welcomed the chance to take some leave with my folks who I packed into the Peugot for the long drive to Livingstone.

On the way we spent a night out near Itezhi-tezhi, a decent waterhole in the Kafue National Park which provided basic accommodation in thatched rondavels with a common area for food and drink. Earlier in the day we had passed by the boma town of Mumbwa where the road had deteriorated to a single track of dirt and sand, causing our progress to slow down. I took a couple of photos in Mumbwa to show Jonas. But much magic was around, my mother had spotted guinea fowl and wild dogs before we suddenly had to stop to avoid a pride of lions occupying the way ahead.

It was unseemly to sound my horn in the middle of nowhere and I was not sure whether the beasts would attack the car, so we sat it out for a few nervous minutes before the massive male rose from his sleep to slope off nonchalantly into the bush, taking his family with him. When the lions had disappeared from our sight, I was able to open the car windows to relieve the heat in the cabin, at which point the sweet and sickly smell of animal kill invaded our nostrils. Now I knew why the lions were so passive with full bellies. Some recent heavy rains had left small pools in the track. The rainwater attracted thick swarms of butterflies which provided us with a magnificent sight of vibrant colour and pure natural beauty to marvel at. Then came the baobab trees, the 'upside down trees' as they were locally known, quite the weirdest giant plants I have ever seen

Rainy season in the African bush is not the time to sight game, the thick undergrowth provides too much cover for mammals and birds alike. On the other hand, we found The Victoria Falls in full flood and went for a walk in the rain forest facing the falls, right in front of the chasm in which the flooding river fell more than three hundred feet to a steamy maelstrom below. It might not be the highest or widest waterfall but for sure it is the world's biggest when measured by water volume.

The turmoil of water surges from either side towards a spot they call the *boiling pot*, where it thunders into the gorge, its only means of escape; it was towards that gorge we walked, through a tropical micro-climate, soaked by the spray over a distance of a quarter mile. My dear Mother dropped all her senses of propriety when she declared herself a "drowned rat". At least she was warm.

At night the Falls were lit up on the Zambian side, but purposely left in the natural darkness by the Rhodesians. The powerful arc lamps attracted a myriad of giant moths and other insects which flew to a gruesome death in the heat of the bright beams of light, their bodies piled high to a depth of almost three feet below the points of illumination, the smell of rotting arthropods contrasted most unfavourably with the damp perfume of the brilliant tropical flora close by. My best experience of the Falls at full flood was at night, rejoicing in the "moonbow", a creation from the hot spray in the moonlight, above which the stars shone in their millions in the dark sky.

By now we were all fully relaxed in each other's company and enjoying our experience together in central Africa. We had a good night talking about the old days and looking forward to the days ahead. Early the next morning we crossed the Zambesi Gorge suspension bridge into Rhodesia, driving the short distance to the small urban settlement of Victoria Falls where we had lunch at the Victoria Falls Hotel. The hotel became famous after hosting King George VI and Queen Elizabeth with their two daughters back in 1947.

The lawns in front of the hotel sloped down to the cliffs which bordered the course of the river from where we looked back to the "boiling pot" and a glimpse of Mosi-o-tunya beyond, about a mile away.

At lunch in the main dining room a hand tapped me on the shoulder. Looking up I could hardly believe my eyes, for there in front of me was Nigel Ashwell, the younger brother of a school friend from my prep school Caldicott who, with his family and mine, had been on holiday together on a retired tea schooner at Salcombe fourteen years earlier. Nigel had become head waiter at the prestigious hotel, and of course remembered Mum and Dad, so we enjoyed a complete tour of the grounds and building, including the "Royal Suite", and were able to enjoy the special hospitality of being transferred for an overnight stay in the quarters of royalty. So it was that we walked in the footsteps of the regal slippers before we headed back to Livingstone and the long drive home via Lusaka. I had arranged for us all to stay with the Carvers, a surprise treat and great fun.

The road from Livingstone took us the breadth of Southern Province, a largely rural area with cash crop farming, the home of the Tonga people. After passing through Choma and Mazabuka, we drove through a massive escarpment with views of the Kafue river gorge. The following day, as we completed the final two hundred miles back to the Copperbelt from Lusaka, I reminisced about my schooldays, prompted, I supposed, by seeing Nigel at Victoria Falls. His brother, Anthony, was a close friend at Caldicott, sharing much of the sporting silverware with me. I was not to know then that twenty years later I would see Anthony again with my future wife and family in Exeter, when, having left his work as a nuclear scientist, he was ordained a priest.

After four years at Durston House and a further four years at Caldicott I left for Aldenham in 1956, aged thirteen. My new school and its many playing fields occupied a large space of land to the north of London in Hertfordshire, where I boarded. Aldenham was first created by a brewer named Platt as an Elizabethan grammar school. That year was memorable to me for the Hungarian uprising, for the Suez War and the subsequent demise of the then British Prime Minister Anthony Eden, and for Jim Laker, the greatest Surrey off-spinner who skittled out a record nineteen Australian wickets at Old Trafford in the fourth Test. The news about Laker reached us at a Boy Scout camp in Snowdonia.

I can't say that that the hard regime at Aldenham was designed to make schooldays the happiest days of life, although there were many happy days along the way, but in surviving everything that was thrown at me, figuratively if not physically, the school generated enough self-confidence in me and made me acquire sufficient general knowledge to feel at home in the company of most people I came up against in later times.

New boys arriving at Aldenham found themselves as little fish in a big pond. We were subjected to the rigours of a code of discipline inherited from an earlier ages The headmaster, Peter "Piggy" Mason and his staff delegated the execution of that discipline to senior boys, who wielded their authority through dormitory beatings for such crimes as laughing after lights out, any slight imperfection to our folded clothes or bed blankets, sneezing and other high misdemeanours. I vowed never to do the same and stayed true to that resolve. True, I was a bit of a rebel, but as one master confided in my father, I was not a bad rebel. I remain grateful for a good education, after which I declined university, viewing it to be an extension of school, wanting rather to use the two years after school, in which I had expected to undergo National Service (which was abolished in 1959), as an opportunity to learn another language, which is how I ended up working in Germany.

We had just two nights back from our trip to Livingstone before we flew on a Dakota to the grass strip at Kasaba Bay for four nights at a game lodge on the southern tip of Lake Tanganyika. The bush along the lake is thick and wild. There was a large space of open savannah on the mile-wide promontory facing the main common room of our lodge and the surrounding compound. Our sleeping quarters were in a group of five whitewashed round houses, each constructed of mud with thatched roofs. The lake was on both sides of our line of sight, to the rear a beach and to the front a grassy shore which partially screened off a bloat of hippos which had taken residence. A mile beyond the hippos was the distant mouth of a fjord which pointed the way to Nkamba Bay, another spot for watching game and enjoying solitude.

The experience of being host to my parents for the first time brought subtle changes to our relationships, for example I could take the lead without question on occasions calling for my initiative and I felt more self-confident as our conversations opened up into topics previously taboo.

That first evening in Kasaba we sat in the dark, looking out to the moonlit lake with the starry firmament above, the cicadas, frogs and crickets all challenging the silence, imagining the secret movements of wildlife all around. The attentive steward wore his starched white coat and red fez impressively, pointing out distant eyes caught in the reflected glare from his torchlight as he kept us happily topped up with tea or whisky, as the genders preferred.

We learned that the staff were restricted from returning to their quarters without cover by the armed guard on duty who carried a loaded Lee Enfield rifle. Indeed, the same guard, an army veteran from the KAR, covered guests returning to their rondavels for the night, taking special care to spot hippos looming out of the darkness to ease their itches by scratching themselves against available hut walls in our treeless compound. The great beasts waited until the sun had gone down before they would emerge from their watery space to avoid the dangers of heat stroke.

At breakfast I grabbed my binoculars and trained them on in the shallows of the lake about two hundred yards from the lodge's stoep where a pair of bull hippos were in combat. The muddy monsters kept up their relentless fight giving no quarter, when all of a sudden the one who did not win, under whatever rules governed their combat, left the safety of the water and risked his life to chase over the grassy isthmus in the direction of the opposing shore. I switched view to see a lone elephant whose path would converge with that of the fleeing hippopotamus if he did not deviate from his present course.

I was more than a little intrigued to find out which of the prehistoric giants would give way, for both were travelling at speeds not far short of thirty miles per hour. I had not long to wait for the answer, it was the shorter animal who veered right to pass by not more than a chain to the rear of the elephant. After the drama of that moment my Mother and I sat with the duty guard as Dad took a dip in the lake on the opposite shore to the hippo clan, watched over by a float of crocodiles masquerading as logs not far away. I knew then that he would be dining out on such a story or perhaps earning a few drinks at the *Jolly Woodman* when he got home to England.

Ignatius Ngoma, a former sergeant in the King's African Rifles, is a name I will never forget. He was the game ranger appointed to protect and guide me on a dawn walking safari, he armed with his .303 and I with my Mamiya camera. Our progress through the dense thorny bush came to an abrupt halt after a mile or so, when the good sergeant put his fingers to his lips, signalling me to freeze. Ahead was a group of Africa's most dangerous animals, the wild buffalos. Thankfully they stood up wind from us. Just like the scratching hippo, the buffalo is not shy about his alimentary smells and sounds, which became more pungent and noisier as the group shuffled towards us. We dared not make a move for fear of giving our presence away, so remained frozen, but hot from sweat, for almost an hour until the danger finally passed us by twenty yards away. My personal reaction to the danger was to empty my bladder, rather than anything more serious, but I came away without a photograph. Now I had a tale for the gang at the Coppersmith Arms, but nothing to show them.

The whole afternoon we spent on the lake fishing from a small boat powered by an outboard motor. I trolled for Nile perch, yellow bellies, and tiger fish whilst we made the journey to Nkamba, where the lodge stood above the lake surrounded by jungle or water, the perfect honeymoon hideaway. The fish were not jumping in my direction that day, they never did, although our guide filled a bucket.

Local fishermen lived from selling their daily catch of kapenta, a freshwater relative of whitebait and a staple food when dried in Zambia. They were caught in fine mesh nets and laid out to dry in the sun before being taken to market. The fresh kapenta was a tasty dish, but the dried variety preferred by the local people smelt high, just like *Bombay duck*. I knew few, if any of my fellow Europeans who found the staple to their liking, but the African population became very unhappy when the fishermen had gone on strike two years before to register their strong objection to a new price control measure imposed by the UNIP government. The fishermen needed a higher price to survive.

Tiger fish were the main natural predator of kapenta, stocks of which multiplied hugely when fishing activity came to a halt. That must have given rise to the recent discovery of a strain of tiger fish they named *the goliath* which could end up weighing over thirty pounds, ten times their usual weight following their relentless feasting on the large shoals of kapenta which had been gifted to them by the strikers.

The break at Kasaba Bay came to an end, it had been wonderful. We returned to Ndola and soon I had to say goodbye to Mum and Dad.

The warehouse was handed over from the architects and work started with the arrival of fixtures and equipment from overseas and more staff training. Jimmy Crawford was not well. I added his duties to mine. I had a staff of over 400 men and a handful of women. Once all the Dexion fixtures were up, we started to transfer stock in from the nine temporary warehouses. The local District Governor started to take an interest in our project, as did the Copperbelt's trades union convenor; I could foresee trouble ahead to be avoided as we were down for an official opening by the President of Zambia himself in early July.

I got word that the five high-tower electric fork-lift trucks had arrived at Cape Town from the UK supplier, a firm called Eaton Yale and Towne of Basingstoke, by now on their way to Johannesburg for servicing by the agent before being transported to us by road. On top of the voyage at sea, the machines would undergo a transit journey by road to us of more than two thousand miles. I felt a great sense of unease, since the functioning of our project was wholly dependent upon the trucks, they were already five weeks late and we could not train staff without them. We had the Presidential opening in six weeks' time.

Despite the hostile stance taken by the Zambian Government towards South Africa, there were no restrictions on telephone contact, which was just as well because I had to get a call through to the service agent's offices to establish contact and ask for the quickest turn round to assure myself and Jim Lafferty that there were no snags nor errors in the documentation, specifically as the freight had to transit Rhodesia in bond. It was not long after that my worst fears became reality when the newly installed telex machine tapped out a message from Heine du Toit, the South African agent, to say that the lorry on which the five trucks were loaded had been driven under a low bridge and all five towers had been smashed.

Thank goodness for my blue British passport, for it took me only thirty-six hours to get all the necessary permits and flights to travel down to the Apartheid state alone, to be met by Heine at Jan Smuts airport. From the airport I was driven to my hotel on Eloff Street, a stone's throw from Hillbrow, Johannesburg's arty student and clubland district.

We had no time to ship replacement trucks from the UK, my task was to persuade Heine's company to divert at least two machines on order for other clients and send them safely north to me. Heine and his family proved to be great hosts, and his directors could not have been more helpful to me once they discovered that I was a family friend of Bill Meddings, whose gear manufacturing company in Slough they also represented. Hello, I thought, what a wonderful coincidence.

The deal was quickly agreed, telex advice sent to Jim Lafferty in Ndola and others that we would have the two replacement vehicles and all fuelling equipment two weeks before the President was due. I then had a day to kill before the flight home to Zambia and spent time discovering Johannesburg. I toured Heine's workshop and warehouse, where I found staff of all colours working peaceably together, as indeed I found black men being served by white staff in the rooftop bars of the President Hotel where I was staying.

The same thing in the two department stores I visited where staff and customers alike were from all colours of the racial rainbow. The many injustices of Apartheid, as Heine and his wife opined at dinner, were that non-whites were paid no more than a quarter of the salaries earned by white people, that they commuted in separate transport and attended separate doctors, hospitals and even cinemas, and were barred from visiting "whites only" housing areas. In short it was nearly impossible to have social contact with non-whites after work other than on the football field. The "immorality" laws banned white and coloured men and women having any relationships with each other, it was all just wretched. It seemed that no-one had an answer other than to keep the lid on the kettle of rebellion and outrage.

"As I see it there is no parallel to be drawn between South Africa and Zambia", I said to my hosts when they asked me about life in the north. "Most white folk who have chosen to settle in Zambia farm the land and seem welcome," I continued, "the rest of us are guests in an African land run by Africans with our help, other than, of course, the many Asians who are involved in commerce and manufacturing. It's different in South Africa, most people here were born in South Africa, this is their home, whether they are white, black or brown or whatever." I was emboldened to voice an opinion that the suppression of the bulk of the population was not only daft, it was untenable, so better surely to bring about its end rather than having its end brought about by the suppressed. I suggested to lighten the mood. I was impatient to get those two fork-lift machines on site so we could bring in the instructors and start intensive training

The day before the official opening, with press and television clamouring for tickets, news came that Kenneth Kaunda would not be coming and was sending vice-President Mainza Chona in his stead. It all went to plan, "all right on the night" said Jim Crawford. I took a back seat to allow our senior Zambian staff to be prominent, after all, it was their big show, and their future. I could not get out of a TV interview with local star presenter Julius Chileshe, everyone seemed to watch it live but of course I could not see it myself, domestic

TV recording devices had not been invented. The project was far from finished and the following months saw the arrival of our rail siding and the first rail delivery from Dar es Salaam, which was in fact a sea container of mixed cargo loaded on a flat-bed railway truck.

One weekend at about that time I joined Brendan and Maurice and the Gillette man John Hadley on a car journey into Zaire, to the capital city of Katanga province called Lubumbashi, formerly Elizabethville. As the border guards were seldom paid by the corrupt regime in the former Belgian Congo, they preyed on travellers such as we for their ration money.

For the sake of free passage along the eighty miles of potholes making up the bush road from the Zambian border post at Kasumbalesa to our destination, and not without a little encouragement from a pair of rifles idly pointed in our direction, we conformed to the established custom of informal taxation, glad to be on our way but wary of what might confront us upon our return tomorrow evening.

In Lubumbashi we found rooms at the *Leo Deux*[11], enjoying a decent dinner before early bed. Breakfast the next morning, it was a Sunday, took place under Martini umbrellas set out to shade the metal tables we sat at on the front veranda of the hotel. Enjoying fresh croissants and *café fine* our table overlooked a cobbled street along which a bicycle road race *peleton* swept past us, led by a rider in a yellow jersey. We could have been watching the *tour de France!*

At midday we made our way to the sailing club beside the reservoir, where we had lunch but not any old lunch, this

---

11. Leo Deux was the nickname for the King Leopold II Hotel built originally in Elizabethville, Katanga, Belgian Congo in 1929. Now it is called the Park Hotel.

one was of grilled dover sole, freshly flown in from Brussels via Kinshasa. I just had to reflect on *la différence* between anglophone and francophone Africa, in the former the food was mundane, and the local women waddled along the roadside, but the utilities worked, and the roads were maintained. In the latter the food was part of the culture, the women floated elegantly by, but the plumbing was a percussion section, the electricity intermittent and the roads required you to drive twice the distance to navigate the obstructions and water-filled potholes, cycle racing routes being the exception.

The darker side of our observations showed evidence of the recent civil war all over the pitted walls of the buildings near the hotel and beyond. Perhaps the folk in the francophone lands set themselves different priorities, rather as if the bush between the Copperbelt of Zambia and the conurbation of Lubumbashi represented crossing the English Channel. Cobblestones, yellow jerseys, and *café fine!* We got back safely despite taking almost three hours to cover the journey to the border post at Kasumbalesa, discovering to our relief that the guards had abandoned their roadside quarters for some more pressing engagement, thereby avoiding any further involuntary *baksheesh*.

On another long weekend a group of us drove in two cars to the small settlement of Siavonga on the northern shore of Lake Kariba. Our journey south over 400 miles took us through the escarpment which rose above the Zambesi River valley. At the bottom of the rocky road we encountered a road block at which we all had to step out of our vehicles and walk through a trough of opaque muddy disinfectant before driving with wet feet through a pool of the same stuff in the car as protection against carrying the tsetse fly, whose blood sucking mandibles thrive on the hides of animals and which can pass on sleeping sickness when biting humans.

The flies can only glide, so the insects climb trees to launch their flight allowing them to cover distances up to a hundred yards or so. To limit their scope of evil, farmers often cut breaks in the forest a hundred yards wide, as if making fire breaks as they do in California and Australia.

In Siavonga we met up with a white boatman and commissioned him to take us seven miles up the lake to *Banana Bay*, where he would drop us with our camping gear and pick us up two days later, leaving the cars in his yard. Unfortunately, half an hour after we had disembarked and were pitching our camp, the single gun boat and crew of the Zambian border force spotted us and hove to. Two armed officers approached us with caution, demanding behind their loaded guns to see our passports, suspecting us to be illegal immigrants who had mysteriously crossed from Rhodesia over the forty miles of crocodile infested waters. Unable to comply, I stupidly volunteered to return with the police launch to the station in Siavonga to retrieve our passports from the cars.

It was Easter and the station sergeant, who alone amongst the staff of the local station spoke English, was away visiting his family, so I was to see him with our passports the next day on his return. Meanwhile, as I was suspected of being an illegal immigrant, it was a night in the slammer for me. An exceptionally long and boring and uncomfortable fourteen hours later the sergeant thankfully reappeared at his desk and all formalities were dealt with affably enough. I resisted the temptation to drive straight back to the Copperbelt and instead got the boatman to return me to Banana Bay, where the boys were fishing and clearly well into party time.

Lake Kariba had been formed twelve years earlier in the days of the Federation by building a dam to hold back the waters of the Zambesi at the settlement of the same name about forty miles east from our camp where there was a narrow gorge ideal for the construction. As the waters filled up over the four years it took to complete the dam some sixty thousand people had to be resettled, and the animals living in the flooded areas rescued. The folk living in that region are Tonga, their river god *Nyami Nyami*[12] being none too pleased at the upheaval and is thought to have forsaken the Zambesi.

Thousands of wild animals became stranded by the rising flood, which gave rise to a huge team being assembled with boats to conduct *Operation Noah* to rescue beasts from the raised grounds to where they had fled. People from all backgrounds wanted to join in the work. Those islands of refuge gradually disappeared as the waters rose even higher behind the dam. At their maintained level on the dam, the waters cover the vast bush forest that once grew in the river valley to a depth of three hundred feet. On the edges of the man-made inland sea the petrified stumps of trees are widely visible and can be both hazardous for boats and yet are home to varieties of lake fish seeking refuge in the root structures, just like the habitat of a coral cluster in a tropical sea.

Kariba is the world's biggest purpose-built reservoir, roughly 130 miles long and 40 miles wide. God help Mozambique if ever the dam would break! The evaporation from the massive surface area of the lake waters has changed weather patterns, more particularly in modern Zimbabwe (Rhodesia) and Mozambique even more so. In the meantime,

---

12. The Nyami Nyami, is the Zambezi River god or snake spirit, possibly the most important god and protector of the Tonga people of Zambia's Southern Province.

the Kariba Dam produces hydro-electric power, not enough for the demands of Zambia's copper mines because at least half the power goes south, which is why the mighty Kafue, a tributary of the Zambesi, whose confluence was downstream from Kariba, was being dammed much further to the north.

I persuaded the boys to let our boatman move us to a better location which I had spotted on the voyage back from my incarceration. There was a pebble beach on the tip of narrow peninsular that jutted out from the bush, with few trees and plenty of stony shore. All was well until the time the light faded, when one of us spotted smoke rising more than a mile away in the bush. We kept a fire lit to ward off game during the night hours, but when we awoke it became clear that the smoke on the lake surface did not come from our fire, rather from a bush fire now raging much closer to us than we had first spotted at sundown the previous day.

Worried that the fire would follow the wind towards us, and with no means of escape, we were cutting down the sparse scrub in a somewhat feeble attempt to make a fire break when an elephant loomed into view only forty yards away, heading straight in our direction. We froze. The great beast was clearly a lone male who was tracking alone looking for jumbo company, in any event he was not interested in us, it seemed, since he turned right onto the firebreak we had been making which provided a pathway to the water on the far side of the isthmus from the campsite. We kept a watchful eye out for our visitor who did not return before the boat arrived to take us back to Siavonga and a long drive home to the Copperbelt, but not before a rain storm swept in from the west, hopefully dousing the fires behind us.

Zambia's land mass which measured roughly three times

that of the United Kingdom could be explored freely and safely, taking sensible precautions against breakdowns on the roads, the seasons' weather, wild animals and insect life, and naughty humans from time to time. The small group of expats I considered my inner circle of bachelor friends found it good for the soul to take time out in some of the places I have described and more. Many of us travelled widely in the pursuance of our work but the real fun came from trips into the bush or on the great rivers and lakes or making camp. We got to know the ways of life of people beyond the urban sprawls, their traditions and, most importantly, their sense of humour. Humour, or lack of it, gives a clue, I believe, to the very nature of a country's culture, and the Zambians certainly possessed it in bucketloads.

Refreshed from our three days away on the shores of Kariba, I returned to the final phase of getting the DC into full working mode helped in no small measure by Peter McManus and the team of supervisors we had been training. Arrivals of imported freight went directly into the new customs bond, an area secured by high level fine mesh fencing with a mesh ceiling. I got the idea for the concession from a conversation I had with the captain of the *Untouchables* cricket team made up of Zambia Customs and Excise staff. We saved a lot of time clearing goods and paying import duties on account. Most of the freight we processed through the bond was for re-sale in our stores, but there were other strange consignments which arrived unbidden.

One day some strange cargo arrived in the form of two unmarked boxes containing over seventy long playing mono records from the Soviet Union, all in plain white sleeves. I contacted the Soviet Embassy in Lusaka, but they declared no knowledge. It was a complete mystery. Jason Ngoma, a trainee fresh from University suggested it must be a tool of espionage but gave no further evidence to support his theory. After the passage of a week and a generous donation to the staff Christmas party fund, I came to own the complete works of Mozart, Tchaikovsky, and Beethoven, upstaging my tennis friend Bunny.

On another occasion a sea container was opened in bond to reveal several cases of Polish vodka, all with screw tops intact but which had either leaked or lost volume by evaporation in the extreme heat of transit through the tropics. A team opened every case (there were about seventy of them), none of which had any shipping marks, lining the bottles on the concrete floor like a battalion of troops on parade within the wire fence of our bond. The men then proceeded to open each bottle and carefully decant the spirit to make up full bottles. We probably lost about ten bottles all told by the time the men sealed the tops using red corks sourced from Northern Brewery and some smart sticky tape.

When I went to check on the work, I spotted one of the men called Silus Mudenda sitting with his back to me, helping himself to some neat spirit from a bottle he had tucked under his overalls. He had been doing so for a while I was later told. In full sight of his twelve mates I crept up behind him and delivered my booted right foot to his backside which lifted him off the ground. It says a lot for the Zambian sense of humour that they saw the incident as hilarious, complicit in my secret approach to present a shock to the boozing warehouseman. By good fortune I had judged the situation perfectly, but I quickly realised that the man had imbibed far more than his body was capable of absorbing, so much so that we bundled him into my car with his two supervisors and drove straight to the Central Hospital, where he received a life-saving stomach pump. Two days later Silus reported back to work, the experience of the stomach pump still fresh in his mind. He received a formal dressing-down in front of his peers by Martin the warehouse manager, after which he was transferred to the staff canteen on tea making duty, a hard lesson learnt but we saved his job and livelihood. Shocked rather than hurt, I was told by Jason the trainee that Silus saw the funny side of his disgrace.

One night we had a bridge four at Jim Whelan's house. I partnered Jim against Westy and Keith Sykes, an accountant working for ZCBC. Since returning to Ndola, Jim's wife had had a very public affair with a journalist on the Zambia Times newspaper and had recently left Jim to live with her hack. Rumour had it that the journalist was two- timing his new girlfriend with his estranged wife, the latter appearing suddenly from a long sojourn in Cape Town. Jim's daughter was asleep in her bedroom as we dealt out the early hands. As the first rubber was won and lost, we heard footsteps passing the card den's open door and I saw Caroline as she calmly announced herself to us, saying "good evening gentlemen" in a steady, friendly voice. I looked querulously across the table at my partner, whose eyebrows were raised high. Moments after we heard a single shot and rushed to the bedroom to find Caroline on the bed, bleeding heavily and very dead.

It was a sudden tragedy none of us could possibly be prepared for. There was no suicide note. It took a while to call the police and ambulance, but they responded quickly once we got through to them. A team of five officers, two in plain clothes, arrived and took charge. We were told to sit down in the lounge area as they would need to take our statements once they had, so it seemed, covered every inch of the property without waking the sleeping baby girl. After securing the scene they finally left with Jim. We were asked to attend the station.

Caroline's limp body was carried out by the ambulance crew who had arrived an hour or so after the law men. Jim's life was shattered, and I was at a loss as to how to comfort or help him. We caught up with him at the police station, where we made formal statements of the bombshell event we had been witness to. It soon emerged that there was a big problem with the gun. Jim had forgotten to register the weapon and obtain an annual licence for it, probably due to his long absence with heart problems. He had left the revolver in the bedside drawer as a safety measure for Caroline should she be alone. It took more than a year for the matter to be resolved by the courts. I recall Jim paid a heavy fine and received a suspended sentence on top of the personal tragic loss of his young wife. Jim left Zambia for his home in Scotland two years afterwards and, sad to say, he never played bridge with us again. I can only imagine that for a young woman to take her own life in such a measured way, she had lost all her love of self.

Not long after that drama, a chance encounter was about to change my life for good. One Sunday I had been playing a four ball at a golf course in Kalulushi not far from Kitwe. We had teed off at dawn and were finished by mid-morning, the air still crispy and the ground dry after the rains had finished. We downed a couple of cold *Castle* lagers at the club house, then drove to join Ron Raymond, who worked as an accountant at Indeco Morison. Ron was caring for a "leave house" made available by one of the senior mine managers.

The grand property had a courtyard swimming pool whose six feet wide paved surrounds were backed on three sides by wings of the extensive bungalow. The house certainly compared most favourably with my two-bedroom bachelor's bungalow in Ndola, although I could boast a mealie patch, two pawpaw trees, abundant bougainvillea, and a bar. There was not one cloud in the sky that day, which had warmed up to a customary 85 degrees Fahrenheit by the time I arrived. Ron was hosting a *braaivleis* (BBQ) by the pool and had arranged for several friends and some British nurses from the Central Hospital to join us.

As the party gained a momentum, a competition appeared to develop whereby he who jumped the greatest distance from the corrugated roof into the pool was adjudged the winner. I doubt that the ladies from the hospital were much impressed by our testosterone fuelled antics, but one of them gave me a smile.

I smiled back, and that is how I met Miss Victoria Gardiner, SRN. Tory and her close friend Tricia Beamish stayed in the nurses' home attached to the Kitwe Central Hospital under the watchful eye of a Miss Kitson, the Deputy Matron. There were more than a dozen British nurses in Kitwe, all of them sent from the UK to work under yearly contracts paid from the UK's Overseas Aid budget, seconded to help run the State hospitals, and develop the Zambian Government's health service along the lines of the NHS.

Over the following months I must have met most of the nurses, they certainly brightened up our social scene, but my eyes from then on were for Tory. So began my life change. It was a round trip of ninety miles to and from where I was stationed in Nodola to the nurses' home at Kitwe Central Hospital. That year I must have driven the length of the equator back and forth to be with my new-found love, mercifully without incident despite the dangers of the Copperbelt Highway.

Once, not long after we had first met, we joined a picnic party in the bush some ten miles from the central area of Kitwe at a spot where the Kafue river ran through rocky rapids. The Kafue seemed to treble its waterflow after passing by the Kitwe copper mines, where vast volumes of clean water were pumped from the deep shafts into the river, but we were upstream that day with the strong currents which always followed the end of the rains. The fast water deterred hippos and crocodiles; the animals only emerged once the water levels dropped. Having swum and slid through the smooth stones and waterfalls that made up the rapids I found myself perched on a monolithic outcrop next to Tory, with others including Westy, digging into the picnic hamper above us.

We were dry within moments of leaving the water, and thirsty. As a bottle of coke was passed to me it slipped out of Westy's hand and dropped onto the rock, bouncing once, then pointed its broken neck into my right little toe, almost completely severing it. It must have been Brendan who drove Tory and me back to the hospital where I threw myself on the mercy of the dreaded Miss Kitson and thence some emergency surgery, my toe later restored to me. Brendan left to clear up my blood from the floor of his MGB.

That encounter seemed to endear me to the Deputy Matron, which was just as well, as a week or so later Tory went down with a bout of jaundice, turning quite yellow and confined to the staff ward for four weeks. Almost every evening of Tory's hospital stay I was able to visit her, long after the official visiting hours, smiles and sometimes flowers directed at the spinster lady Kitson, whose office overlooked the ward entrance, her guard duty perch. We will never know how Tory contracted the hepatitis, it could hardly have been the Kafue, for none of us were ill. I suspected it was something water-borne she had picked up when visiting Malawi with Tricia just before her D-day at Ron's pool. It was then that I really knew I had met the one.

9

Kippers

(September 1971 – April 1972)

By September 1971 the new distribution centre was fully up and running, my project had come to its conclusion; Jim Whelan had been sent on long leave back home to sort his life out and make arrangement for his lovely little daughter; Jim Lafferty had retired and Lionel Wharrad had been recruited by Bookers from the John Lewis Partnership to take over. My new boss wasted no time to send me back to take over from Jim at ZNWC for a second time, at least for the time he was away, re-joining Denis Sakalla. Tory had moved out of the nurses' home for a month to look after a leave house with her friend Tricia.

The housemate left us discretely alone the evening I visited with my bags packed in the boot of my white Peugot, ready for an early morning departure for Chipata. The round trip would cover twelve hundred miles and take me away for five days, so knowing just how much I was going to miss Tory for even that short time, and convinced as I was that our relationship could only go one way, the moment had come to dive in the deep end and propose marriage.

Now, I have long been told I am impetuous, and there is some truth in that accusation, but this was not just a job to be completed and move on to the next one, this was about our two lives, for goodness sake. "Do you really mean that?" said Tory. She needed time to think. Taken aback, downcast but undaunted, I hoped that when I was back in five days' time, she would have her answer. That is how I left it, but it became a constant a distraction from the work in hand, *"will she, won't she?"* resounding in my head every mile of the long drive to the East. Come on, I said to myself, no time for faint hearts. Had I made a mess of it, after all I had never proposed marriage before, never had met anyone like my blue-eyed nurse before? And why should I have expected an immediate 'yes'.

The week dragged by, I did some useful work, and drove five hundred miles non-stop on the return to arrive back in Ndola late on Friday, long after sundown but ready to murder a few beers from the fridge and eat up a feast prepared by Jonas. Tory had told me in some detail about her parents' failed marriage, her three older siblings, her devotion to her nanny Jill, her father's misdemeanours, and her mother's travails. My relatively stable family background contrasted completely with Tory's, which made me think that her indecision in the matter of my hand might be another uncertainty in her fragile take on life.

As a child she had been handed over when she was ten days old to a young nanny of eighteen called Jill. At the age of six Tory's mother arranged a job for Jill at the home of two spinsters, a Miss Drewe and her companion Miss Brotherton, who ran a residential nursery at Castle Drogo on Dartmoor, the prized possession of Miss Drewe's father who was a tea shipper and founder of the *Home and Colonial Stores*. The two ladies took Tory along with Jill, who would work for them, to join their family of displaced youngsters.

Jill Congdon's parents lived in an old stone cottage on a farm beyond the moor. They became her dearly loved adopted grandparents who provided the little girl with some stability. Jill's father was Churchill's preferred Royal Navy chef on *HMS Prince of Wales* when he met FDR in the mid-Atlantic, a brave man three times rescued at sea during different phases of WWII.

Later Tory had to witness a tug-of-war between Charles and Dorothea Gardiner, her parents, with Charles taking his four children to a house he had rented in Exmouth. Whilst her sister was at boarding school, Tory and her two brothers, Christopher, and Peter, went to school in Exeter. As soon as she could, she had left home to take up nursing, ending up at the John Radcliffe Hospital in Oxford where she gained her final orthopaedic qualifications and made many friends, the closest one being Tricia, who, like Tory, had been assigned to Kitwe Central after first landing in Lusaka only six months earlier.

The long drive from Chipata had worn me out. After a good sleep I sped off with hope in my heart, first to a jeweller's shop in Ndola to pay for an engagement ring I had reserved, then over to Kitwe to meet Tory for lunch. Tired after a night shift on her busy children's ward she gave me the answer I had hoped for, oh joy! She tried on the ring, three tiny diamonds set in white gold, and began to laugh. The ring was far too big for her finger, despite my estimate that a fit to my little finger would match her ring size, how little did I know of female digital anatomy. No, I had to return the ring for adjustment immediately. A week later I collected the ring, with its diameter substantially reduced, for re-presentation to my new fiancée. It has remained in place ever since.

Getting engaged did not change the vivid colours of our lives under the skies of the tropics in central Africa, but it certainly enhanced my enjoyment, for once now sharing experiences and making friends together. I went to see the Chairman Wally Lewis, whose permission I had to seek to approve my move from bachelorhood. Earlier, after he heard my news, Maurice Widdowson had joined me in Ndola on his promotion to be Head of Retail, asked if I would move to Kitwe on Jim's return, to be General Manager of the department store where I had first started. I would be replacing Brendan, who had accepted a move to the flagship store in Lusaka.

I readily agreed, solving several problems in so doing, for one the certainty of a second contract for two more years, the next to live forty miles closer to Tory and the third to reduce the huge amount of travel by road and air and thus get back to a steadier social life outside work. The added attractions were that I liked Kitwe where I had many friends, despite its wild frontier character, and the house in Freedom Avenue, where I had spent my first Christmas in Zambia with the boys, would be mine to start our married life, sometime the following year.

It felt as if I was making a job application when I wrote to Charles Gardiner, formally asking for his daughter's hand. A positive reply arrived by airmail two weeks later, what else could he say, poor fellow, except to warn me of the dangers posed by Idi Amin. Charles's knowledge of African geography took little heed of the fact that Kampala was fifteen hundred miles away up the rift valley beyond the great lakes of Tanganyika and Victoria. I replied to the effect that we both felt safe in

Zambia, far from the Ugandan demagogue, notwithstanding the unrest and bush warfare in Rhodesia to our south.

When Jim got back from leave, I transferred to the house in Freedom Avenue, joining Brendan for a while before he left to take charge in Lusaka, and began to get to grips with my new job in Kitwe. I met up with Mike Delaney, once again my ultimate boss and fellow cricketer who quietly instructed me to carry out sweeping Africanisation of all but the top management jobs in the store, and to weed out non-Zambian Africans[13], without making waves, as he put it. He was following a directive, I was told, from Andrew Sadanis, the State House appointee who led the country's Industrial Development Corporation (INDECO), our major shareholder, you might recall.

Before I wound up the house in Ndola, I had asked Jonas to come with me to Kitwe, but the prospect of working for an *umfasi* once I was married was not for him. I found him a job at the Distribution Centre I had left some months before as a driver's mate and paid for his training to qualify for a heavy goods vehicle licence. It was a better life for him, there would be fewer jobs managing expatriate houses in the future, and fewer still the number of bachelors under contract. I handed back the Company Peugot and drove off in the brown Vanden Plas Princess saloon I had bought from George Wright, a golfing partner.

I had resolved to keep my active links with Ndola at the cricket club and with the Lions, regardless of the inconvenience of the Copperbelt Highway. Tory's friends at the hospital added to the dimension of our social life, there were many

---

13. Non-Zambian Africans were mainly Malawians and Rhodesians left in Zambia after the end of the Federation and subsequent independence.

impromptu parties and gatherings at the Theatre Club where my membership was still intact, and Tory was in the cast of a Gilbert and Sullivan production. Westy and I moved our weekly bridge school to Kitwe, finding new opponents to flex our skills against.

Tory contacted Jennifer Owen, a friend from Devon who had stayed on in Zambia after working as a nurse three years earlier. She had married John Blackburne, who farmed a large ranch he had bought outside Kitwe. John had first arrived in Zambia as a VSO. He gave a new name to his land and dubbed it *Mfubu Ranch*, after the many neighbouring hippos. The Blackburnes became our close friends. John had even more chutzpah than other young British expatriates in the new republic who, like him, were setting up vibrant enterprises and a lot of jobs for the people. Of course, we were all trying to make a good living, but in so doing reduce the country's reliance on copper and the "white" economies to the south.

The transfer of power from the Colonial Office in Whitehall via the failed Central African Federation to majority rule under a fragile, but sustainable, democratic parliamentary system had been achieved peaceably in Zambia, but the way of life continued as it was before independence for many years. The Sikh wedding was just one example of a separate culture working within the new nation state, as were many the Anglican churches, the Roman Catholic church, the Salvation Army, Rotary, the Lions, the Plymouth Brethren, the Freemasons, cricket, football, rugby, bowls, tennis, squash and golf clubs, the Legion, Hinduism, the Buffs, the ZSPCA, the ZSPCC, Synagogues and Temples, Young Farmers' clubs, the WI and much more. There was little to doubt that the Republic of Zambia was then an energetic fellow member of the Commonwealth.

The various ethnic groups worked, and to some extent, worshipped together, but they still lived in separate spaces and enjoyed sparse social contact. Why was that so, I wondered, it is easy to suggest that people are more at ease within their own culture, and there remains much truth in that theory, but what keeps them apart? I concluded that fear was an overarching factor, fear of the unknown, fear of being misunderstood or seen as being ignorant, fear of strange food, fear of violence, fear of responsibility, fear of failure, of fear itself. We say without thinking words inviting *"the fear of God"*. Equally we exclaim those other, wonderful words *"the love of God"*. Was that the clue, that we could retain our separateness but come together in the love of God, in the recognition that all men are born equal, are equal beings under God's sky? I was happy then, that in Zambia I was offered a fulfilling but equally indulgent life at work and play, and I can truly say that along with my friends and acquaintances I was able to look people of other races and cultures straight in the eyes inviting equality, and whilst that worked to some extent in forging bonds, the legacy of history still invited fear, amongst Africans, to step up alongside on equal level.

On Mfubu Ranch there were seven traditional African villages, each one had their own UNIP Party representative, and collectively the Party named the grouping as the *Bwana John UNIP Branch*, thus showing their acknowledgement of the source of their well-being. John found he could solve most labour problems by talking to the Party men within the formality of arranged meetings, but on moral matters of honesty and behaviour, he dealt with the village head men, who always achieved the best results.

That was then. Now I am able to attest that when I was visiting the country thirty five years later I discovered a generation of self-confident young people who exhibited no signs of the fear that worried me, nor had they any experience of either the good or the not so good aspects of life in earlier times. And I felt at ease in their company.

Tory and I were married in Exeter Cathedral on 15th April 1972, a sunny day, in front of a hundred and thirty friends and family. Before that we had been apart for six weeks between the end of her contract and my earliest leave date. Whilst away the house at Freedom Avenue was to be refurbished and refurnished by Moira Wharrad, Lionel's wife, who busied herself in a design and care role on behalf of the fifty or so occupiers of Company property at ZCBC. Bless her, she wanted it to be fit and ready for my new bride. The four weeks leading up to the wedding day were a busy round of meeting Tory's family and catching up with my dear parents, my brother John and his wife Wanda and my youngest brother Andrew, along with many friends I had been apart from for so long. My younger brother Adrian was in Versailles, Kentucky. Make sure you pronounce the town's name correctly!

I had had two stag parties before my flight back from Ndola, one in Kitwe at the Theatre Club, and a blast at the Cricket Club in Ndola. Now I was faced with one to be hosted by my old cottage mate Peter Brawley, inviting pals from much earlier times to his house in Bristol, conveniently on the way to Exeter where I was to be married by the Archdeacon of Totnes two days hence. I remember little of the final stag party at which a certain Cardinal Puff was an honoured guest. My team of ushers comprised my brother John and his erstwhile flatmate Jim Hatchett, author of *The Samurai Slayer* novel, who were supported by Keith Harvey and Chris Williams, both good friends I had once worked with in Birmingham. My best man was John Lurie, who had shared the house in Tockington when we were working in Bristol. They all travelled with me the next afternoon for the Cathedral briefing and a final night of bachelorhood at the Clarence, the landmark hotel within the Cathedral Close; meanwhile Tory hosted a party at her mother's house, attended by at least six of her nursing friends from Kitwe.

As tradition had it, I was not to see the bride on the morning of the marriage, but we did sneak a tryst the evening before. Back at The Clarence the bar and its piano had been taken over by the wedding guests, with Charles Gardiner stroking the ivories and leading the singing, sharing double billing with Wilfred and Diana Homer from Burnham, all of us in full voice, but when my bride's brother Peter started to conduct the chorus he found himself invited to take to his bed by the watchful management..

The wedding took place in the choir of the Cathedral, with our guests behind and facing me, smiling encouragement as I sat with my best man ready to take our position facing the high altar to the right when the organ gave notice of Tory's late entrance. I was not to know that as soon as I moved up to receive my Bride in front of Bob Newhouse, the Archdeacon, my knees would start trembling. It got worse as the service progressed, tears began running down my face. Looking up through those tears as the ring was presented, I saw that the priest was weeping with me. Tory was all smiles and joy, blissfully unaware of the unmanly knee knocking taking place to her right. It seemed that everyone except me was full of joy, but emotion had taken over and bossed me all the way to side chapel for the register signing. I was for once overcome by the collective love I felt from all the friends and family who were smiling and wishing us well.

Our reception was held in St George's Hall, a simple finger buffet and champagne; John read the telegrams, I made a speech, then the time came for farewells and the car ride to a secret destination, or so I thought. Clearly the decorations daubed on my car and the attachments hanging from the rear bumper were proof of my inability to hide anything, but worse was to follow. Moments after we checked in to the bridal suite at our secret destination, the switchboard operator of the Grand Hotel in Torquay announced that she had a call from my wife, and would I take it? "Steady on", I said, as I cleared my throat with a swig of the hotel's gifted bubbly, "that's impossible, she's with me right here!", but too late, the call came through. "Ha, Ha, found you" sniggered so called chum "Jimbo" Hatchett and usher extraordinaire, amidst sounds of laughter from the crowd behind him in The Clarence telephone booth. Yes, my friends, I had fallen for an old stunt and both of us just wept with laughter at Jim's ingenuity, the tension of the day well and truly overcome. We both wished we could have stayed behind to enjoy the party our friends were having in Exeter, in those days that was not the form.

One night at the Grand was about as far as my pocket would stretch to; after Sunday Communion at St Luke's in the centre of Torquay, we set off for The Castle Hotel in St Mawes for the remainder of a week's honeymoon. My new mother-in-law put us up for one last night at the Elms before we headed back to Holyport in Berkshire where my parents now lived after the sale of South Ley to Bill and Margaret Meddings. The following day we took the flight back to Zambia and our future life together.

Landing once again at Ndola airport we were met by Brendan, Maurice, Westy and their various girlfriends who treated us to a champagne reception in the car park they had kindly driven my Princess to in readiness for the onward drive to Kitwe. Sent off on the final leg of our long journey by our laughing friends, we had driven not half a mile when the smell of fish filled the car. No cans on the bumper, no "just married" signs in lipstick on the car windows, but carefully wrapped kippers tied to the manifold. All along the way the locals waved to catch my attention, pointing to the clouds of smoked perch mist emerging from under my car. "Nice chaps", as my father would have said!

10

Mark Phillips

(1972)

Moira Wharrad had done us proud, the parquet floor of the spacious split-level lounge of our sprawling bungalow now restored to a high polish, hiding all traces of the previous resident's spilt drinks around the L-shaped corner bar he had installed. The choice of upholstery was a bright pink, trendy at that time, no doubt in honour of my new Bride. We used the guest annex as our master bedroom, the four other bedrooms variously furnished with my old *katunda*[14] from the house in Ndola.

Before leaving for the UK I had installed Esther, wife of Clememt Chileshe from the store's display department to cover the housework; Clement had no place to live because his earlier digs in his cousin-brother's mine house had been lost when the said relative had been fired, no reason given. Clement was a cheerful soul and was glad to have temporary use of our servant's *kaai*[15] rent free for as long as Esther worked

---

14. Katunda, meaning possessions, luggage, bric-a-brac
15. Kaai means a small house, general word for servant's quarters.

for us, her wages paid from my pocket. To look after the grounds and garden I had brought Friday and Andrew across from Ndola, they lived with family in one of the townships.

John Hurn invited us to his Sunday breakfast party, never to be missed, the giant fry-up prepared and served in the garden by Roundy, his legendary cook. For entertainment we listened to recorded tapes of *Top of the Pops* from the BBC, posted out from England each week by John's father. John had a similar reel-to-reel tape recorder as I had, blasting out the sounds of Alan Freeman and the latest chart-toppers. The brightly coloured birds and lizards of the garden seemed unimpressed as they pecked and hopped around us.

Our first "at-home" was only a week later to celebrate my 29th birthday combining it with a cup-final party the following Saturday. We all listened to the live commentary on a Zenith shortwave radio. It proved to be a big day for Maurice, who hailed from Morley and supported Leeds United, who beat the Arsenal 1-0 to win the Cup for the first time in the Centenary year of the competition.

Not long after, Tory tested her cooking skills on our next door neighbours, Jim Murphy and his wife Molly, a middle aged couple from Dublin, a meal with the unlikely outcome of me agreeing to buy Molly's pale blue Opel shooting break for Tory at a knock-down price. Tory had already enrolled for driving lessons. Jim, who was a solicitor and advocate, had decided to retire to their cottage in Wexford after more than twenty years in the territory. Like at least two other Irish legal men serving in Zambia, Jim had been offered a post as a judge in the High Court but had no desire to move to Lusaka.

Clement Mambwe and his wife Veronica were early guests for dinner, Clement had spent four years on a Canadian government bursary at a university in Toronto. On return to his homeland he had been recruited by our firm and fast tracked up the management ladder to be General Manager of our store in Mufulira, about thirty miles distant from Kitwe. I had been asked to keep a watching brief to support Clement. They were both good company and confirmed to me that travel broadens the scope of our minds, regardless of our original backgrounds. Clement was a beneficiary of the generous Canadian aid budget I have previously described. It was his sense of humour that endeared Clement to me, just as it had been with Denis Sakalla; maybe the fact that they had both assimilated the western mind set, through a daily contact with *"mzungu"*[16], enabled them to switch cultures, just as I had found I was able to do in Germany, that country's humour being far more cynical and lavatorial than mine, but funny none the less.

Suffice to recount that work in the store went apace. Sales grew with the country's economy still fired by strong commodity prices, not least copper, which had reached £1,400 per tonne on the London Metal Exchange. President Nixon was forging strong links with China, hoping to bring about an end to the hopeless war in Vietnam. The Conservative government of Ted Heath was making little progress in controlling the powers of the Trades Unions in Britain. The bush war In Rhodesia was taking its toll on the resources of Ian Smith's government, the same could be said for the turmoil felt by Portuguese colonial regimes in Angola and Mozambique.

Tory and I made a weekend trip to Salisbury, managing not to repeat the woes of a previous trip I had made with the boys when we were turfed out of a comedy club after I had

---

16. Mzungu is a general word for white men or strangers, like the Arab word "kafir"

loudly chastised the stand-up comedian on the stage for ridiculing life and people north of the border. The Rhodesian youth took a dim view of us red-necks fraternising with the locals, as did a certain Mr Jenkins, an officer of the Rhodesian Customs at the border post in Chirundu. We had managed to leave the Copperbelt that Friday evening just an hour after sundown and had reached the border at Chirundu just after midnight, planning to drive through the night. Having cleared the Zambian side and crossed the river, we parked to clear Rhodesian border formalities. The said Mr J required me to open doors, boot and bonnet, then remove the rear wheels, suspecting, he declared in his Geordie sing-song, that we were smuggling gemstones or whatever; Jenkins' reputation was legion with us expats, he just could not stand the thought that we were working for the "enemy". Of course, the weasel faced demi-god found nothing, and at last I had the car off the jack ready to roll when I called back to Jenkins "was there anything else, sir?" Getting a negative reply, I told him that he might find it interesting to know that on our side of the border we had local Zambian Africans qualified to do his job. I was a marked man thereafter.

As we passed through the Huringwe game reserve before reaching the southern Zambesi escarpment the dawn was breaking to the east revealing a layer of mist hovering six feet or so above the ground, causing the treetops to appear disembodied from their trunks. It was a magic hour when game such as elephant, lion, various bush buck, and baboons came close to the road before the giant golden sun popped up to provide a fiery backdrop to the forest. We were driving along a road which took us through the farming settlements of Karoi and Chinoyi before we reached Salisbury ready for breakfast at the Red Fox Inn, our destination.

This was 1972 and an air of normality still pervaded the city centre, the presence of the khaki clad[17] British South African Police Service taking a high profile. We had lunch in the famous Meikles Hotel on Jameson Street. Meikles to Salisbury was like Raffles is to Singapore, Reid's is to Funchal, The Norfolk is to Nairobi, The Hotel Ivoire is to Abidjan, The Oriental is to Bangkok or The Peninsular is to Hong Kong, famous watering holes one and all. By now Rhodesia was in a state of civil war, so in a way it was understandable that the oafish young men in the night club or the assertive officials such as my favourite border officer, ignorant of life beyond their boundaries, led them to take the view that the governance of African countries by whites as being good, and by the native blacks as bad, allowing for no shades of grey (working together), despite Ian Smith's declaration that Rhodesia was a meritocracy.

The war had driven people to be incapable of providing the space for an adult negotiation or exchanges of views. Our trip south had been less enjoyable than it was informative. The Rhodesian Front (RF) missed a trick when not taking the warnings of Nkomo in particular, and others, including the South African leadership under John Vorster. They found conflict when another way would have been possible, after the break-up of the Federation. Had they done so the RF would probably not have come to power. As it was, I supposed, they could not do that, as they would be seen to have "betrayed" their white constituents. The latter held the UK Foreign and Commonwealth Office in low regard, imagining they could go it alone, and for a while they did, to the extent that BMW started production of the Cheetah, a model saloon car

---

17. British South Africa Police service was in fact the unchanged name of the Rhodesian Police, originally formed in 1889 as a paramilitary mounted security force by the British South Africa Company.

well adapted for the bush roads, and a lot of other import replacement production received investment.

Universal conscription of white males became compulsory, leaving farms in remote areas poorly defended against marauding gangs, and the bloodbath began, at first with more fatalities suffered by the black people, many of whom supported the white government. A visitor to Salisbury might have thought that all was under control, but as events later proved, the whole edifice was doomed, although the death of the RF would take several years yet. What eventually followed was a story of horror beyond imagination then, so heart breaking to me, knowing as I did a lot of people of goodwill who lived in that once wonderful country.

Back on the Copperbelt I had been diagnosed with giardia lamblia, a parasite invading the gut. I had just had a call from Tory to say she had arranged a dinner party that evening to entertain friends who had not long arrived in Zambia from the UK. We liked home entertaining, always have done, it was a way of life for us; ever since moving to manage the largest department store and supermarket in the city I had found guests would often bring up something they had experienced as part of dinner conversation, something I did not encourage, indeed my stock in trade reply was to invite them to bring their complaint or query and have tea or coffee with me the next day in my office, which usually put the matter to bed.

That afternoon I turned up for my appointment at the doctor's surgery where a pretty dark-haired British nurse called Nina put a needle into my bare buttock and smiled sweetly with embarrassment as I made some unnecessary remark about dropping my trousers on our first acquaintance. There was a meeting with the Trades Union officials later, which went on and on, as they always seemed to do, until I brought matters to a close to deal with a cash shortage case. I then rushed home to shower and change clothes and set drinks out in readiness for our guests, a Doctor from the Rhokana mine called Nigel Burgess and his wife, who duly arrived with another invited couple. I found I needed no introduction to Mrs Burgess, the said nurse Nina. The lady's blushes were a sight to behold.

Many place names in Zambia were derived from the tribal chiefs of the area, for example our copper mine was on the land of Chief Nkana and another, not so far away, the one visited by my parents called Mindolo Deep, was named after the Chief's mother Mindola. Words from the local African languages crept into our English, as indeed did some South African or Rhodesian expressions, for example traffic lights were known as robots and food was scoff which, if you liked it, was deemed to be lecker. If someone was in big trouble with, for example, their wife, they were facing *maningi ndaba*[18].When I was at home in England on leave before our wedding my brother John had accused me of adopting a (Northern) Rhodesian accent, which I denied, but on reflection I felt was an inevitable result of exposure to folk who *"porked the cor"*, rather than parked it.

After Zambian Independence the annual bank holidays of Rhodes and Founders days in early July were re-named Heroes and Unity Days. Taking advantage of the break from work a group of our friends made up a party with us to go by car to Livingstone. After checking into a guest house belonging to friends, we proceeded to make a day camp about three miles upstream from the Victoria Falls. We had already borrowed a boat with a powerful outboard motor and water skis.

---

18. Maningi means much or a lot of or big and Ndaba is a word for trouble or discussion

Being dry season, the game viewing within the Livingstone Park was quite stunning, as it had been in the Kafue Game Reserve on the journey down. We could see there were hippos nearby. All over our chosen spot were elephant droppings in which we found vegetable ivory, white indestructible kernels of the fruit from a type of palm tree which flourished along the banks of the Zambesi. The little balls of "ivory" passed through the digestive tracts of the mighty animals and were easily washed to be used as a decorative top to the souvenir walking sticks sold by vendors to the many tourists visiting the Falls.

Tory and the other girls took over the task of organising a barbecue, we had brought all the supplies and gear we needed with us from Kitwe, including cold boxes full of beers and water. As the meal was being thought about, if not yet in the preparation stage, I set off in the boat with Brendan and Westy heading for the fast running open water at the centre of the mile-wide river. We navigated around the many islands and rocky outcrops identified only by the frothing water of the river not so far from the big drop downstream at the falls. Finding some good open stretches we took it in turns to ski behind the boat. I had learned to water ski in north Wales at Abersoch in a protected seawater bay, but the waters of the Zambesi presented a considerable variance on that experience.

It was on my second ski-run, when we had drifted to a point about seven hundred yards above the Falls that the boat arced around to head away from the dangerous drop, responding to my urgent signal when I heard Westy shout what I heard as "crocs" (he actually called out the danger of "rocks" gesticulating without a bottle of ketchup this time). I ditched the skis and swam as fast as I could to the safety of the boat, where I remained for the next hour until we returned to the barbecue site, having recovered the skis as they floated downstream. Crocodiles prefer placid waters, so my sudden fear of providing a meal for some monster was totally without foundation, and I became the butt of several jokes whenever the subject of water skiing arose.

The country's foreign exchange reserves had been depleted over time because of some profligate government spending and support of the freedom fighters of ZAPU, FRELIMO and the MPLA in the neighbouring territories. My Company's ability to import depended first on acquiring foreign exchange and secondly on obtaining licences for the categories of merchandise we needed for the stores. Luxury goods became the first victims of shortages. At our HQ in Ndola Mike Delaney and his buyers were working hard to secure import licences, we were coming into a time when import substitution through local production had to be stepped up.

For my part in Kitwe I had been working to set up new product or service areas in the store, and to secure our sources of fresh product for the supermarket. In conjunction with a cleaning business owned by an Indian named Ravi Ranshaw, I was able to establish a laundry and dry-cleaning service. Zambian and Congolese artists and artisans began to offer us their finer pieces enabling the store to set up a department to promote local arts and crafts. At long last we had managed to get real support from the city police to remove the hawkers and unlicensed vendors from the broad stretch of pavement running the length of our storefront, about two hundred feet, which helped me make far better use of the display department and their efforts to provide excitement in the store's windows. I had meetings with Ernie Rogers who owned the Rhokana Mine Mess, the outcome was to offer a range of six kinds of pre-prepared frozen meals from our freezer cabinets; our butchery and meat supplier, Franz Werner, an émigré Austrian came up with a range of salamis and other charcuterie to compliment an expanding delicatessen section. John Blackburne took over the fruit and vegetable supplier's role from Cedric Whitimore, who was upping his egg and chicken production under his *Eggs for Africa* brand from his farm on the Kafue, upstream from John, who appointed another John, his clever Zambian foreman, to manage buying-in stocks of fresh vegetables from local farmers, thus expanding the range of our offer.

At Mfubu Ranch, John Blackburne had installed new mushroom production, not previously attempted in our part of the world. His citrus orchards and banana fields were to be enlarged twofold and I agreed with Mike to provide financial certainty to our major supplier of fruit and greengrocery by giving John a contract. I thought that might allow him to borrow to increase his investment in irrigation equipment and other plant.

The climate provided challenges, not least to the passage of local pigs and cattle through the government abattoir, thence to Franz's butchery and into the store. New chiller and freezer cabinets had arrived from Italy to replace failing equipment that we had to scrap, in part, and sell on the serviceable units to local traders in the peri-urban areas beyond the city centre. In all this I had the support of Neil Eccles our food manger from Sheffield and his deputy John Songolo.

There was an Afrikaner farmer called *Van*[19] who called me out of the blue on the telephone from his home in Southern Province. Neville Hoets, a friend of mine and business owner in Kitwe, who had launched Hellmann's Mayonnaise in

19. Van, so many Afrikaners had that nick name, taken from their family names, for example Van der Merwe, as the French "De, du or de la" or the German "Von", it is similar to calling a Scot "Mac".

central Africa and whose claim to fame was that he had been at school with the author Wilbur Smith, had apparently given my home number to Van. It transpired that Van was coming by pick-up truck to Kitwe the next day, on the back of which he had twenty five sacks of locally grown Irish potatoes, in other words he was growing Murphy's where none had grown before. I gave Van directions to the house in Freedom Avenue since he would be arriving after business hours. He arrived on the dot at six o'clock the next day with his spuds and collie bitch, who had to be housed in the *kaai*, a safe distance from my amorous dog Sammy.

After a few beers I had reached an agreement in principle with Van that I would get the firm to advance him two thousand Kwacha to buy seed potatoes provided ZCBC had first call on his crop. I called Maurice and Mike, who gave me the OK for the deal, and so it was that for the coming two years our store had a monopoly on four seven ton truck loads of a staple food at a time when spuds could not be imported for lack of foreign exchange. By the third year the potato crop failed due to blight and our two thousand kwacha rolling deposit disappeared with Van over the border into Matabeleland or wherever, but we had already made a satisfactory return on the good crops.

Our Company held the Marks and Spencer franchise for Zambia and stocked St Michael products within the clothing and food departments of our stores and shops. It was not a major money spinner for us but added some prestige to our image locally. We had what was billed a courtesy visit from the boys of Baker Street, although I suspected they wanted to check our displays and the state of stocks on their arrival, after travelling thousands of sea and land miles from Britain. I had long felt the packaging was insufficiently robust for non-containerised handling in Dar es Salaam and the rough road transportation by ZamTan, indeed whilst the soft goods were largely unharmed, many cans and dry food packs showed dents and spoiling marks.

Several of us questioned our ability to allocate valuable foreign exchange to support the import business with the UK's leading retailer. As things turned out, M&S took the decision out of our hands by deciding, rightly in my view, to pause the franchise contract until better freight arrangements could be achieved. They never did, at least not in my time.

Being head of a prominent business in any town or city brings with the job a raft of social, community and legal obligations, some enjoyable and many not so. If a big wig from the Lusaka body politic visited town I was expected to turn up to a reception hosted by the Mayor or the District Governor. The events were largely good humoured with some raucous back slapping and seemingly endless speeches, oh boy, how they liked to talk!

My attendance at the Magistrates' or District Courts was a regular occurrence, not just to fulfil my duties as a licencee which, as in the UK, was a function of a responsible individual not that of the company, but more often in criminal cases involving shoplifting or theft where we chose to support a police prosecution, which was our standard policy. Some cases were open and shut, others more complicated and a few got the attention of the local or national press. One such case involved a shoplifting arrest of a European woman by Snake Lungu. Following procedure, Snake called me to his "interview room", the woman claiming she knew me and was sure I would let her go, and yes, I did recognise the lady, she was the girlfriend of the Secretary of the Nkana Golf Club at the mine, of which I was a new member.

After a short conversation I picked up Snake's 'phone and dialled the police who duly pitched up, arrested the felonette, to coin a word, taking her away for charging at the station. Less than an hour later I received in my office a delegation from the Golf Club comprising the Club Secretary, the Club Captain and a couple of Committee members, demanding the case be dropped. "No way, gentlemen", I had to tell them, "we have no separate rules for Club Secretary's companions, nor anyone else for that matter, just last week I had to prosecute the girlfriend of the UNIP Convenor who had leant on me a lot harder than any of you guys could do". Hateful stares confronted me and after some silent seconds I added "No, we leave it up to the Courts to make judgement, so will you please leave".

Privately I could never undermine my African security staff for the sake of a white person, it would be unthinkable. The lady duly went to Court and got a suspended sentence, but I was blackballed from the Golf Club and I did not bother to attend the extraordinary meeting of the Club Committee I had been called to, and never played on that course again. Fortunately the Courts only called me as a witness if something to do with company policy had to be explained, the Chief Accountant Jacob Mbewe or the Training Manager Laston Kaluba would usually deputise or on some occasions the Assistant Store Manager, a chap who had been recruited from John Lewis called Bob Loose, would act in my stead.

October was fast approaching, bringing with it heat and humidity ahead of the rains. Tory, who had been carrying our baby, was coming to the end of her term, proving herself an excellent timekeeper as Andrew arrived spot on the day, or night as it happened, he was due. We subscribed to CIMAS[20] who provided

---

20. CIMAS, acronym for Copperbelt Independent Medical and Ambulance Service, a private medical insurance service

clinics for its members in most of the Copperbelt towns, so when her contractions became regular after sundown, I rushed Tory to the clinic. Our GP, a Doctor Jenkinson, was playing a match at the Squash Club where he had been alerted by telephone from the nurse in charge.

The open windows of the ward were fitted with mosquito gauze, as were most metal framed windows in Zambia, but Tory's brow was aglow under the slow spinning ceiling fan, and still no sign of the Doctor. It was the hottest night of the year, and humid to boot, the rains only a few weeks away and I was getting a bit frantic, behaving like any inexperienced first timer. I tried occupying the time by soothing my wife's brow in the ninety degrees October night heat, even at this late hour, when the said Doctor Jenkinson arrived at last carrying his squash racket and clad in white shorts. A reassuring smile as hands were washed, he bade me stand aside, took a stethoscope to various parts of the panting anatomy of the mother to be, and urged her to heave and push.

Within minutes of the Doctor's arrival our baby son was born, and his father passed out.

I wanted to tell the world about the birth, charged with raw emotion as I was, but it was midnight and the only person I was able to call was John Hurn, who appeared within ten minutes with two bottles of *Taittinger*. Good old John! Young Andrew Charles was well whetted by the morning.

The following weeks were all about the baby. The bar I had won was put to better use as a layette counter, Tory and I had moved our bedroom to be next to the little boy in his well-prepared nursery, thus freeing up the guest wing. As visitors came and went, I realised the extent to which our circle of friends had expanded since our marriage. Anne Ball-Foster and Gay Johnstone, whose husbands were both called Mike and worked for Indeco Morison, provided motherly advice proving a great help to Tory, fussing, and running errands.

I had little day time away from work, but rushed back not many days after Andy's birth when I was told we had a special delivery of a shining black billy goat which had just arrived in our driveway, tethered on the back of a flat truck driven from Solwezi by the brother of Alice, my secretary. It was her gift, as was fitting for the son of a Chief, but what to do with such a magnificent animal in our urban garden where I had let him roam on a short rope? To start with he had to be named, so we chose "Mark Phillips" after the recently wed husband of the Princess Anne. Then we needed to find a more suitable home for MP. Step up John Blackburne, who collected the gleaming coal coloured stud which would be cared for by one of the villages on his ranch.

We used the nickname *"Picky"* for young Andrew, derived from the diminutive *piccanin* referring to an African child, although his blond baby hair confounded such origins. By the time he was three months, Picky was a regular in our swimming pool and could swim without wings when six months old. Somehow his specific gravity allowed him to bob to the surface and float, he was quite fearless of water. Picky was a star guest at our next cup final party, when to the utter chagrin of Maurice, the second division side Sunderland beat his beloved Leeds United 1-0. Once again, my Zenith short wave radio did not let us down.

Mike Foster joined us when on a camp for two nights at Baluba Hill, a rocky *kopje*[21] on Mfubu land, the home of a troop

---

21. Kopje, a small isolated hill or rocky outcrop, a not uncommon feature in the bushland of central Africa, the word is taken from the low Dutch or Afrikaans "koppie".

of baboons, who made sure we kept our fire going throughout the night. In the morning I collected water from the nearby Baluba stream and gave Picky a bath in a plastic washing up bowl. Our son was a healthy boy, the light of our lives.

11

Midnight Cowboy

(Late 1972-'74)

Now that 1972 was coming to its close we were looking forward to spending our first Christmas together as a family, the word "home" now meant where we were at, no longer with our parents or even in the UK. The warm climate held the prospect of two days splashing in and out of swimming pools at our house on Freedom Avenue or at Mike and Anne Foster's home in Parklands, a mile distant. The department store had been exacting in the run-in to Christmas, our business being the main retail attraction taking the lead role in the city's preparations for the great festival, with an exciting Santa Claus Grotto we opened following the dramatic arrival of Father Christmas.

By popular acclaim we had chosen one of the store's cleaners, a Mr Lovely Chishimba, to be Santa. Lovely's mother must have had a cruel sense of humour, for his countenance no way matched his name; mind you, behind the white beard and red robes was a man full of the kindness as reflected in his eyes. Lovely made his grand entrance from the back of a flat truck driven by Yandikani Mumbwa, our senior driver, which had been adorned with a wild splash of bright glitzy carnival colours by his workmate Joseph Mpundu[22]. Joseph was one of those guys who seemed to find a solution to any problem, a gifted handyman. A band played, then one by one other floats drifted by the store front, all with their own themes and music, some downright loudly out of tune, others serene such as two choirs from township churches.

Clement from the display department was appointed Lovely's deputy, allowing for meal and comfort breaks. Over three hundred youngsters passed through the grotto wonderland each day. On the second to last day before Christmas Eve Bob Loose had not been told that Clement had reported sick, so come the close of business a red missile was seen to fly across the still crowded ground floor from the grotto, making a bee-line for the staff rooms. It was Lovely, of course, our faithful Father Christmas, who had sat unrelieved in several senses since the early morning. What a lovely fellow he was by name and nature if not by good looks, he must have been desperate.

By Christmas Eve we had sold over a thousand frozen turkeys imported by air from England on a special licence. Further birds had been supplied through Franz, our butchery master who presented me with the largest turkey I had ever seen, all thirty four pounds of it which he had placed in my car parked in the service alleyway at the back of the store. I drove home after close-down ready for the welcome two days break, bringing the Princess to a halt outside our kitchen door where Abram, our house servant emerged to greet me in his as usual

---

22. Mpundu, a twin, common name in Zambia. In previous times if twins were born, it being too much for the poorly fed mother to sustain two babies, the twins were left in the bush after birth, the one died, the survivor was nurtured.

way. Not knowing the word for turkey in ChiBemba (if there was one) I used *nkuku*, the word for chicken, and asked him to pick up the fast unfreezing avian from the car's back seat. Poor Abram, a chicken so large stopped him in his tracks, I swear his bulbous eyes stood out on stalks like a comic character from the Beano.

As we feasted on one leg of the monster roast the next day, I looked back on the tumultuous year we had just lived through. Back in the UK the miners had been on strike in January and February at a time when Edward Heath, the Prime Minister, was more concerned, it seemed, to sign the Accession Treaty for the country to join the Common Market of Europe. We had married at a great cathedral. We had managed to get down to Salisbury only days before Ian Smith decided to close the border of Rhodesia with our country, protesting at the support he alleged that Zambia was giving to "terrorists". Now, at the end of the year, we had a son.

In January 1973 Britain signed the Treaty of Rome and joined the Common Market. Harold Wilson, he of the wage freeze and leader of the Labour opposition regarded the terms of Britain joining the Rome Treaty as derisory and demanded a renegotiation. Prominent politicians from right and left agreed with Wilson. As Wilson and Heath were shouting at each other the oil price started to jump, and President Nixon signed the Paris Accord to end the terrible war in Vietnam. Two months later Nixon started the sell-off of metals and other commodities from the US Stockpile[23], having already caused mayhem two years earlier by taking the dollar away from the gold standard, bringing to an end the Bretton Woods

---

23. The US stockpile described the outcome of the policy adopted by successive US administrations to conserve domestic stocks of essential raw materials along with minerals and commodities in favour of importing from foreign resources.

international money accord set up in the aftermath of the Second World War.

The copper price dipped on the London Metal Exchange, I guessed because every bullet and bomb fired or dropped in Vietnam contained that metal which was no longer needed for armament production on such a grand scale. It did not take long for the price to drop below the cost of extracting and refining the ore. Zambia, a major copper producer, was in trouble, as was Zaire, now under the thumb of General Mobuto Sese Seko; Salvadore Allende's Chile in another continent, also a major producer of copper, suffered the same plight.

In February 1973 Ian Smith told the world's press that he was re-opening the border, suggesting that by closing it he had forced Zambia to stop supporting ZAPU and others, quite untrue, but Kenneth Kaunda announced that he was keeping the border closed. All of a sudden I saw that our trade routes from the south were shut, some said Kaunda had cut off his nose to spite his face, but I saw it was a clever gamble to put the pressure on Britain to sort out the Rhodesia problem, the main cause of Zambia's economic difficulties.

As the rains came to their end in March, Tory's mother and stepfather arrived for a month's stay. Very quickly the couple took to walking young Andrew in his stripy buggy. They trekked through the African market and trading areas, causing quite a stir, clad as they were, Dorothea in a flamboyant flowing dress with matching wide brimmed sun hat, and Tony in his WWII baggy khaki shorts and pith helmet, an article of dress I had not seen since meeting the Lewanika in Mongu three years before.

I took a week's local leave and borrowed John Blackburne's Land Rover for another adventure through the Kafue Game

Park and on to Livingstone and the Victoria Falls. There we stayed in two whitewashed mud rondavels with grass roofs at a tourist encampment. I took a liking for Tony who had an interesting life story. He had served as a pilot in both the Navy and RAF, and as a support officer on Churchill's staff. I did not know that he suffered unusually badly from vertigo and claustrophobia when I took our visitors down the deep mine at Mufulira, learning about it later from his wife once we were safely home and the ordeal was over for him. Their stay was otherwise full of fun, it had provided time to get to know my new family and for them to be at ease with us, and for Tory a chance, for once, to be hostess to her mother.

It was not so long before we saw them again. We took Andy on leave back to Europe to meet his other grandparents, cousins, uncles, and aunts for the first time, and for us to have a holiday in June. It also provided the chance for us to join Tory's sister Katy and her husband Richard Sale, then a barrister in BP's legal department, to have Andy and their son George baptised together at Barkham Church near their new home at Longmoor Lodge in Finchamstead. The isolated property was situated close to an army garrison known as Longmoor Camp and its functions were a bit *hush hush*. It had been a training unit for bomb disposal soldiers. My boyhood chum Derek Merrell's elder brother had worked at Longmoor in the '50s as a Major in the Royal Engineers, he told me some years afterwards, in charge of a cold war project they were hatching up with the Americans.

Nonetheless, Longmoor provided a wonderful venue for the large family and friends party which followed the Baptisms, affording us a rare opportunity to see folk without having to travel the length and breadth of the British Isles. Time was always short when taking leave.

We left our newly Christened son in Exeter with his grandparents for a week and took a flight to Germany. Hiring an acid yellow Ford Taunus (these were the seventies, cars were brightly coloured, men sported *gaucho* moustaches, side burns and bell bottoms, ladies still wore mini-skirts over bottle tanned legs) we drove from Dusseldorf to Bad Homburg to stay with my friend Uli Hummel and his wife Elizabeth. Uli's father was a doctor in general practice whose home I had lived in as a paying guest for nine months in '61, now their three-story house in *Brendelstrasse* had been inherited by Uli. I had missed Margaret Lumsden's Teutonic kitchen since moving to Kitwe, but Elizabeth had delighted me with her generous helpings of *leberkaes* and *ribchen mit sauerkraut* at dinner.

The following day it was lunch up the hill at the home of Heinz Begere and his elegant wife Eva. Heinz was my mentor and former boss at Arnold Becker in Frankfurt. Lunch became dinner as my German fluency returned, glad to do so using the informal manner of address in the second person, something the Germans would not have allowed when I was a mere trainee. Heinz and Eva spoke English to Tory using me as interpreter from time to time when words failed them, thankful that I could still do so, particularly when asked about the glow worms which lit up the warmth of an early evening on the terrace as we sat looking out at the garden, drinking *kalte Ente*, a delightful white wine spritzer with the twisted zest of a whole lemon suspended within the liquid from the silver cap of a crystal jug.

When I first arrived at Frankfurt's *Hauptbahnhof* I was barely eighteen years old. West Germany, then the *Bundesrepublik*, had been formed in 1949 by the Western Allied Occupation Forces after inviting each of the Occupied German States to join a Federation, holding elections under a new Constitution which was won by Konrad Adenauer. The "old fox", as he was affectionately known, was an academic who led the Christian Democrat Party. Adenauer had survived imprisonment under the Nazis. He proved a most capable leader, unifying the western parts of the country despite the historic and strongly felt rivalry between the States, or Lands as they became better known.

The new Constitution provided for two thirds of the seats in the *Bundesrat* (Parliament) to be elected as in Britain, first past the post. The remaining third were allocated to outsiders, usually experts in one field or another by the Parties in proportion to the votes placed for them, eliminating any Party which had not achieved five per cent of the total votes cast nationally. Not a bad system, I thought.

Adenauer had appointed Ludwig Erhard as Finance Minister (Erhardt succeeded Adenauer in 1963 as Chancellor) who was lauded as the author of the *Wirtschaftswunder* (economic miracle) setting Germany on a course of post war economic success and fiscal discipline, although it is my view that without the American Marshall Plan that would not have happened. Bad Homburg is a spa town built around the open spaces of its *Kurpark* which plays host to Europe's first Casino, a short distance from Frankfurt-am-Main in the northernmost Land of the American Zone of Occupation, called Hesse.

The firm I was to work for, a distributor of textiles called Arnold Becker, was managed by Heinz, and employed several hundred people in its in five branches. Heinz had been a cavalry officer in the *Wehrmacht*. I learned about his war service, first on the western front in France, where his regiment captured a British supply train lost in the rush to Dunkirk. He was relocated to the eastern front joining the vast army assembled at Stalingrad, a disaster for the German cavalry which the troops survived only by eating frozen horse flesh. After the retreat from the Soviets he was sent to Italy, where he ended up on General Kesselring's Staff, before being taken prisoner of war by the British army.

A small package reached Heinz some four years after his arrest and subsequent interrogation by the British Army Intelligence Corps in which Jim Lafferty had served. Marked "OHMS" , the brown paper parcel had been forwarded eight times before reaching the addressee. It contained his watch and other valuables in a package under cover of a letter signed personally by Field Marshal Lord Alexander, which he showed to me. "What country other than Britain would provide a cubby hole somewhere in Whitehall to store a watch which no longer worked and pay for it to be returned to its owner?", he wondered one evening when I had asked him why he wore two watches. "One to tell the time, the other never to forget the act of kindness" he had said. I felt proud of my country.

Working in Frankfurt as a trainee I had few hours of spare time. I would begin at half past seven in the morning, not knocking-off until five in the afternoon. I travelled by bus for half an hour from Bad Homburg to the company's building in the *Weserstrasse* near the *Frankfurter Hauptbahnhof* where I had first met Heinz. On Saturdays we worked until midday, which was good, because I had time to play tennis at the club I had joined near my digs. Sundays I often spent with my school pal Peter Norman, who had arranged a six-months internship with a shoe business in the south of Frankfurt on the other side of the city.

Peter had ridden his BSA Bantam motorbike from England. On several occasions whilst Peter was with me we drove the bike on the autobahn and local roads to Geisenhem on the Rheingau, home of Lo Siegert, who had been an *au pair* at the Norman's home in Northwood some years before. Lo lived with her mother, who had taught me to play *skat*, so useful on the trip to Mauritius you might remember, and her elderly grandmother. Her father had died during the war in East Prussia, where the family had an estate before the Soviet occupation.

On one occasion two German friends I had made playing tennis asked me to go overland with them to West Berlin. As a British passport holder I would have no problem crossing through East Germany by the autobahn corridor, although my West German mates might have problems on the way if stopped by the Stasi or Soviet military, a matter hotly debated with their fearful parents. The parental problem was solved for them when news arrived the day before our planned departure that the Ulbricht Government in the Communist East had started to build a wall to divide the city out of barbed wire and bricks, ostensibly, so they said, to keep out marauding Fascists from the West, but in reality to stem the tide of escapees from Communist brutality. I never did get to visit Berlin.

It was Heinz who insisted I stay on for a spell at his Company's branch in Munich after a home trip in December to be with my family for Christmas. I fell on my feet with free digs in Munich at the family home in Gauting of the owner of a prominent printing *Verlag*, in exchange for giving his three children lessons in English. Further duties included escorting the printer's wife to the Bavarian State Opera every week in formal dress, coincidental to his poorly camouflaged weekly dinner date with his mistress. During the five months of winter I spent there I leaned to ski and enjoy the beer, food, and culture of Bavaria's fine capital city.

It was fun sharing memories and impressions of Germany with my dear fellow passenger as we drove the yellow Taunus from Bad Homburg, made famous by the hat which Teddy, the Prince of Wales had bought there in Queen Victoria's reign, to the Black Forest in southern Baden-Wurttemberg to stay with Lo and her husband Bernd.

Bernd Eger had worked for *Matteus Mueller*, the famed producer of *sekt* made in Wiesbaden, but had moved south to take charge of a schnapps distillery in the Black Forest. After sampling much of Bernd's production we made our way to the Biehl's house where I had lived in Gauting, from there we travelled on to Salzburg in the Austrian Tirol, which had been an earlier haunt of Tory's. At last we returned to Exeter for an emotional reunion with our little son.

For once I enjoyed a trip down Memory Lane with Tory who had met a few of the main characters of my late teenage adventure in Germany. I missed my old work colleagues in Frankfurt, war widows like Frau Meyer and Frau Weber who mothered me when I could barely speak their language, who got me to copy their infectious Frankfurt dialect. Then there was Georg Lind who took me to the Eintracht Stadium to watch some top soccer, a tragic fellow who had been conscripted at sixteen in the dying months of the war, taken prisoner by the Soviets and released sixteen years later from a peasant farm in Siberia. He was billeted as an unpaid labourer, effectively a slave, working for people who did not use a knife and fork, nor a spoon, nor could they read or write a word. Georg was thirty-two when I met him, but he looked twenty years older, poor chap, a wonderful man with no bitterness in his heart.

There are few if no winners in a war, those sent to fight emerge dead, emaciated, deranged, mentally maladjusted or plain crazy, permanently scarred in mind or body or both. Even the heroes and unwounded survivors carry bad memories, which they can sometimes carefully compartmentalise out of memory or for selective recall on the rare occasions when in the company of those who shared their experiences.

We used the few remaining days in England to stay with friends, an experience that caused me to realise that whilst in my imagination we were all as we were four years earlier, time had moved on. I was utterly disinterested in what I termed their "pelmet talk", being regaled with endless descriptions of their home redecoration projects. In the same way my stay-at-home pals and their wives showed signs of sleep as I recounted stories of our life in Africa. A lesson learnt for life, to enjoy the things you have in common with people, and to talk about other things only when your friends show an interest.

Leaving the UK, we had a week with my brother John and his wife Wanda May in a rented apartment at Cala San Vicente on the north coast of Majorca, where Dad had bought a holiday home. Andy was yet a crawler, but Simon and Zoe, John's kids, ran around us riotously. My brother Andrew, by then in his early twenties, joined us at the apartment, then Brendan arrived from Zambia on his way to Liverpool and a period of leave. John, a surveyor, had formed a partnership with a Spaniard called 'Lito Lopez to market residential properties in that part of the island, principally near Pollensa. They quickly found a holiday flat for Brendan to buy.

'Lito was a lovable scoundrel, who later reverted to type with some of my brother's money a few years after the pair had sold us a plot of land. We later sold it with a small loss to a Frenchman who had a lighting business in Paris and a factory near Lille making post boxes. He is forever remembered as the "French letter-box man"[24]. I had to make a special trip to collect

---

24. A French letter was the commonly used slang to describe a condom.

his payment in cash, because the prevailing exchange controls restricted moving money out of Franco's Spain. I believe that Brendan made a small profit when he sold the second-floor apartment at Puerto Pollensa some years afterwards.

In between he had found it to be a convenient venue for holiday trysts. My heart went out to 'Lito's lovely wife Pilar when news reached me of her husband's arrest and subsequent incarceration by the judiciary serving the Generalissimo Franco. We resolved never to buy property abroad again, local laws and customs need to be learned and respected else you fall foul, and in any event, who wants to keep going back to the same place? "I do", you might scream, but I am not so sure!

I was happy to be away from the UK. Our lives in Zambia were not affected by the three-day working week introduced by Mr Heath in response to the power shortages caused by the oil crisis of '73. There might have been long queues at our Zambian petrol stations, but we had no need for central heating oil.

We made good friends with Stephen and Mary Pedley. Stephen was the new Anglican vicar of Kitwe who was a couple of years older than me, we first met when we attended Ron Raymond's wedding to his Scottish girlfriend Eileen, a popular nurse at the Nkana mine hospital. Both Stephen's and Jenny Blackburne's fathers were then newly retired clergymen from Exeter diocese. John's father was still active in the Church in England as Bishop of Thetford. We were later to meet all three men together when Matthew, the Blackburne's second baby boy, was Baptised by Stephen in a little bush chapel on Greystone's Ranch close to Mfubu. The sight of those three elderly priests clad in their crimson cassocks (Bishop Blackburne was a Queen's Chaplain) in that remote spot in darkest Africa remains an indelible memory.

After Ron's nuptials and Jenny's family baptism I joined Tory at a Sikh wedding ceremony of two young hospital friends, both doctors from India. I discovered too late that headwear was *de rigeur* and managed to adorn my head by tying the four corners of a not so pristine white handkerchief to produce a skull cap of sorts. Just as the long formalities had come to their close and I had removed the absurd fake *chapeau*, I received a tap on my shoulder, accompanied by the words "hello, Derrick, what brings you here?". The speaker's face I failed to recognise immediately, but it turned out to be that of Justin Robbins, who at one time shared a desk with me at Aldenham. Justin was one of those fresh-faced chaps at school, I was quite unprepared for the composed handsome adult now in front of me, but happy to make the extraordinary reunion after thirteen years.

It turned out that the now qualified Dr Robbins worked at Tory's hospital as a registrar under another Commonwealth aid scheme. I wondered if Justin had also seen the film *"If"* showing at the Nkana Bioscope, a movie shot at Aldenham and much acclaimed, but I had no inkling of that when to my ultimate surprise and shock I was confronted on screen with the familiar portrait of the school's sixteenth century founder, Richard Platt, a brewer, whose traditions we were quite unable to toast together since Sikh weddings are free of alcohol and, it seemed, also free from any glasses to drink the proffered bottles of Coke and Fanta, the only libations on offer.

As the rains subsided in early '74, I had to consider my future once again. My second work contract would be ending in September. I had overcome the task of staff reduction at the store, the head count had gone down from 450 to 250 in two years, shedding twenty or so jobs previously held by locally employed European. Laston Kaluba, now our Personnel

Manager noted we had recruited and inducted almost two hundred new staff in the two years we had been working together, which meant I must have fired nearly four hundred employees in a period of eight hundred days or so. There were a few people who had retired or resigned of their own accord, but the scale of our personnel work was mind blowing. I recall one chap who lost his job with us after several warnings about his poor work standards who had admonished me at interview, saying that he recognised his failings, but he was honest. "Honest?", I replied, "why, we take honesty for granted, that's no reason to excuse bad work".

No sooner had I digested Laston's analysis of our staff work I received an anonymous letter accusing me of being a "tribalist", yes, me, a *mzungu*, a tribalist. I showed the letter to Jacob Mbewe, proud owner of my once beautiful Vanden Plas Princess, and Harry Chibesakunda his colleague who showed no surprise, indeed they left the room to return with a register of staff comings and goings from the salary records. "Look at those names", Harry suggested, and sure enough the penny dropped. Despite my carefully crafted policy of recruiting purely on merit and suitability, there was no doubt that well over one hundred incomers hailed from the eastern *Ngoni* people whose language *Nyanja* they shared with Malawians. And yet, here we were in the centre of the Copperbelt, home of the *Bemba* people. Guilty as charged it was open and shut, although I never did discover the author of that letter although Jacob, himself Ngoni, had his suspicions.

Great news filtered through to the bar at the Kitwe Club, one of the few places we would go for a meal out. It was Friday, a night to enjoy Botswana beef from the steak counter and grill; John Hurn let it be known he had a girl friend called Liz who had arrived from a village near his UK origins in

Norwich. Liz was to stay under Roundy's care with John. The lady inevitably proved a big hit with the boys so when the time came for her to return home, no rings on her fingers as yet, we organised a breakfast party at the club before she was to be driven to the airport in Ndola. A three dimensional pyramid of wide brimmed champagne glasses, twenty five at the base and one on the fourth (top) level was constructed by Julius the barman, the top glass then filled with crème de menthe into which bottles of champagne were carefully emptied. As the frothing liquid cascaded down the pyramid, the colour changed until all the glasses brimmed a cool light green. With not a drop spilled, the assembled company raised a toast to Liz (and John) in what was dubbed *"Liz fizz"*. Liz, my love, you will never be forgotten.

Another piece of good news, it seemed at the time, was that Cathy McGregor, she of lobster thermidor fame, was to marry Westy. Malcolm's parents, who we had met on a past visit to Salisbury, found a way to get up from Rhodesia to join the reception which was held at our house. I had plans to use the swimming pool as a centre point for the party, identifying strategic victims for an unwanted splash, but as things turned out, the pool's filtration unit broke down and our attempts to mend the system simply resulted in the backwash depositing the contents of the filter cylinder back to the pool, turning it a murky green. The only thing to do was to allow guests into the pool area once darkness followed sundown, circulating paper dishes as floats decorated with bougainvillea and lighted candles. That romantic Plan B solution prevented some smart dressers from getting soaked under the original provisions of Plan A.

Mike had called me in the office to schedule a meeting. "Sounds serious" I mused. "Clearly not to discuss the cricket match next Sunday?" I went on to ask. Mike made no comment, but when he arrived the next day, he had Roy (The Pipe) Ritson with him, so this was going to be personal, I thought. Indeed, it was nothing to do with my new-found tribal criminality but rather about a new contract. Before we started I had to tell Mike, and asked him to alert Lionel Wharrad, that I had taken a 'phone call the previous evening from Stavros, the Cypriot owner of a supermarket in the suburban Parklands Shopping Centre, following our arrest of his mother for shoplifting. Stavros demanded we drop the case. It was another Golf Club Secretary's girlfriend situation, only this time no committee delegation, but a bold statement telling me I had a fair-haired son and they knew where he and my family lived. I had put the 'phone down without comment.

The facts were that the steely grey haired lady had helped herself to a handful of underwear which she had put into a shopping bag, walked from the ladieswear department at one end of the store, past the home furnishings, giftware and food departments, made a diversion to the dry cleaning department, then wandered through menswear at the front as if butter would not melt in her mouth, leaving the store by the first of our four customer doors. She had been apprehended in Matuka Avenue at the front of the store, taken to the interview room, confessed her guilt and departed with a constable from the local nick. Her case would come before the magistrate a week or so hence.

I asked Roy and Mike to record my report in case Stavros and his heavy gang gave me any trouble. That done, we did cover a new contract to start in September, four months hence, which would involve our moving back to Ndola HQ to take charge of the Buying Office, taking over from Ray Broad. I knew Tory would be happy to stay in Zambia, there was no reason not to as far as I was concerned, and the new job would be a great experience with bags of scope to accelerate the import substitution programme we had embarked on. I made one condition once salary levels had been agreed, namely that I take over Ray's house at Nyimba Crescent in Kansenji, the house occupied by Roy and his wife when I first arrived so long ago. I could not wait to get home that night to tell Tory, resolving not to trouble her with the threats from the thug with a mother.

As things turned out at the Courtroom, Mrs Varoufakis was given two years jail suspended for two years and a stiff fine. I heard nothing further from her son.

Having settled matters for the future, at least for the time being, I received news that our Group General Manager would be leaving in June to be replaced by a man recruited by Bookers called Gerald Sterck. Tory and I completed our move in time to be part of the Party sending off the Wharrads with our good wishes for their retirement back to their home in Britain. By now I had started a complete reorganisation of the Buying Office, which included redesigning the internal building, and the recruitment of a secretary, Christine Law. By coincidence, Christine had a little daughter the same age as our son and was known to Tory through play groups, her husband Jim was known to me through David Seaman, his boss at Mobil Oil, Africa.

David, who was a close pal of Brendan, lived in Kitwe, and had sadly lost his wife to cancer not long before. Christine, who I beheld as an English rose in all her glory and bubbly blonde hair, had been working for me for a couple of months when she suddenly announced she had to go on leave to London. I felt a bit miffed as I was shortly to take my end of contract leave and needed Christine on board, but news came no more than two weeks later that the young mother had died in hospital with inoperable breast cancer. Her husband Jim returned, a distraught and inconsolable widower, opting to cut short his employment so that his mother could care for the baby girl. I had no clue that Christine was ill, her loss was so sad, a stark confirmation of the complete uncertainty of life. Unwanted lightening had struck twice at Mobil.

Soon it was my turn to go on long leave. Tory and I travelled with Andy by air to Durban to embark on the SA Vaal of the Union Castle Line on a voyage back to Southampton which lasted nineteen days. Our journey was routed through the Botswana capital city, Gaberone, and Johannesburg to avoid Rhodesian airspace. The trip became memorable for the events on board and the people we met, as well as the route taken, calling into port at East London and Port Elizabeth before staying two nights at Cape Town where we used the ship as our hotel.

It took us more than a week at sea to reach Las Palmas and then a day steaming to Funchal, where we were banned from landing because of the outbreak of revolution in Portugal only two days before our arrival. Before that we had enjoyed discovering Cape Town where we had taken the cable car to the top of Table Mountain through a thick morning mist which eventually dispersed to show that the tabletop was far from flat.

Our trip in the mist was coincidental to the first ever jump by hang gliders, two pairs of young enthusiasts who we met and spoke to before they leapt forth from the table's edge for their historic flight which ended up taking them forty minutes of frolicking in the up draughts. We got down and back into the City in time to greet their safe landing in open parkland, we had beaten the press and TV crews who pounded in on the scene.

As everyone knows, the South Africans take their sport seriously. As we had left Durban at the outset of our sea journey, so the first Rugby Football Test had kicked off between the Springboks and the visiting British Lions led by Willie John McBride, the doyen of Irish Rugby folklore. The Lions won, as they did the next two Tests. By then we were passing the Skeleton Coast off Namibia on our way to the Equator. The day of the fourth and final Test arrived. I placed bets on the outcome with the heavily partisan South African deck officers and the tension aboard became manic as the match commentary was relayed to us through the ship's radio and public address system, only for the match to be drawn. Willie John and his team had survived unbeaten on tour but had to share the final spoils. The South Africans claimed the draw as a victorious winning bet seeing they had not lost which was Afrikaner logic at its best. I did not fall for it.

During the journey up the west coast of Africa we held three further "Test Matches", but this time it was international deck cricket. An eleven raised from volunteer passengers accepted a challenge from the officers, all South Africans. I had worn my garish MCC tie at the Captain's table which gave me some credence with his sporty corps of officers, so I think that might have been the cause of me being asked to captain the passengers' team for the first "Test". The officers had not been beaten in fifteen voyages. We lost the first match. Getting the hang of the new (to us) sport, we threw down the gauntlet for a return Test.

The second match we won, I think they had fielded a reserve team as there were many new faces in the line-up but, of course, the *Vaal* men could not take a defeat lightly. So it was that we were challenged to a decider. My team, by this time, had trained hard and were a determined bunch, but alas, the match proceeded to the final over of eight balls with the officers needing twelve runs with four wickets in hand.

The game was played with a hard ball but there was a long net enclosure which prevented the ball from striking the ship's superstructure or dropping into the sea. I took the players to one side, purposefully holding the game up to distract the guys with epaulettes, brought up the wicket keeper and asked Daniel, an Englishman living in Lusaka, to bowl full length if not Yorkers at the batsman's legs. First ball, lbw and out. Next came a four past the bowler to the end of the netting twenty feet beyond. The next two balls were dots, no runs scored, then Dan thrust down a bouncer, against orders, got a snick which the wicket keeper held above his shoulders. Out! Two wickets and eight runs left for either side to win in the last three balls, the first of which was despatched for another four. Two balls left, four runs needed, two wickets had to be grabbed by a now desperate Dan.

We staged another team huddle to ensure further distraction for the batting side and I asked Dan to slow down. Sure enough, the big hitting batsman mistimed his shot, playing far too early and popped a catch to me at mid-on. All to play for as the number eleven officer came to the crease, the very man who had been bragging about how the Springboks would thrash the Lions when we were still in Durban. Imagine our joy, therefore, when Dan clean bowled him on the last ball, and we won. Whether or not there was an Honours Board in the *Vaal's* wardroom I do not know, but it would be gone long ago as the ship was finally scrapped in 2003, renamed the *SS*

Festivale of the Carnival Cruise Line when bought In 1978 from the ultimate owners Safmarine. It was the passing of an age of mail boats when Union Castle, who leased the vessel, could no longer compete with the airlines. The great ship, which had started life as the *Transvaal Castle*, is no more.

When we left Cape Town I was press-ganged by the entertainments officer to be the auctioneer for the daily run, whereby I had to convene a passengers' get-together in one of the lounges at 11.00 am each day, manage a team of volunteers who would take wagers of one Rand per punter to bet on the number of miles steamed in the past twenty-four hours. The actual mileage was announced each morning by the ship's captain on the tannoy system a few minutes after eleven o'clock. The profits from the daily auctions went to a seafarers' charity. As we neared Southampton on the final day of the voyage I was presented with a pewter mug by the crew for my troubles. I still have it.

After our departure from Madeira the ship held a fancy-dress ball, with competitions for young and old. Tory, who by then was six months into another pregnancy, clad herself in a Union Jack and donned a bicorn naval hat, her entry read "England Expects". Andy we dressed up in a white pillow case with mock laurel leaves on his almost white mop of hair dubbing him "Junior Caesar", he won his category, and I wore a dressing gown, Stetson and rider's scarf as "Midnight Cowboy". I failed to get a prize.

Both sets of parents came to the port in Southampton to greet our arrival for the start of five week's holiday, the last week of which was spent in Majorca where John, my brother, and his wife Wanda had once again rented the split level apartment at Cala San Vicente. We were on our journey back to Zambia. but before flying off via Barcelona and Rome, on to Nairobi and Lusaka, I had to sign a disclaimer to the Spanish Airline releasing it from any responsibility, in the event my wife should go into labour during the flight. In return, the Spanish aircrew placed us at the front of the queue to board and in the front row of the 'plane, avoiding the rude pushing and shoving of the other Iberian passengers. There was no pre-allocated seating then and queuing politely was not something known to the Spanish. We arrived back home safely, our new baby daughter Christy-Anne was born in Ndola a few weeks later.

12

Chinese matches and a burning crocodile

(1974-'75)

The big international event of the late summer of '74 was the resignation of the American President Mr. Richard Nixon. Even the mighty get bitten when they expose their backside. The new US President Gerald Ford seemed a steady pair of hands, but for most of us outside America it seemed a pity to say goodbye to "Tricky Dick Nixon" who had done well on the international stage, easing relations with China and ending the war in Vietnam. Mind you, the Zambian economy was finding it hard to recover copper production given the reduced demand and depressed price of the metal.

My job as Head of Buying became more difficult insofar as we had little foreign exchange to cover necessary imports of manufactured goods, making it even more important to get local producers to support us. Mike Delaney handed me the project to get our own stores group label established across all merchandise ranges, setting incredibly low retail price targets and high quality specifications, modelled on M&S,

not *"St Michael"* but rather simply *"a ZCBC Quality Product"*. The buying team responded with astonishing enthusiasm. Within three months we had stocks coming into the stores and shops, all one hundred and fifteen of them, in all clothing departments, home furnishings, toiletries, food, ceramics and most importantly, school uniforms; as the months went by new lines were added as we spent our import licences on overseas sources of raw materials and componentry for local production. I had to spend more time than I wished travelling away from home checking factories and quality control arrangements for production schedules.

The CIMAS nursing home in Ndola was situated at the top of the hill on Broadway, where Tory had been overnight in readiness for our baby to have an induced birth, should it fail to present itself naturally. The baby was already a week late. It was in the late morning of 22nd October that I had an urgent call from Sally, wife of "West Ham" Sam who we had met aboard the *Vaal,* and who worked for our Medical Service, urging me to get up to the clinic at all speed as things were beginning to happen. "Baby's coming" I shouted as I rushed through the office, across the quad and out of the front door where my newly acquired yellow Cortina, a mirror of the hired Ford Taunus from Duesseldorf, was parked ready for a fast getaway. I smelt burning rubber and saw smoke in the wing mirror facing my wake as I sped up the hill, arriving just in time to scrub up and post myself at the bottom of the hospital bed where Tory was obeying the call to push. A moment later, there she was, our little Christy-Anne.

It was to Margaret Lumsden's house that I made for after the birth. Margaret, who was now working for me as buyer of children's wear, stood on the front stoep of her house, ready with a bottle of bubbles and a wholesome meal. Dear lady and stand-in grandma, we had long ago dubbed her *"from whom all blessings flow"*. I just sat and grinned, as I had done the night Andrew was born two years before in Kitwe.

It was not long after that Andrew proudly showed his new sister off to his chum Lescon Sutton from next door, and to Judy our maid who lived on the premises in the house in our back garden. Tony Sutton ran a clothing manufacturing business in Ndola. His wife Penny, like her husband a wizard squash player, had quickly become a close friend for Tory and had given birth to a second boy, Ewart, a couple of months before our new baby girl.

The walled front garden shielded a tear drop swimming pool which quickly became Andy's favourite play space, secured as it was to be safe for children by the ironmongery which I had installed around the front of the veranda. The garden, ably managed by Howard our gardener, was otherwise dominated by a large rubber plant tree whose shiny dark green leaves and protruding cerise and yellow flowers caught everyone's eyes at the many weekend afternoon pool parties we were to host for friends and their families. A large Avocado tree shaded the house to the rear, producing the largest and tastiest pears I have ever eaten. Half the size of a rugger ball, the giant fruit would drop on to the tiled roof above our bedroom breaking open as they fell onwards to the ground, to the delight of Sammy, who would roll his back and sides in the squishy green-yellow flesh of the fruit. It was his way, we decided, to deal with the ticks which were the purge of pets in that part of the world.

It was wonderful to have two little children to celebrate Christmas with that year, Christy-Anne only two months old. Only eight days after her birth I witnessed the wonders of black and white TV communications by satellite to watch the famous fight between Cassius Clay aka Muhammed Ali and George Foreman, staged in Zaire's capital Kinshasa, the notorious *"rumble in the jungle"*. Clay knocked out Foreman in the eighth to regain the world heavyweight crown amid a frenzy of worldwide interest not least in neighbouring Zambia, where those few of us who owned television sets opened our doors to those who did not to watch the so named *"fight of the century"*. Well done Zambia Broadcasting Company for its technical achievement and money forked out to bring us such excitement. It was a great improvement over the usual boring reports of visits by foreign dignitaries to State House or of a Government Minister opening a new school room in Petauke, for example. Zambia Television newsmen made a report about a new model tractor at a factory in the Caucasus by Soviet State TV seem like gripping high drama.

The general absence of restaurants and cafes encouraged us all towards home entertainment. Our children were no barrier to dinner parties out. Andy had his little car seat and Christy-Anne travelled in her Moses basket propped safely between the rear and front seats of our cars. Molly Murphy's blue Opel still ran well for Tory, who had passed her diving test whilst we lived in Kitwe.

Our dog Sammy took well to the move back again to Ndola, his presence a discouragement to any would be interlopers, house theft being a permanent call to reality for most of the expatriates and our Zambian neighbours. Sammy was a big dog, he ate almost anything that was chucked at him, a canine dustbin; he was our guardian and friend. Our house was located behind a high whitewashed wall on the corner of a residential road and the main Kwacha Road leading north to the large township of Chifubu. Opposite us was the open space of the Kansenji School playing fields. The driveway from Nyimba Crescent was protected at night by wrought iron gates. A smaller iron-grilled gate filled an opening on the long wall parallel to the Kwacha Road leading to Chifubu.

Notwithstanding the bus service out to Chifubu there was always a long stream of people walking or cycling in both directions during daylight hours with most Chifubu residents thinking nothing about having to cover distances on foot up to five miles to get to their place of work, a fact of life learned in their schooldays. *"Flying Pigeon"* sit-up-and-beg bicycles, which had been imported from China through our Zambia National Wholesale, gave witness to a successful commercial enterprise, they were cheap and easy to repair. As more bikes were imported using the ongoing trade credit provided in the Uhuru railway deal, so the demand for tyres increased, but with lack of foreign exchange the bush mechanics would replace inner tubes with anything they could find to stuff the punctured rubber rather than patch them. The improvisation of the young bush mechanics really worked.

We saw little of the Chinese workers. I recalled an occasion in Kitwe at the time staff were cashing up in the supermarket at closing time when it was reported that one of our checkout tills was a thousand kwacha short. It was the till which had accounted for a large purchase of groceries by a delegation of the Chinese construction workers, on a rare visit to town from their bush camp. I remembered seeing the three men in their Chairman Mao suits not long before Neil Eccles had overseen them loading boxes of cans and bottles to a parked field-grey truck. I had no alternative but to suspend Elias Mudenda, the till operator, pending a full audit, although he was otherwise an exemplary worker.

He had not long to wait for me to reach a verdict on his employment prospects. Early the next day the three men with their little red books and grey suits asked to see John Songolo, Neil's deputy manager of the food hall. The interpreter had a wad of one thousand kwacha in notes which he presented to John along with the original till slip showing how they had totted up by hand. They wanted to show us that the total of their purchases was exactly a thousand kwacha more than had been charged. The NCR cash registers provided totals printed to three figures, our man had simply guessed the thousands never having had to handle such a big sale before. The honesty of the Chinamen impressed all of us and got Mudenda off the hook. No harm had been done and a big lesson was learned.

In the office our menswear buyer Norrie Greig, the chap who met my father and traded naval stories at the Coppersmith's Arms, and our food buyer Jack Gibbs were being briefed for another buying trip to China arranged in part by Mike through the Ministry of Trade, and by me with the Chinese Embassy. The pair were to be joined by Bert Craig from ZNWC, my old outfit, and would be away for three weeks.

We had to advise the Chinese authorities of our purchasing requirements in advance so that moneys from the Uhuru deal could be properly allocated to different trading corporations in several Chinese Provinces. Chinese delegates from the regional corporations would travel to Canton and Peking to complete contracts with our boys so that all could be signed up before the trip ended. The way business worked in Communist China in those days was essentially like this: Mr Woo had a factory which made shirts somewhere in Province X. He would be given an annual target and a guaranteed price for his production subject to quality approval testing by the Province X Textiles Import Export Corporation, who would provide him free of charge all the componentry, raw materials and machinery he needed to meet his production quota. Once he had delivered his goods he would be paid by the Corporation after deduction of the costs he had accumulated for all supplies made to him on credit. The stocks he produced would now be sold by the Corporation, who would negotiate with the overseas buyer in US Dollars or in our case in Chinese Renminbi. The Corporation would be financed by Central Government through a master national corporation covering Mr Woo's specific trade or product sector (Food, Textiles or whatever) in Peking (Beijing), to whom each provincial corporation was answerable. Our Mr Woo was not allowed, officially, to produce more than his quota, but inevitably some additional "back-door" trade covered the costs of Mr Woo's peccadillos.

The products we bought were relatively unsophisticated, being merchandise made for the Chinese domestic market. The Cultural Revolution under Chairman Mao Tse-tung was still holding his vast country in fear. Our buyers would negotiate only to the extent of selecting and advising their target cost price, following which the officials of the corporations would get into a huddle and ask the chaps to come back tomorrow. The confirmation of each order followed a tortuous process of referral to higher authority by the officials, contracts being drawn up and presented days later containing at least four sellers' signatures but only one of our buyers' autographs.

The boys were given a day off to get over the thirty-six hours of travel back to Ndola, whereupon Mike and I held a debriefing session. I asked Jack how he dealt with the boredom of time wasting. "The hotel was basic" he told me. "It had a well-stocked bar offering local beers and spirits, even wine, but there was a limit to how much of the foul tasting high proof

Maotai we could handle". These were well practised drinkers in their early fifties. They presented us both with complimentary bottles of China's favourite liquor, a spirit fermented from sorghum I was told. It takes all sorts, and taste is a matter of personal preference, but how anyone could actually "like" Maotai remains a mystery to me to this day. Bottled halitosis is my personal description of the vicious brew. "We went for long walks" Jack continued, "tailed by our two minders and Sooksook our young lady interpreter". Norrie added that he had been taking pictures and had inadvertently left the camera on the top of a stone railing. The three colleagues returned the next day to find the camera exactly where it had been left, reminding me of the honesty the Chinese had shown in the case of Elias Mudenda.

The Chinese conjured up wonderful brand names for their products, such as the *Flying Pigeon* bicycles I have told you about, *Great Wall* corned beef, *Double Happiness* matches and so on. Indeed, we became weary of the matches when it was reported to me that we were receiving complaints from all over the country that the *Double Happiness* were not striking alight, engendering much unhappiness. "Maybe the idea is to strike two together", some wag in the warehouse had commented.

This occasioned a product recall, no easy task in Zambia, followed by a visit from the Chinese Commercial Attaché from Lusaka to our Distribution Centre where Jack and I met them to discuss the problem. The Attaché had brought six staffers with him. He requested that our forklift drivers gather all bulk stocks of the matches on their pallets and to line them up in the despatch bay area, whereupon the Embassy staff diligently took random outer cartons, then inner packs, then individual match boxes, opened the boxes and laid out sample matches on the concrete floor in a manner and order best known to them. The ranks of matches made me think of the terracotta army only recently discovered in Lintong near Xi'an in central China. Once done, they proceeded to strike the matches, making note of the success rate, a process which took an hour or so. When they had finished, the six men formed a well-practiced huddle, not unlike a rugby scrum around the Attaché, babbling away in Mandarin (I think) for some minutes before the delegation's chief approached us to give us his verdict that the matches were *"shitty"*. He would make his report to Peking, who would take up our claim with the offending factory. I feared for the factory owner's prospects, let alone those of the quality control men from the trading corporation, but no matter, we would get a full replacement shipment by air. The Attaché had lost much face so would likely rattle his cage to redeem his dignity.

I was sharing a beer with Mike after a home cricket match against a club from Luanshya. Mike's job title by then was Head of Supply and Distribution, one of three principal heads of functions under a new management structure established by Gerald Sterck. Maurice Widdowson was Head of Retailing and Jack Freemantle, a man not long off retirement age was Head of Administration, a job which included all finance and accounting responsibilities. I sensed that Mike was encountering some frustration in his dealings with Sterck who, it seemed, was taking a back seat serving his time. My father would have called Sterck a *"cuff shooter"*, airs and graces and little substance, at least that is how I viewed the man and could understand Mike's feelings. We had a big problem brewing with the Ministry of Trade in Lusaka over import licensing and with the Industry Ministry, which was indirectly our majority shareholder, and Mike was bearing the brunt of these tussles on behalf of the Company. Brendan had returned to Ndola and was working with Maurice in charge of Department Stores with Joseph Chishimba running the two shops divisions.

Not long after Christmas, well celebrated at the Cathedral of the Holy Nativity and with friends, we asked Dean David Elliott about a Baptism service for our little girl. The service took place a few weeks into February conducted by Bishop Jack Cunningham. Christy-Anne's Godmothers were in Britain and represented by proxies at the service, her Godfather Brendan carried out his duties with confidence as he cradled the little bundle of womanhood who was dressed in the same christening robe as had been worn by her brother, her mother and countless ancestors. Abandoning any thoughts of using the garden for a party after the church ceremonies, because of the rain, we entertained the forty guest adults and children in the house, overflowing onto the protected veranda which overlooked the pool.

At the same time the sporadic fighting continued south of the Zambesi. Harold Wilson had replaced Edward Heath for a second stint as British Prime Minister in February 1974 and was trying without success to talk Ian Smith into some sort of resolution of the bush war but made the mistake of insulting the Rhodesian Front leader. Feelings in the UK were mixed, some seeing Smith as a war hero (WWII), having bravely served the mother country as a fighter pilot, others as a rebel and a racist who should be brought to book. Fuelling the latter cause was the Liberal Party leader Jeremy Thorpe, who suggested that the RAF might bomb the Rhodesians into submission. During his first term as PM (1964-'70) Harold Wilson had held conferences with Smith aboard Royal Navy ships HMS Fearless and HMS Tiger with no gain. There was a lot of diplomatic activity taking place in early 1975 about which our newspaper, *The Times of Zambia,* reported the Zambian Government line. We listened to the BBC World Service on our shortwave radio and the Rhodesian Broadcasting Service, the latter not officially sanctioned, in our attempts to find true reports.

Michael Ball-Foster of Indeco Morison, our friend from Kitwe, whose UK parent Company Morison Son & Jones Ltd had been recently acquired by brewer Arthur Guinness, joined us with his vivacious wife Anne for another weekend camping at Baluba on Mfubu Ranch territory. Guinness was then under the chairmanship of Lord Iveagh, who had appointed Morison's Chairman Michael Ogle as his new deputy, based at the Guinness London Head Office in Albermarle Street off Piccadilly. As we shared a case of Castle beer around the camp fire in sight of roaming baboons from the kopje behind us, Michael reported a meeting he had had with his boss in Zambia, Bob Ring, a man I had met on several occasions and liked.

Apparently, Mr Ogle's Devon country home was in Jeremy Thorpe's parliamentary constituency. The two men had shared accommodation when at Oxford University together. Ogle had asked Thorpe to become a Board Member of Indeco Morison due to JT's longstanding friendship with Kenneth and Betty Kaunda, to the extent that he had become Godfather to two of the Kaunda sons. Mike went on to say that Thorpe would soon be coming to Lusaka on a private visit to attend to the business, but he asked us to observe a blanket news blackout. Thorpe was well known to have homosexual proclivities and was dubbed with the nickname "Bummer Thorpe" in comic reflection of his Westminster label "Bomber Thorpe", given him by some newspaper columnists on hearing of his simplistic incendiary proposals for solving the Rhodesian problem.

Thorpe attended the business meeting in Lusaka after staying at State House with the President. I doubt that KK thought the Zambian Airforce could do much to further Thorpe's aggressive cause. The ZAF's Russian Mig fighter 'planes were grounded at Mbala (formerly Abercorn) on the south shores of Lake Tanganyika, having landed on their arrival in Zambia on a runway too short for their further take-off. Thorpe's attendance at the board meeting was rewarded by a gift of a stuffed elephant's dildo, mounted on a large wooden shield, procured by the enterprising Enga-Enga, a man providing Bob Ring with his *mister-fix-it* services. It was to be Michael's understanding that some months later that the trophy held pride of place on the wall of the inner sanctum of Thorpe's London flat.

On return from Baluba I was called to Mike Delaney's office and given twenty-four hours to get on a 'plane to Johannesburg. The Company had been "given" an import licence and letter of credit finance approval for one million US Dollars which I was to use to purchase bully beef and canned pilchards from Southwest Africa (now Namibia). I was given the name of the supplier, who I was instructed to contact if he failed to meet me at the airport. I caught the early morning Zambia Airways flight on a BAC1-11 to Lusaka, transferring to an international carrier to take me to Jan Smuts in Jo'burg. I was met at the barrier, carrying an overnight case and a bottle of duty-free White Label by a short, swarthy bloke with dark wavy hair who introduced himself as Ralph Weinberg[25].

---

25. Weinberg and Honig are assumed names to protect the identity of the actual SA government officers

Weinberg drove me first to my hotel, a small guest house in Sandton to check in, then on to an office of the South African Tourism Industry, where I met a fascinating lady of mixed ancestry called Honig. Mrs Honig welcomed me to South Africa, explaining her role at the Ministry of Agriculture and asking me to confirm my credentials, which were my UK passport, the fiscal credit issued by the Bank of Zambia and a letter of introduction I had been given whilst in transit at Lusaka airport. Satisfied that I was her man, we took another car to a branch of the Standard Bank in Rosebank, a nearby suburb on the northeast side of the city. I had little clue as to the purpose of all the mysterious procedures other than to understand that it was my job to place an order through the Bank on behalf of my Company on the authority of both the South African and Zambian governments, which duty I duly performed and signed the contracts.

The following day I was back on an aircraft heading home via Lusaka, clutching a copy of a contract to supply two and a half million cans of fish and meat protein food to be transported to Zambia by rail through Bulawayo and Livingstone from Johannesburg. It was not long before Gerald Sterck emerged from his office retreat to fill in the gaps, namely that I had been sent to South Africa as a white man with British nationality on behalf of the Zambian authorities to buy strategic foodstuffs, which he understood were to be supplied to the ZAPU camps between Chirundu and Kariba, in other words to fighters opposing the Smith regime in the escalating war south of our border in Rhodesia. I was struck by the irony of the South African government having knowingly transported supplies for Smith's foes by rail through Rhodesia itself, secretly I suppose under false manifests. After all, Southwest Africa, from whence the food was supplied was still under the mandated control of South Africa, a legacy of war, the territory having been a German colonial possession before the League of Nations transferred its governance to the charge of the then British Dominion. I never discovered which body had financed the purchase.

I was back at the airport two days after getting back from South Africa to greet Dorothea and Tony for a second visit. We were happy to have them both with us but distressed to see that Tony was declining in health. They joined in our life in Ndola. No sooner had they settled in when a 'phone call came out of the blue from Johannesburg. My childhood friend Derek Merrell was on the line to say that his mother, affectionately known to me as Aunt Vera, had booked a flight to Heathrow via Ndola to see me, having spent a month with her son. Derek, code name *"Goldfinger"*, was the leading gynaecologist at the giant Chris Hani Baragwanat hospital in Soweto. I had not seen or heard from Derek since my leaving party in '69, during which time he had married and divorced the socialite daughter of a rich Armenian banker in London and was not a happy rabbit.

We loved having visitors, so what the heck, I thought, it will be company for Dorothea and Tony to have someone else of their own age to share tales with for a week of their stay. Little did I know about the jealousy of some folk, for dear Vera, always talkative, came from a different world to our relatives from Exeter. I feared Dorothea was determined not to find any common ground with our surprise guest. A lesson thus learned was to avoid mixing friends or relatives from different circles, they might have your acquaintance in common, but that is all.

The next bombshell to hit me, figuratively speaking, came a week after our guests had all gone when Gerald Sterck called me at home for the first time with the appalling news that Mike Delaney had been declared a Prohibited Immigrant and had been deported to South Africa. To be *"PI-ed"* was not uncommon as government sensibilities frayed due in part to the foreign exchange deficit and the war in the south, but the Company was given no reason for Mike's surprise departure.

Lorraine, and their daughter Susan were still in Ndola unable yet to travel to join Mike. Indeed, much needed to be cleared up in their personal affairs and with their possessions, given the added complication that Susan had no passport. Mike and Lorraine were British, he born of English parents in Ceylon who were tea planters, and Lorraine born of parents who worked in the Rhodesian colonial service and who had now returned to their homeland in retirement to live in the south of England. Since both her parents were born outside the UK, Susan fell afoul of the immigration regulations introduced to stem the flow into Britain of ethnic South Asians fleeing Idi Amin's Uganda. By the time she and her mother were ready to join Mike, holed up in Johannesburg, United Nations temporary travel documents had been secured for the eight years old Susan.

It was quite uncanny taking over Mike's job, as well as his secretary, his dictation recorder with two hours of his voice, and his confidential files. Having no predecessor to hand over to me, I had to help myself and of course I discovered a raft of interesting information but no clue concerning his PI order. I had to make a few management changes, not least to bring in one of our top Zambian store managers, William Mvula, to replace me in the buying office alongside Alan Marples. Peter McManus had replaced Jimmy Crawford at the Distribution Centre.

Sadly, my friend Maurice came to the end of his contract. Sue Griffee, Maurice's girlfriend, left for California whilst he was given a move to Bookers' new acquisition in St Lucia. Brendan succeeded him as Head of Retail Operations. With me in charge of Supply and Distribution the Company was now in the hands of we two former Kitwe neighbours. I must not forget the avuncular Jack Freemantle who ran his team of bean counters on the side-lines. Little would the original Diamond Flats duo have imagined in 1969 that in less than six years they would be running the whole shebang, all three thousand employees and all thirty percent of the country's retail action. Work had never been more exhilarating as we took on the daily challenges which confronted us whilst still trying to forge changes to boost the Group's profitability.

I stepped down from the cricket club, joining a Saturday afternoon sixteen ball group at the Golf Club. Our highly social team comprised chaps from the Standard Bank and ZCBC/ Bookers. That secured my Sundays, away from all activities to be together with family and friends. The wonderful climate in Zambia encouraged an outdoor life which we certainly did not want to miss. We always took the view that our life in the tropics was a gift to be nurtured, that normality, if it existed, was life in the UK.

My brother Andrew arrived for a month's stay in April with his Bahraini girlfriend Munira Isaq. They had been globe-trotting since leaving the LSE, missing out on their finals although Munira was already a graduate of Beirut University. I managed to get some local leave during which we took our guests down to Livingstone, not only to see the Falls but to join Manu Patel, a friend met through both business and cricket, whose offer to drive us in his Mercedes to the Chobe game reserve in Botswana we could not resist.

The Kazungula pontoon and the border police huts with their grass thatches loomed into view. We had been through another Tsetse fly dip along the dirt road which took us by the north bank of the great river from Livingstone to the crossing place. There was an all pervading and distinctly medicinal aroma rising from the encrusted muddy underside of Manu's limo. Border protocols were tougher now due to sensitivities associated with the bush war. I offered to collect all five passports to take across to the officer sitting at his makeshift desk swatting flies in the shade under a thatch parasol, noticing that my brother's document bore another name and claimed Irish nationality, he had apparently established a different identity for himself but why he should have done so only became apparent after several more years. I pretended not to have noticed, thinking he would tell me about it in his own good time. Cleared through all formalities, the car was driven onto the pontoon to be hauled across the wide river by a mechanised wire cable. We were located at the confluence of the north flowing Chobe River and the east flowing Zambesi. Our landing spot was in Botswana territory; had we gone two hundred yards left we would have landed in war torn Rhodesia.

The dirt road from the border post to one of the *Southern Sun* Hotels in the Chobe Reserve, where we stayed for two nights, was of much lighter fine sandy dust. It ran almost due south for an hour to our destination with rising bush to our left and the swampy river to our right. Large herds of elephant came into view aside the pods of hippos which were wallowing in the green waters. The elephants were being watched by flocks of large black and white wading birds, the saddle-back herons. The smell of animal kills wafted through the open windows, signifying the presence of predators, almost certainly lions, close by the point of our arrival through the fenced approaches to the game lodge.

In the spacious open-sided reception lobby, pictures of Elizabeth Taylor and Richard Burton adorned the walls, vying for prominence over a larger portrait of the leader of Botswana, Sir Seretse Khama with Ruth, the equally well-known Lady Karma. The Hollywood stars had spent their second honeymoon at this exclusive spot not long before, booking out the entire hotel to assure their privacy. I quickly agreed that they had chosen well, for the wild game and birdlife were everywhere and easy to spot although the bush remained thick from the rains now coming to their seasonal end.

An afternoon car run led us to rhinoceros before we made our way towards the river swamps to look at the evening ablutions of an elephant herd. There our little group found itself in a spot of danger. We had no guard nor a game ranger with us. Our way forward on the dirt track was blocked by a bull on sentry duty about thirty yards ahead of us. The elephant was flapping his huge ears, which signalled anger. Manu managed a quick seven points turn in the narrow way, only to see there was another guardian bull, about one hundred and fifty yards in front. A steep earthen bank bordered the track to our right, the incline down to the swamp lay to our left, and behind us trundled the massive beast from whom we had just fled, still flapping his ears. There was no easy way of escape. At the wheel, Manu was thus left with no alternative than to show aggression. "Come on" I said to Manu "turn the lights on and full steam ahead". Now an elephant can make short work of a car, even a big one like the German tank we were in, and I knew that the it was unwise to show headlamps, but the gamble paid off, mercifully, with the animal facing us taking evasive action up the steep bank, leaving space for us to pass and escape with beating hearts, ready for nerve settling drinks before dinner.

With rice, flour, salt, cooking oil and other basics along with a lot of imported foodstuffs in short supply in Zambia, it was a joy to feast ourselves on the unrestricted menus of the *Southern Sun*. After a dream-filled sleep facing attacks from wild rhinos and elephants, we took full advantage of the buffet breakfast, then made an early start to the drive back from this delightful, and as it turned out, exciting break with Manu and our family guests.

Half a mile short of the Kazungula pontoon we took a right turn and crossed into Rhodesia. At the border post, manned only by a pair of Rhodesian Army conscripts, we accepted their offer of a stamped piece of paper to avoid having a rebel mark in our passports. We joined an army escort vehicle, which had appeared from behind a clump of anthills for the drive to Victoria Falls township, the armed Land Rover keeping a watchful station behind Manu's Mercedes. A few miles into our journey a gleaming black sable antelope came out of the bush to our right and ran alongside for what seemed half a minute before he spurted forward across the front of Manu's car. The beautiful creature disappeared into the forest on the opposite side of the dusty red road, leaving an indelible memory of such a magic moment.

By the time we reached Vic Falls it was time for a mid-morning coffee which we took at the famous hotel we had stayed at four years earlier, but no sign of Nigel, the Head Waiter we knew. There was no border crossing open at the Falls, so we had to return to Kazungula by the same route, taking a gamble to leave without an escort. We encountered no fighters. Once across the river, the formalities started all over again, one of which was to present the yellow inoculations records books we were obliged to carry to the government medical orderly taking shelter from the sun under a grass thatched canopy. My own records showed that I had no up-to-date cholera jab, but instead a letter from my doctor to say that I was excused having one on the grounds that I had an intolerant reaction to the serum.

I doubt he could read English, for the duty medic insisted he must give me the missing jab there and then, with no argument, after which he got out another needle to pump me with a generous amount of adrenalin. We had been on the road to Livingstone only ten minutes when I started to shake uncontrollably, the effect of the adrenalin shot pumping up my heartbeat. I was still quivering when we arrived under the spray of the great waterfall, grateful that I was not driving the car. By dinner time I had recovered enough to collect my car from the town and say a farewell to my generous friend Manubhai Chaganlal Patel.

A walk before breakfast the following morning led us down through the rain forest for a thorough soaking in the warm spray. Memories of my Mother having acted out as a "drowned rat" came back into sharp focus when the four of us reached the end of the trail which overlooked the boiling pot. From our vantage point we could see the rail and road bridge suspended above the deep gorge which separated Zambia and Rhodesia. Little did I then know that we were looking at the place where later that same year, on 26th August 1975, John Vorster and Kenneth Kaunda would broker a meeting between the Rhodesian Front and the African Nationalist groups ZANU and ZAPU. The parties met each other in a railway carriage mid-way across the gorge in the forlorn hope of reaching a settlement to the long running insurgence. I wondered if the freedom fighters remained well fed on my bully beef.

Whilst the bush war was being fought relentlessly in Rhodesia, it brought about a draining effect on Zambia's economy. Bank transfers of our contract remittance allowances, as well as end of contract gratuities were being delayed in a foreign exchange queue at the Central Bank. It used to take only a few days for my money to arrive to credit my savings account at Lewis's Bank in Bristol but was now taking a few months.

Expatriates were leaving as contracts ended, farmers were finding it difficult to get supplies of imported stocks of fertilisers and feed additives although in my view they were coping well by finding all sorts of alternative compounds from within the country's borders. Kenneth Kaunda began pressing his new policy of *"Humanism"* by publishing tens of thousands of copies of his *"little green book"* on the lines of Chairman Mao's little red one. KK was diverting his attention away from the travails of his own country to act out a prominent role, indeed an energetic involvement in the non-aligned nations movement led by Pandit Nehru, the Prime Minister of India.

The Indian Congress Party leader had coined the expression *"Third World"* to describe non-alignment. In further pursuit of his new-found status as a major world statesman Kaunda played up his standing with fellow African leaders in the Organisation for African Unity (OAU). In turn the OAU were losing friends in the West as their spokesmen courted support from the East, blaming all ills which befell the dark continent on the USA and the former colonial powers, more specifically France and the UK. In their carefully crafted propaganda onslaught, the African leaders were egged on by the Soviet Union, in particular, and by the usual elements of academia and pressure groups enjoying the comfortable freedom of Western capitals whilst beating their breasts in a frenzy of writing their revisions of history. It seemed to me to be dishonest to ignore the damage being done to the prospects of the citizens of the young nations of free Africa through the corruption and mismanagement of the some of the ruling authorities.

The crunch seemed to come when the not-so-subtle shift in policy manifested itself when a ban was imposed overnight on private medical care and clinics. Reading between the lines of statements by Ministers reported in the pages of *The Times of Zambia* and *The Zambia Daily Mail*, the time was approaching to quietly dispense with expatriate management, certainly in the public sector, partly because government coffers were nearly empty and partly to please their new friends from the Eastern bloc. Curbs on foreign exchange practices and salary levels were hinted at. None can be sure what really brought about these changes in the Governments line. It was certainly not manifest in the day to day lives of everyone working and playing together but was certainly in the air and brought an unwelcome slant to my feelings of security, not so much on a personal level, but for the aims of the country's progress and its economy for which we were all working.

The CIMAS branch clinic in Ndola was closed by gun-toting soldiers and its patients were crudely manhandled on several occasions. The surprised and fearful patients were transferred in their hospital gowns at the point of a rifle to the General Hospital wards in army trucks. News got through to Tory that Peter's wife Sue McManus, expecting her first child, was one such victim. The expectant mother was likely to give birth at any time, being a few days overdue. She was denied familiar food and had to lie in a bed in full view of not only twenty or so other African mothers but also ZA soldiers carrying arms within the ward. My wife decided to don her old nursing sister's uniform and enter the hospital as if she owned the place, to deliver a basketful of fruit juices and sandwiches to the beleaguered Sue under the soldiers' watch and thankfully pulled off her brazen ruse. Katy McManus was born safely the next day.

The good news of a new birth was followed by sadness. Ernie Rogers, who I had worked with to develop the ready-cooked frozen meals we sold through our supermarkets, and who had run his *Rhokana Mine Mess* since 1950, had been killed when his car collided into a ZamTan truck at night. Ernie was much loved; his funeral was watched by a thousand people surrounding the church for lack of space inside.

I had to come out of cricketing retirement when Terry Jones from the Lions Club called on me to play in the annual cricket match against the Ndola Rotary Club, always keenly contested. We won the toss and elected to bat. I was joined at the crease by my opening partner who was captain of a 20-over league side called "The Untouchables". It was Chris who helped me set up the bonded store in the DC, site of the vodka saga involving the unfortunate Silus.

Chris was out with a score of 42 when the total on the scoreboard showed 114. I followed him the next ball and the rest of the team made a further five runs! Tortoises and hares, I thought, but we got the Rotarians out for 56 and won the day. I never did play another cricket match in Zambia, but it was good to end on a half century and a win. I loved the game of cricket but still remember that match against Rotary ahead of all the others I have played because it was for the sheer fun of the game.

John Hurn and Brendan got kicks from boating and water skiing on the dambos outside Kitwe and Ndola, but by June the dry season left the water levels low. I had just returned from Mfubu when Brendan pitched up at our door strapped in bandages across his shoulder which he had dislocated after coming a cropper off his powerful trail bike, doubtless enjoying rides through the dry bush as a substitute thrill to dambo skiing. Brendan's accident was another one of those vivid episodes of expatriate life in Africa and, having a good tale to tell myself, I poured him a scotch and related the drama of burning the mortal remains of a huge crocodile.

The story began a week before when a young girl from one of the riverside villages on *Mfubu Ranch* was washing herself in the Kafue. A crocodile had risen out of the green depths to grab her, the whole act taking seconds and so swift that the girl had no time to scream. The headman Mpundu appealed to Bwana John for his help just as Tory and I were making a family visit. Mpundu was distraught, to say the least, and his wives were ululating loudly in his wake, making the distress all that more heart breaking. John resolved to lay a trap for the croc using the blood from a slaughtered veal calf to seed the river close to where the wretched reptile had done his dirty stuff, taking the calf's dismembered head securely tied to a long rope, so letting us cast it into the slowly running waters as bait.

Standing guard with John in the dark of the early evening I waited two long hours, periodically dripping the seed blood from the bucket into the river. I kept a grip on a double barrelled twelve bore shot gun which was loaded and cocked ready for any action. As luck would have it, the croc suddenly appeared not more than ten yards before us, its eyes clearly visible in the beam of the mobile spotlight John had rigged up. We pumped four barrels of shot into the open snout of the brazen beast, but it quickly disappeared into the depths.

Now you should understand that the villagers had actually found the body of their ravaged youngster with her leg missing, so in accordance with custom and despite the humid heat, her body could not be buried incomplete if the girl was to have a safe journey to the place of her ancestors.

Days after the riverside fusillade, whilst on patrol alone on the river in his *Avon* outboard, John had spotted a crocodile's corpse caught in the branches of a tree about two miles downstream. The body was in an awkward position, five feet above the water. Noting the spot, he made it back to tell Mpundu his news, quickly returning to the spot with a party of men to secure the croc's corpse. John told me on the 'phone that the village men had laid into the beast, cutting open its underbelly to find the undigested female leg which they removed and placed in a blanket so that the lonely limb could re-join its owner.

A burial had proceeded back at the village without any further delay, leaving John with the problem of what to do with the remains of eighteen feet of a long dead murderous reptile. I suggested on the telephone that we could burn the carcass by moving it this way and that over the fire until it was all turned to ash. I then drove over to the ranch from Ndola to help with the gruesome task, at one stage I reached into the carcass to pull out one of the loose vertebrae, which I slipped into my trouser pocket. The dead croc's loss was my bonus , an interesting paperweight in the years to come.

Our garden at Nyimba Crescent was an ideal setting for another cup final party, this year between Fulham and West Ham. We just had to ask Sally and her husband Sam, fellow passengers on the *Vaal*. Sam won the sweepstake draw for the correct score making him doubly happy as his team beat the club from west London, which my father had supported since he was a boy. I recalled the last time I was at Craven Cottage on the Middlesex bank of the river Thames. It was in the spring of 1969 when I had gone to the ground with one of my brothers to see the game against Liverpool. That day the Scottish forward Ian St John slid purposefully into a tackle to take out fullback George Cohen. I heard the crack of Cohen's leg, the complex break ending the career of the heroic veteran of England's World Cup victory three years before.

From far away Westminster, in June 1975, we learned that Harold Wilson was campaigning to get the British voters to endorse the Heath government's accession to the Treaty of Rome through a referendum. Living abroad I had no vote, but my dislike and distrust of both Heath and Wilson, supported by the slithery Thorpe, none of them conviction politicians, caused my opinion to incline towards Peter Shore, the Labour minister, and others who advocated leaving the Common Market altogether. The result came through in an evening broadcast over the BBC World Service, still our lifeline to the world outside. Few of my colleagues took any interest in the event although Mike would have, had he been still around, I thought at the time.

13

Malaria and a Job

(1976)

I was able to get up to date with events in the UK through Booker's Personnel Director David Taylor. This David had become more of a friend since the days when he handled my recruitment. His upcoming visit was now important insofar as along with several of the other senior expats in the Company, I felt justifiably concerned about the future, particularly since the demise of the private health clinics and the recent UNIP government announcement that salary scales in all nationalised industries such as ours would become aligned to Zambian civil service rates of pay. I had less than a year to run before my third contract expired and would certainly not stay on if I had to take a seventy percent cut in pay, my position at ZCBC being set at a pay level on a par with a deputy permanent secretary in one of the Ministries, so I had been informed.

With that in mind, David asked me if I could take on a trip to Nigeria on Bookers' behalf to assess a business they were looking to acquire with the help of a Chief Jonathan in Kaduna, having cleared his request through the generally invisible Gerald Sterck. By now, five years had passed by peacefully in Nigeria since the frightful civil war, the government of General Gowan had showed political skill in its reconciliation with the rebellious Colonel Ojukwu's Biafra, restored as the Eastern Region of the Federal State.

By the time my visa came through, Bookers' plan had been changed and my trip was cancelled. Nonetheless Bookers, David told me, were on the lookout for other investment or management contract prospects in Asia, Africa and the Caribbean, where they had recently set up shop with *Minvielle & Chastanet* in St Lucia, to which Maurice had transferred to, and in Trinidad where they had bought a department store called *Stephens* and a pharmacy chain called *Ross Drugs*. In Malaysia they had become involved with *Pernas Edar*, a state sponsored business supporting ethnic Malay traders. The new business sought to help the Malay *Bumiputra*[26] compete in a market dominated by ethnic Chinese businesses, a similar concept as that I had experienced with ZNWC. David's message to me was to hold fire and watch the space. Our problem was that we were a long way from being able to job hunt.

By 1976 it was as clear as daylight that our days in Zambia were numbered. I had a task to secure the best possible succession in all the departments under my control. I brought William Mvula into my office to work alongside me. At home we stepped up the entertainment of friends with several weekend braais around the pool and dinner parties. Poker and Bridge were both sporadic since Westy had moved to the Lusaka store six months back, but we had Dominic Eedle who had arrived on his first contract two years previously to take the vacant

---

26. The bumiputra are the sons of the soil, the natives of Malaya.

place. My reel to reel tape recorder now played eight hours of music, an anthology of all our favourites, making ideal background music for card nights at our house. Our friend David Seaman of Mobil Oil had also joined in. He must have been in an expansive mood one evening. Out of the blue he invited Tory and me to spend a week at his company's vacant beach villa on the north shore of Mombasa, an area of Kenya already familiar to me, remembering the stay I had had at the Nyali Beach as a *rich smoothie* more than six years in the past.

Our flight to the port city took a long transit stop in the humid coastal heat of Dar es Salaam. The airport bar at Dar had only canned mango juice for the children, who we struggled to restrain from running or crawling on the dirty airport floor during the long four hours we had to wait.

Once in Mombasa we were greeted by the grinning face of Shiraz Janmohammed who worked for *Kamyn Industries*. Kamyn was a supplier of knitted hosiery to our stores. I had met Shiraz two years before on a business trip, he was a bubbly character who exuded human kindness. He handed me the keys to a well dented but mechanically sound red Series II Ford Cortina and gave me his telephone number and directions to the north shore. That night, having found the villa and unpacked, tired from the journey but with food we had bought from a small shop a mile or so distant, the children started to cry.

It was obvious to us that they were both not just distressed but unwell with rising temperatures (thank goodness we travelled with a thermometer). It was dark and we had no telephone at the villa. The children were fast going downhill with burning fever. Tory decided to seek out the lights of a building about six hundred yards along the shore which turned out to be the Dolphin Hotel. There she was able to get willing help. The hotel staff rang their doctor in Mombasa who agreed to come out straight away, his immediate problem being that the bridge from the city over the river was closed at nightfall, which meant he had to drive for half an hour by car to reach us by taking the inland route.

The headlamps of a car flashing by the window of the children's bedroom were followed by the crunch of wheels on the stony space next to where the Cortina was parked. Tory, by now safely returned on foot from the helpful hotel, rushed to greet the turbaned doctor whose voice and presence closely matched the persona taken by Peter Sellars in *The Millionairess*. The wannabe Ahmed el Kabir administered jabs and liquid medicine from his Gladstone bag saying little but waiting for thirty minutes to watch both youngsters fall into calm sleep; we were instructed to attend his morning surgery in the city to which he gave us directions and told us to ring the bell three times to indicate we were patients and not naughty street ruffians playing pranks.

From the doctor's surgery I called Shiraz at his office in the Kamyn factory who expressed great concern, immediately instructing us to await his arrival. I put Tory and the children into my friend's car after only a brief consultation with our doctor of the night before and followed behind in the bright red Ford to see his younger brother Ali, a paediatric consultant at the Aga Khan Hospital. The children were admitted to the hospital straight away, where they spent one night whilst Shiraz and his family took us to their home, lifting our spirits and allaying our fears for Andy and Christy-Anne. The two spent the night in the care of the hospital's children's ward. By the afternoon we were able to collect the kids from the hospital in the Vanga Road.

The Aga Khan Institute was, and is, wholly financed by the Ismailis, a branch of Shia Islam. Our children had contracted a strain of malaria prevalent on the East Africa Coast, which has only hours to incubate in babies but is easily treated if diagnosed in good time.

The rest of the holiday was just wonderful. I used a harpoon gun to fish with little success but saw wonderful coral and fish as I snorkelled on both sides of the reef. We feasted on a giant lobster bought from vendors who called at the villa. We discovered the *Two Fishes* hotel on the south shore with its labyrinth of canals to connect swimmers to several pools in the hotel's floral grounds. In the afternoon we showed Andy the famous tusks on Kilindini Road and visited Fort Jesus, then went on to see the Royal Navy ships in the harbour. On our last night we went once again to Shiraz's family house and spent the evening in endless chatter sitting under the stars of the tropical night feeling wonderfully at peace on the rooftop where a whole sheep had been cooking on a spit, suspended above a trough of glowing charcoal, which we shared with a dozen people of all ages gathered to meet us. There were tearful farewells as we took our leave for the final night of our holiday.

We were just arriving home at a late hour from Mombasa to find that the telephone was ringing as I frantically unlocked the front door. The caller was Brendan, with the ghastly news that John Hurn had been killed four days earlier. He had been in a head-on crash with yet another ZamTan truck on the Kitwe Road, in just the same way as Ernie Rogers had his life taken from him. Poor John! He had been a friend since my early days in Zambia. What a terrible homecoming. I asked all the questions and yes, the notice would be in the paper tomorrow. John's body, or as much as could be removed from the wreckage, was with the undertakers pending a pointless but obligatory autopsy. His parents had been told. He would be flown home for burial in his home village in England. What a bloody mess. Poor parents! Poor Liz!

The children went to bed. I grabbed our two pillows and placed them, as usual, in the top-loading ice cream freezer I had brought to Ndola from the Kitwe store. I had discovered that a head laid on a frozen pillow was a sure way to get to sleep quickly in the heat. None of our houses had air-conditioning.

When sleep came, I had terrible dreams from which I awoke in a hot sweat and thumping headache. It got worse. I felt delirious and gasped for water. I remember nothing until three days later I came to. Tory sat on the bed to hand me a cup of tea. I remain convinced to this day that manoeuvring the teacup from Tory's outstretched hand to my mouth was the most difficult physical and mental problem I have ever had to solve; I had had malaria. Ravi Kalideen, our doctor, came to see me some hours after waking and before I had a chance to glimpse in the bathroom mirror. He diagnosed the same strain of malaria as the children had contracted in East Africa, it was virulent, but it was not a repeater.

The bathroom mirror presented my haggard and unshaven face, but I felt too weak to bother about anything beyond a soapy wash. Sleep followed, doubtless helped by Ravi's pills. By the evening I was sitting up in bed enjoying holding hands and sharing jokes with Tory, who had begun feeding me with chicken soup and scrambled eggs. By the next morning I felt well enough to have visits, the first from Alan Marples and his wife Pat who came to say farewell; they flew out the following day having completed three successive contracts. As they left, Brendan dropped by with more details about John which included a copy of a death announcement in that day's edition of *The Times of Zambia*, wishing John peace and eternal happiness in his heavenly dambo, or words to that effect. I made it into the office the following morning with much to catch up on after Mombasa and malaria.

John Mayes, our Group Training Manager came to see me unaware of my illness. As usual, his horn-rimmed specs had been repaired with sticky medical tape. His normal owl-like appearance seemed more sheep-like today, and I soon discovered why. John, a quiet and methodical backroom boy had taken the daring step of secretly marrying a British nurse. Secrets are difficult to keep secret at the best of times, but for John he faced a disastrous penalty on two counts, number one his wife had lost her free air passage back home from the government and had been fired for breaking contract rules (to remain single during the contract term) and number two, he had broken his contract terms with our Company (he was employed as a bachelor, so not entitled to wifely fares and married accommodation).

Recalling my stilted conversation with Wally Lewis to ask his permission to wed Tory, and learning that John had not yet announced his new predicament to Gerald Sterck, I advised him to do so immediately and throw himself at the mercy of our cuff shooting head honcho. John's contract was due to end in a few months. I knew that John was too valuable as an asset to the Company, he was a highly effective trainer at a time when the successful and speedy Zambianisation of many jobs required John's deft hand to accomplish, and so it proved. His contract was unaffected, but he was to remain in his small bachelor bungalow and would be responsible for his wife's airfare home. I could see the Company's point of view, that *"rules is rules"*, but the decision was made *"pour encourager les autres"* although there were clearly no others by now! The future salary scales put paid to any further contract employment unless they proposed to bring in qualified personnel from eastern Europe or elsewhere, for whom the Civil Service pay bands in Zambia bested their pay prospects at home by a considerable margin.

A month or so after my bout of malaria Brendan threw a lavish barbecue party one Sunday afternoon, making it known that he would be leaving at the end of his contract in late May, only six weeks hence. His guests seemed to me to provide a good audience to advertise his possessions. Quite naturally he was angling to sell anything he could not or did not want to take with him.

He had had no job offer, he confided, and was planning some business enterprise once back in the UK. My own plan at that time was to stay in my job as long as possible, hopefully until the end of my contract in September, and had given that assurance to Bookers in London, making the same points in a rare conversation with my time serving boss.

Tory and I decided that when the time came for our departure we would use the company fares to cover most of the cost of a less than direct route of travel, by taking in stops in the Seychelles, to where our friends Wilfred and Diana Homer had migrated, and to Tunisia where we had never been but had the chance of a special holiday deal. So much for my plans; it was late evening at home after Brendan's showroom event that my brother John came on the telephone line. He never called for a chat, indeed international telephone calls were so expensive then as to be prohibitive for social use, so this had to be ominous.

My father's cancer had spread faster than expected. He was not expected to last beyond 12 weeks. I called Roy Ritson in the morning to discuss bringing my leaving date forward by commuting all my paid leave entitlement and then booked an appointment with Gerald Sterck. I had to get home somehow to have time with Dad. A date in late June was agreed, and messages were sent to London.

Sterck was for once sympathetic, even friendly, and certainly unusually talkative, no doubt needing as much support from me until my final departure, now only four weeks off. In the space of three weeks he would be losing both operational heads of function on top of concerns about the now frayed relationship Bookers had with Indeco, whose ability to keep up contractual payments remained in doubt. The matter was clearly critical because Booker's new Chairman, Michael Caine (not the film star, rather the man who married Emma Nicholson, the MP), was down to attend a board meeting with Ministers and Indeco appointees in Lusaka' four days before I was now due to leave the country. On top of that, a man employed by Bookers as consultant on overseas appointments, Thornton Hawkins, would be accompanying Mr Caine.

In the same way he had behaved recruiting all the other expatriate managers, including Gerald, Thornton had applied his own rather strange methods of interview on me when I first applied to work in Zambia. Each one of us had experienced his obscure line of questioning at one time or another. "Why was Mr Hawkins coming?" I asked of Gerald who replied "he's coming to say goodbye". "What, to me?" I asked innocently, to which Gerald said that I had been accorded no such honour, Hawkins was retiring at last (the words *thank God* were mouthed but muted) and no doubt would have much to say for himself.

I guess it was fortuitous that Bookers had been told about my new departure date and end of contract because later that morning I had another call from overseas, this time from David Taylor in London. David was the one person who had the measure of Mr Hawkins, but that was not his purpose today. "Would you consider an appointment to manage retail operations at Minvielle and Chastanet in St Lucia?" he asked, and he went on to explain that because Maurice Widdowson has resigned, the Group needed to replace him. It lifted my spirits to think that I might have a job to go to without the grind of finding one, which I could only do in practice once back in the UK. I asked David to give me a day or so to talk to my family, remembering my own twenty-four hours rule, which was to do nothing, wait a day, and things generally worked out.

As I had taken the call in my office, it took me about twenty seconds to slip into Brendan's office along the corridor to get his opinion and to find a telephone number to call Maurice on, news of his resignation not having yet filtered through to his erstwhile best friends in central Africa. If we called our Caribbean chum early that afternoon, we might catch him at home before breakfast, taking account of the six hours lag in time.

I had just returned from lunch at home when I had told Tory about David's call, to find Brendan already on the 'phone to Maurice. Giving me the thumbs up sign Brendan passed the receiver across to me. Maurice's crackly voice urged me to only accept the job, which was no easy ride, unless Bookers would give me the authority of being on the local company's board. He explained why and went on to tell us both of his plan to set up a batik factory in the island of St Kitt's. He had resigned because of his frustration with the unceasing interference in his work by the previous owners, who had been retained as executive directors, an act of madness by Bookers in his eyes. I discovered how right he was to warn me, but that is another story for later.

Tory and I poured over atlases and encyclopaedias to find out more about St Lucia and the West Indies before we would receive the mass of background material promised by David to be sent in the post. I had given David a positive response, subject to being appointed as Director of all retailing operations along the lines Maurice had advocated. A formal letter setting out the terms of the offer would follow, I was assured.

14

Moni wokondedwa Africa

(Farewell dearest Africa – 1976)

Now it was our turn to consider the practicalities of closing our home in Ndola and moving across continents to a changed life. Brendan's home showroom had not proven very successful mainly because he was never there, so we agreed to combine his items with ours in a sales stall we would put up on the main Kwacha Road to Chifubu beyond the iron grill door in our garden wall. The stall was managed throughout the daylight hours by Tory and our maid Judy, who together moved most of the clothes and small household goods within a day, raising over one thousand Kwacha (£750). After three days the take had doubled. Our cars were advertised (I was given the option of using a company car by Roy the Pipe, should I need wheels). I had to find jobs for Howard and Judy, and a good home for Sammy.

We had swung into action with good results. Jacob Mbewe arrived unannounced with a cousin in my old Princess to tell me he had heard we were leaving Zambia and why couldn't we stay? I am not sure if that fulsome compliment was the intention of his visit but like to think so despite his request to buy my Zenith Radio and the Grundig reel-to-reel tape recorder he had previously admired in Kitwe. I readily agreed, two less items to sell, I thought, and since Jacob was such a good fellow, I flung in all the pre-recorded tapes as my gift. The week rushed by, then on the Friday the Stercks held a party for Brendan and the next day he was gone.

Seeing Jacob again caused me to think back on the incident of the tribalist accusation thrust on me in the anonymous letter I had received at the Kitwe store. Tribalism is accentuated in large parts of Africa; actually, it is a quite normal facet of human nature. We all want to belong to something. Nomadic Arabs trust no-one but family, and sometimes not even kin are worthy of being confided in, which might explain the plethora of intermarriage within families and the need to protect their women through polygamy.

In Britain, tribes are called clans and have elephantine memories. When the written word is not there to pass tales down generations, the spoken word retells the sagas across the centuries, witness the Campbells and MacDonalds. In the massacre of some thirty clansmen in 1692, the result of strife and religious conflict on both sides of the Irish Sea, a tradition of the obligation to despise each other has been long established. In Africa the tribe is not just a name, it is a structure of headmen and chiefs, of laws and traditions, of enmity over centuries once more (witness the Shona and the Ndebele or the Xhosa and the Zulus) but also, and here is the defining difference to the European clan, of language. Most Zambians speak at least five or six languages. How many of our highly educated Europeans can claim such linguistic mastery? And boy, how they love to use their God given talent of speech, *maningi ndaba*, always *too* much. The Zambian women are the loudest mistresses of the art, giving notice of their presence from afar as they converse one behind the other in well-spaced single file order.

The Zambian woman, at least in her traditional role of motherhood and comfort, seemed to be conditioned to produce babies and having done so, to carry the youngest on her back slung in a *chitenge*[27] cloth which could be easily manoeuvred to swing the passenger into a position of mouth on nipple for feeding on the hoof. The sad part of this, I believed, was that the baby always faced its mother, so had little view of the world until it could walk.

I was able to tell my brother John that our flights had been booked and the frantic winding down was keeping us busy. There was no change to Dad's condition. Calling from our parent's flat in Bray, John passed me over to my Mother with whom I had not spoken since our last leave in Majorca, and who exuded the trait of her generation to bring the call to a swift conclusion for fear it was costing a fortune. We were little the wiser about what to expect once we got back to Britain.

It slowly dawned that the leaving of Africa was becoming emotional for us both. As the number of the days we had left in Ndola diminished, we spent almost every evening with friends saying our goodbyes, often tearful. Friends apart, I had to get around the stores with William but first made a visit to the Distribution Centre on the south side of the city. On arriving in the car park next to the transport bays I eyed Sam Phiri, one of our long serving lorry drivers, a small wiry man now going grey on top. Sam had taken on Jonas as his driver's mate after he left my house service back in '71 and took personal credit

---

27. The chitenge is a length of fabric, usually a Dutch wax print of Indonesian design, which is wrapped around the lower body of a woman, as if it were an ankle length skirt.

for getting Jonas through his HGV driving test. As usual he had a big grin on his creased face. Sam was now a real *"madala"*[28] living many years beyond the average life expectancy of forty. The only times his smile disappeared were when he spotted a scratch or dent in one of the lorries, whereupon he would launch into a diatribe of hurled insults as he chastised the offending driver.

That day Jonas was away on a run up to Kasama, so I left a greeting for him with the *madala* and walked with William past the storage and picking bays, the first aid room, the siding platform and other parts of the operation Peter McManus and I had played leading roles to set up five years previously, finally reaching the staff canteen. The finality of leaving Zambia really hit me as I was greeted by many familiar faces, faces of my team of workers who brought the whole warehouse project into being with me that I would probably never see again.

The smell of the day's hot relish[29] wafted from the canteen. It would be served with large dollops of *nshima*, a stiff porridge made from mealie meal, formed between the fingers then used to scoop up the *mphodza* (relish). At the outset we had decided to provide hot meals for the staff to see them healthy and well fed, the meals sold for a peppercorn price of ten ngwee (about eight pence in Sterling then). I spied Silus Mudenda of stomach pump fame, lording it with his prominent "Canteen Supervisor" name badge, who stood behind the serving counter. He greeted me like a long-lost friend, much to William's apparent amazement.

That simple act demonstrated the special relationship that existed between people like me, guests in a country from far

---

28. Madala, a venerable old man
29. Relish is a generic term used by Zambians to describe a stew of meat, vegetables or both

away Britain, and the locals wanting to get on in life, grateful for the opportunity to do so through the jobs they valued, jobs created out of the ingenuity and capital we brought to the table. Silus, Sam and all the others were prepared to work hard for the reward of being able to provide for their families and stand tall amongst their peers.

Things had been going well at ZCBC and ZNWC, due in large part to the progress we had made with Mike's import substitution programme. The own brand products ranges had much increased so that, with the notable exception of hosiery still imported from Kamyn in Kenya, we could clothe men and women and their children from top to toe in our locally manufactured quality products. A year had passed since Mike had his PI order; I had received word that he was now working for Edgars Stores in the Transvaal.

The country was already showing signs of economic struggle. Unrest in the Lusaka and Copperbelt townships was being reported along with more crime, some of it serious and life threatening. We had dinner with Mike and Gay Johnstone. Mike had left his job as number two at Indeco Morison to become MD of Reckitt and Coleman in Ndola. Gay was in floods of tears after hearing that a mutual friend, a recently widowed British architect, had been brutally murdered at his isolated farmhouse eight miles to the north of Ndola and close to the border with Katanga. The self-same chap had been at our house for dinner only a week before.

Mike had cooked up his speciality that night, a boozy gourmet dinner, which included carrots in gin, coq-au-vin, pumpkins in a Grand Marnier sauce and more than that I cannot remember, so the show had to go on , but it was in a sombre and sober atmosphere that we left them behind at the end of the evening.

The Government response was to step up police road checks. Criminals, on the other hand, set up their own phoney roadblocks. Steve Smith had been caught in one such trap on the road between Ndola and Mufulira, where he encountered a felled tree across the road. He had tried to reverse but three masked hoodlums stood in his way, one armed with a tommy gun. He escaped unharmed after unloading his wallet and emptying his pockets. The Zambian authorities blamed the crime wave on foreigners from Zaire, a claim we all wanted to believe. Sad to say we knew there were several gangs operating protection rackets in Chifubu in open defiance of the police. At least, that was what our gardener Howard reported, he lived in Chifubu and I knew he was scared.

With only two weeks left I was joined on a Sunday after lunch by William for the drive to Lusaka. The road south was a journey of two hundred miles, as I have said before, the first town on our way was Kapiri Mposhi where the Great North Road branched off to our left. We encountered two police check points before reaching Kapiri. Unlike the days down in Siavonga, I carried my passport with me everywhere, so out it came, despite the eminent presence of William Mvula, whose new appointment had been headlined news in *The Times of Zambia*.

The press article had featuring his photograph, a copy of which lay on the back seat of our Peugot. Just over halfway we passed through the old mining town of Broken Hill, recently renamed Kabwe after the name of a prehistoric man whose skull was found in mine diggings in the early 1920s. The town had been named Broken Hill for its elemental likeness to the more famous mining district of that name in Australia; it still had large mine workings and the railways in Zambia had now made Kabwe its headquarters. Those mines produced many metals although the main orebodies were of lead and zinc. I had learned a while back from my Kitwe friend Neville Hoets, now somewhere in Spain with his wife Kirstin, that the author Wilbur Smith had been born in Broken Hill.

From Kabwe we passed only one further police check that day and arrived at our digs, checking in at Lusaka's Ridgeway Hotel. William went off to meet some friends whilst I met up with Malcolm Westmore for a quick beer in the hotel bar. We set a plan for the following morning which would allow us to get away by eleven at the latest as we had to call in to the new Kabwe store on the return trip. Westy left me to spend the rest of his evening with Cathy and I grabbed dinner in the restaurant where I spotted Jonas Savimbi, the Angolan leader of UNITA wearing sunglasses in earnest conversation with some Zambian officials in dark suits. *The Ridgeway* was one of two international hotels in the city, the other being *The Intercontinental*, about half a mile distant, both regular watering holes for the comings and goings of political grandees from home and abroad.

Having arrived back in good time the following evening, I got in a couple of hours at the office before going home for a swim under the stars and a catch-up with Tory whose sales stall was now about empty. I put a call in to the UK to check with John on Dad's cancer. There had been no change.

With William I finished a tour of all the Copperbelt stores. I had a request from London to get a police clearance for work permit formalities in support of the application Bookers were making for me in St Lucia. Keeping my appointment at the main nick behind the store off Independence Way, I was escorted to the cells where they took my fingerprints. I must have made a strange spectacle to the fifty or so men on remand who peered at me through iron bars watching my dabs being taken, my thumbs and my fingers following the controlling hand of the duty sergeant. I guess they expected me to join them. Thankfully, I was able to escape, I had little wish to use the galvanised latrine buckets let alone share the air with the poor unwashed prisoners sweating in ninety degrees of Fahrenheit heat. Back at the Station desk I was assured that co-operation between Commonwealth police forces guaranteed my report reaching Castries directly, and that a copy would be sent to me at our PO Box 2162, which arrived only two days later.

On Saturday, the Sixteen Ball group at Ndola Golf Club had a party for me in the nineteenth. George Wright presented me with a wood-lined copper desk box depicting a roan antelope on its embossed lid, on the underside of which was a specially worded plaque dated June 1976. I still have it. George was renowned for his comments on the course, reacting to every shot. A good drive from the tee might be accompanied by words such as "long and low, like a barmaid's bust" or if someone missed a putt and started to chastise himself with "if only…", George would retort "C'mon lad, if my aunt had balls she'd be my uncle". His sayings were legion at the club.

Earlier in play I had partnered Bob Syder, the Standard Bank manager where I held my account. Bob, a South African, was a few years older than me, fair haired and built like an athlete and played off a five handicap which bettered me by nine shots. I confided with Bob as we were coming up the final four hundred yards fairway, an uphill expanse of fine grass which was watered every evening after play in the dry season. Water was never in short supply, pumped through extensive underground pipes from abundant aquifers.

The gist of my confidence with the Standard Bank's manager was a confession that his bank had made an error in my favour, namely that the most recent transfer of eight hundred Kwacha to my bank in Bristol under the contract remittance scheme had an extra nought added to the sum. I had been struggling for several months what to do, my UK account had a handsome surplus of funds, much more than I would have had if playing monopoly, with interest being paid monthly at seven percent.

Bob looked me in the eye and declared "I knew about that the day the mistake was made, so I'm glad you came clean". So was I so glad! Bob was a decent fellow, but I guessed he was loath to confront me although frankly I had expected his bank to do so. Bob suggested that I repay the surplus when I got back to Britain, which I did, in instalments and over the next three years. That might seem harsh, my reason to string it out and thereby earn some interest was in reaction to the time being taken in the queue for foreign currency transfers at the Zambian Central Bank.

My plight was not on the same scale as John Blackburne's farm sale proceeds, but a hard-earned sum the equivalent of twelve thousand pounds Sterling remains stuck in Zambia in my name permanently. Back in the clubhouse Bob, George and the others generously bought me a succession of Castle lagers in the hope that I would lose at the dice game *Max and Jacks,* which by some tradition led to the winner having to buy the next round. Being a good loser has its benefits sometimes.

Before removing my spikey golf shoes in the locker room for the last time I said a fond farewell to Hilarius, my regular caddy. I had called over the acting caddy master to witness my gift to Hilarius, a box of used but good condition golf balls and two spare clubs, a putter and a spoon along with a blue ten Kwacha tip, I wanted to make sure my caddy avoided being challenged for stealing. Many caddies played a far better game than we Members, almost all of us being once-a-week hackers, a fact recognised by the Club's Committee which arranged regular mid-week caddy competitions to encourage the playing of golf by local people.

The Ndola course was host to an annual tournament of touring professionals, largely but not exclusively from the UK, on what was called the "Sunshine Circuit" which featured a succession of open tournaments in African countries such as the Ivory Coast, Kenya, Malawi, Botswana as well as Zambia. The Ndola event was known as *"The Cock of the North",* whilst the actual *Zambian Open* was played at the Lusaka course. Two days before the "Cock" the Club held a Pro-Am competition over eighteen holes, with much prestige attached to those Club Members who qualified to join the ranks of amateurs playing with two of the touring professionals in three ball groups.

By some quirk of good form, I had qualified the previous year, drawing professionals from Scotland and Ghana. The poor Ghanaian had contracted an awful cold and was clearly feeling uncomfortable in the dry air of our high altitude, coming as he did from the humid west coast of the vast continent. He returned a nett score higher than me, so for once I could brag that I had beaten a pro.

The arrival of the golf pros was an occasion to look forward to, the travellers, about forty in number, would be billeted out to stay with Members. Many home parties were arranged to celebrate their company. At our home in Nyimba Crescent, Tory and I had hosted a young Scot called Sam Torrance who had willingly helped with barbecue duty, manipulating boerewors and steaks on the grill atop an empty oil drum which had holes punched in its sides to allow ventilation. The hot fumes rose up from the charcoal fire at the base, the circular end panel of the upright drum had been removed and replaced by a heavy mesh metal grill which overhung the sides, thus providing a hot spot for cooking with the overhanging warm areas for storing cooked food, ready for eating as guests came to help themselves in a long drawn out convivial gathering combining food, drinks and ceaseless banter under the bright stars of the tropical night sky. Away from the fire, a sweet perfume from a frangipani tree wafted slowly into the still night air.

The frangipani's scent seemed to me to represent a cross between the fragrances of the honeysuckle and a jasmine flower, quite delicious and once experienced never forgotten.

With a week left the packers arrived. We had sold most of our household goods and clothes, indeed Tory had a buyer who insisted paying thirty Kwacha (£24) for my plain blue lightweight two piece suit, bought originally from C&A in London four years before for nineteen pounds, complete with holes in the pockets.

The Company furniture would stay in the house as would our survival kit to cover meals and bedding for the final days, the latter would be given to Judy to take to her new home. We had assembled everything we wanted to take with us to St Lucia, which the freight people packed into three tea chests to be held in bond once they had arrived in England for onward shipment, to which would be added most of the boxes containing our wedding presents, left behind in the basement of The Elms, Tory's mother's house in Alphington.

Michael Caine flew into Ndola with Thornton Hawkins, having had a testing time in Lusaka. He had managed to close a deal with Indeco which secured the management contract for ZCBC, my understanding being that all top jobs other than the chief executive (Gerald) would be held by Zambians and that the Bookers office in London would continue to confirm all international buying for the Zambian business. Anything Michael said was calculated carefully to assure shareholders, wherever they were, lest it should get out that Bookers stood little if no chance of getting future dividends or capital repayments from a cash-poor Zambian government.

I knew then that despite the best will of my peers and me, our business was not yet that ready to be managed by people who had not worked their way up from the bottom but owed their responsible appointments to academic prowess or, by association, to political power. I hoped that I was wrong. I thought of Agnes Banda, John Songolo, Telephone Mvula, Alice Sakuwaha, Dennis Sakalla and so many others whose future I could no longer play a part in, left to fend for themselves against the wolves. A good reason to pray.

The Stercks flung a farewell party for Tory and me, there were forty or more of my Zambian colleagues as well as remaining head office expats such as Neil Eccles, George Wright, Dean Wright, Norrie Greig, our fashion buyer Gwen Powell, Chris Chapman from Esquire, Alec McPhail from the Ndola store and his deputy Dominic Eedle, Tom Welsh our Canadian buying manager and Jack Gibbs, head of food. There was Kit Falwasser, our elderly lady home textiles buyer and Agatha Christie lookalike, and Margaret Lumsden our dear friend and buyer of children's clothing, and others, all who would be leaving Zambia within a few months.

Despite her age, Kit had a boyfriend of many years standing called Malcolm who made good men's silk ties in a small factory off the main shopping street in Ndola. Malcolm had an office above the workroom, in which he employed half a dozen women. His building stood next door to a bar on the ground floor, affectionately known as the lower office, where *"Alchy Malchy"*, for that was his nickname, could usually be found after eleven in the morning. Kit and Malcolm planned a life together to enjoy their pensions, having bought a small house in Alicante, Spain.

Michael Caine called order by clinking his glass and said a few words about his journey to Lusaka which gave some comfort to our Zambian colleagues, most of whom had told me how much they regretted our going away. Next up was Gerald Sterck, who proceeded to eulogise about the oddball Thornton for several minutes and made a toast to his retirement. He sat down without a word spoken of my time in Zambia, his speech was greeted with a few muffled claps from his wife and then an awkward silence. Michael Caine, who suffered from a stutter, broke the ice by saying "Ge-Ge-Gerald, the p-p-p-presentation?" William Mvula interrupted the proceedings with a short but kind speech about the man he was about to take over from and proceeded to raise his glass to Tory and me, after which the Zambian guests dropped their inhibitions and the party went with a loud swing. I never did find out what presentation there might have been but had my doubts that I was one to be on the receiving end. In any event, it was one of many emotional moments in the farewell grind. Dear Thornton, he had failed his masters terribly in his selection of Gerald Sterck, I cannot think of a man less suited to the ingenuity of collaborating to good purpose with the men and women of his host country.

Two days later our little family boarded the flight to Lusaka in transit for London on the Zambia Airways DC8, the same 'plane I had travelled in with Sam Kelly seven years before. Having checked in for the London bound flight I was approached by a uniformed policeman and asked to accompany him to the basement offices. The officer gave no indication why I was wanted below, and my thoughts turned to the Standard Bank overpayment or some other crime I might have committed without knowing it. I had left Tory and the children to walk up the stairs to the departure lounge, Tory's worried face was foremost in my mind as I wrestled with the prospect of being retained in gaol.

Our hollow footsteps became silent as the policeman and I entered a carpeted office where a man in khaki uniform and pips on his epaulettes stood up to greet me. In his hand was a white envelope which I imagined might be a court summons or worse. "Derrick Swain?", he enquired. My affirmative but croaky response sealed my identity, I was about to find out why I was there. "This is for you" he said, as he handed me the envelope, a farewell card signed by William and fifty others which had been handed to the pilot just before we taxied to the Ndola runway with instructions to give it to me in Lusaka. The pilot had passed over the task of finding me to a policeman on his way out of the airport.

As I was explaining to Tory what had happened in the police zone below, I saw a familiar female face looking at me from the far side of the lounge. It was Carol Blunt, a girlfriend from my teenage days in Burnham, friend of Lisa Brunowski and alumna of Cheltenham Ladies" College, on her way to Mauritius with her new husband who held back with their baby daughter, gazing at us from a distance. Our flight was called, I got a peck from Carol and then it was time to go. On board the aircraft I took my seat and broke down in tears.

Much has been written about Empire, much of it being revisionist twaddle and some of it fair and truthful, and much also has been written about contemporary conflicts in Africa. Perhaps it is because the Colony of Northern Rhodesia morphed into the fully independent Republic of Zambia in an orderly process, without bloody conflict, that little has been written about those early days which give credit to people working under the flag of the Union and the green, gold, black and red flag of Zambia with its golden fish eagle emblem. Those days were particularly exciting for us post-colonial expatriates, who not only took part in the events of the first ten years or so of the Republic, but also benefitted hugely from the life experience we gained there

Zambia inherited healthy finances from its colonial government, including eighteen months foreign exchange cover, a well-developed and expanding mining industry, a network of well-engineered road systems, railways connecting the major towns with each other and with neighbouring countries and their sea ports, two international airports, a small but well drilled army and a police force devoid of serious corruption, general hospitals and regional clinics, the rule of law and a democratic structure for its future governance. I could go on. It was never going to be a perfect hand-over, the new rulers were in a hurry to take over and the old rulers post Federation had little desire to resist them. What was inadequate was an education system to carry children beyond Form Three into secondary and tertiary learning.

There had been only sixty years since the first missionaries arrived on foot through Angola into what was a protectorate of Britain known as Barotseland-North-Western Rhodesia, later combined with a second protectorate of North-Eastern Rhodesia, both territories administered through its charter by the British South African Company from 1924, just forty years before independence. The sheer scale of enterprise and energy under the various stages of British responsibility that had brought the territories to the reality of an independent nation state in that short time is truly and deeply impressive.

A love for Zambia and a caring interest for its people remain together in the hearts of almost all of us who spent time there. It lives on in the twenty-first century through organisations such as The Zambia Society, The Friends of Northern Rhodesia and Zambia, the various Commonwealth agencies, many churches and through charities and educational organisations. Most of us, when we left Zambia, planted trees and shrubs for the enjoyment of future residents, having ourselves benefitted from the wonderful plants found growing in our allotted properties, such as the glorious rubber tree, candelabra cacti, poinsettia, peach tree, avocado and bougainvillea at number one, Nyimba Crescent.

15

Rain

(August and September 1976)

As things turned out It was probably not such a good idea to have taken the job in St Lucia, but I was not to know that when I started out. Not many would turn down the chance of working in paradise, as we have come to call the West Indies, and certainly not when you are thirty-three, fit in body and supported by someone like my Tory, ready to share in the new adventure. I walked into two big problems not of my own making, rather I was not forewarned nor was I well informed. But I run ahead of myself. In any event and despite all setbacks, the experience was worth it, every moment spent with wonderful folk under those sunny skies.

Our British Airways VC-10 was resplendent in its new BA livery. It had touched down at last on the tarmac of Hewanorra Airport on the south shore of St Lucia close to the small coastal town of Vieux Fort. It was late August 1976. The huge airliner towered above smaller light aircraft and a single Dakota, parked close to the new terminal building. Having set down the twenty or so passengers who departed their flight in St Lucia, the crew took off for Port of Spain in Trinidad, the aeroplane's destination that day. Little Christy-Anne was taking a ride in her mother's arms behind her elder brother Andy, who was still proudly clutching his *BOAC Junior Jet Club* passbook. More airmiles had been clocked up and signed off by the pilot. An hour before touchdown he had been woken up by a glamourous hostess, his personal escort for a private tour of the flight deck.

As I looked curiously around, I found we were still in sight of the blue ocean, its surface whipped up by winds, white horses seen through the gaps between the waiving palm trees which surrounded the new airport's perimeter. A hot breeze blew through the open sides of the terminal where we had to stand in line to complete immigration formalities and then collect our luggage. A smartly dressed customs man in similar white uniform to his Commonwealth counterpart in Zambia scrutinised our bags to his satisfaction. After he placed a chalk mark on our suitcases, he looked at my passport and then pointed to a blackboard where there was a message in bold white script which bore my name. I found a note of welcome from the Company in a white envelope asking us to take a flight north to Castries. There were four flight tickets enclosed. We quickly discovered that the silver Dakota on the apron bearing the name of *Saint Lucia Airways* in bold navy-blue script was our transport to Vigie airport near Castries, the island's capital. St Lucia is less than thirty miles long so it would not take long to reach our destination, I thought.

I had not bargained for a flash storm which raged for twenty minutes, filling up the sky with ominous black clouds. We sat watching the wind-driven rain, then hung around for two hours before we were able to take-off. I just loved Dakotas

(DC-3s), they first flew out of the Douglas Aircraft factories in California in 1943 to serve the US military and quickly became the world's most prolific means of air transport. Stepping into the 'plane at the port side rear door a passenger had to walk uphill to reach the vacant free seating, a comfortable leather bucket seat awaiting him or her. The aircraft levelled out as it gained speed on the runway for take-off. Years later, in May 2008, Tory and I flew on the final flight of a Dakota in Europe, from Manston in Kent, the aircraft type finally grounded by a diktat of the EU in Brussels which claimed it to be unsafe. How could they say that, after 65 years of faithful service and millions of flights the world over?

The Dakota sped over the ocean at its cruising speed of 200 mph, its altitude could not have exceeded two thousand feet as it passed the famed Pitons on its starboard side at the volcanic Soufriere, two peculiar and unique conical mountains clad in dark green vegetation which rose two and a half thousand feet out of the sea. Then, quite suddenly, the sky cleared and minutes later we set down in bright sunshine. At last I felt we had finally arrived in the West Indies, where a steel band was playing its tuneful percussion outside the small terminal building, and there, behind the wire perimeter fence, frantically waving his arms, was Maurice Widdowson. He had two other people in tow. The tiny airport was set beside the sea on two sides between which I saw a hilly promontory with generously spaced houses perched on its steep hillsides. This was the area called Vigie, after which our landing strip was named.

Our greeting party comprised a cheerful but urbane chap named Rodney Broughton, who had been sent out from London to keep my seat warm at Minvielle & Chastanet (M&C for short), with his wife to keep Tory company. They were to take us to the nearby Malabar Hotel where we had beach front accommodation booked for a week while our company house was being redecorated, or so I was told, which was just as well since our packing cases would not arrive on the *Geest* banana boat for another four days. On the way we passed a large cemetery on our left, with ornate wrought and cast-iron graves, some were obviously built to accommodate for several generations of the dead. Maurice told me that last October he had witnessed the spooky All Hallows celebrations, when conga trails of people danced slowly through the eternal resting place bearing fiery torches held high, an annual tradition with its roots in Catholic and West African culture.

Maurice insisted he have the honour to be the first to buy me a West Indian rum punch, which certainly eased the hotel check-in procedure at the desk next to the bar. One punch turned into three before the party left with promises to return at seven o'clock for dinner.

Finally reaching our beach chalet I found that Tory had the young ones settled. In front of us was the Caribbean Sea, facing west into the dying sun, the water only a short distance across the light sandy beach, itself fringed with palm trees rising out of a carpet of thick spongy vegetation. The warm and placid sea, now gold in the reflected light of the setting sun, beckoned us irresistibly for our first swim in the West Indies.

By the time we had unpacked and changed for dinner the children were fast asleep. Tory had arranged for a lanky security guard to sit outside our digs to keep an ear out for the children before we joined our friends in the open-sided beach restaurant. The earlier storm left no evidence of its passing as the gentle shore wind, taking its temperature from the warm sea, made the table candles gutter happily in their glass storm-proof holders. Maurice was as keen to hear news of Zambia as we were to learn about our new surroundings, although the advice I needed most urgently was to describe the local menu. I settled for callaloo soup and salt fish ackee whilst Tory skipped the starter choosing breaded flying fish. I thought, if we are to stay at the Malabar for a week, I will have time to test out most of the mysterious fare on offer, my lifetime weakness for tasty eating now well exposed.

Our fellow diners left us for an early night although it was late on my body clock, which was ticking on British Summer Time. Despite tiredness and all the excitement and emotions of our arrival in a new land, sleep evaded me, my mind still thinking about the past two months in England. My father had died in early July, less than three weeks after we had arrived home from Africa. I had left the family with my sister-in-law to make the short car journey with John from his house on Maidenhead's Castle Hill to our parents' flat by the Thames at Bray. Dad was sitting quietly in his favoured chair facing the window. His warm greeting had been followed by a host of questions about the children, my new job and how things had been in Ndola. He talked of getting better and of his plans to visit us in St Lucia, which pulled on my emotions, knowing the prognosis of a few weeks left for him at best, but tried to behave as if that elephant was not in the room. Why was it that we always seem to veer away from confronting the subject of death? As we talked so we played and enjoyed a few games of cribbage and scrabble together, proving that despite Dad's dimming life, he remained the avid competitor he had always been. After a couple of hours, a male nurse arrived to conduct the end of day and bedtime tasks, so I bade goodnight with the promise to return in the morning. John and Mother had remained in the kitchen to give Dad some private time with his returning son.

There followed a week in which the little ones got to know their grandpa and I was able to spend a few hours each day in the sitting room sharing the odd cigarette and glass of scotch whisky with my father as our conversations relaxed and took on intimacies long forgotten, tales of his childhood and family, his business life but little about the war. Eventually we had slipped away to see Tory's parents, and it was while at my father-in-law's flat in Bournemouth, that Tory got the fateful call from John to tell us that Dad had gone. He had died in his bed at home, sedated from pain by a cocktail of opiates in the company of his doctor and his wife.

There had been little if no rain for several weeks before the funeral, the good weather continuing throughout the two months we were in Britain. Bray Church was full to bursting; at sixty-nine my Father was the first of his generation of friends and relatives to pass on; I felt emotionally drained after the service and in no fit state to make conversation with others, however much I wanted to talk to people I had not seen for seven years or more. Adrian came in from the States, he had arrived a day after Dad died but in time for the funeral. Our youngest brother Andrew, who had been with us in Zambia a year back, was sadly missed. He had been out of contact for several months travelling somewhere in Asia.

The hot days after the funeral were spent sorting through Dad's files then writing to everyone in his address book. Dad's office was in a room above the detached garage. It felt I was invading his private space and that he should be there helping me, instead It dawned on me that with Dad gone, no longer did I have a fall-back, the buck now stopped with me. I must have drifted off to sleep because the next thing striking my conscience was a shaft of bright sunshine through the bedroom window at the back of our chalet. Time for an early breakfast and getting my mind set on the day ahead.

I remembered what I had learned in London and also at last night's dinner table, that Saint Lucia had been a self-governing Associated State within the Commonwealth since 1967, which meant that the British Queen was Head of State, her authority exercised by the Governor. The young nation's defence and external affairs were handled by Whitehall, but most other responsibilities were those of the government in Castries, whose leader was the Premier, John Compton. Mr Compton had been appointed by the majority St Lucia Workers Party of an Assembly of seventeen elected Members. The island's population was about one hundred and forty thousand.

The UK Government in Whitehall was represented by the BGR, or British Government Representative, a career Foreign Office diplomat. Both the Governor and the BGR lived in fine wood-frame mansions in spacious gardens on high ground above the Port of Castries. Indeed, the Port of Castries was a natural deep-water harbour. At one time before the Panama Canal was built it had been the world's fifth biggest tonnage port, being then a coal bunkering station like Valparaiso in Chile, for refuelling the vessels which steamed between the West and Northeast coasts of the USA by way of Cape Horn. Nowadays its wharves handled ocean freighters, banana boats and cruise ships, the latter tying up at the end of Bridge Street, the main drag and shopping street so that passengers had easy access to the town's shops and businesses.

We had driven in from the Malabar by way of the John Compton Highway, a straight stretch of tarmac road leading from the airport past the national football stadium. Further on at the head of the harbour's waters lay a huge rubbish dump displaying the wrecked remains of boats, cars, lorries and detritus of all kinds, only a hundred yards from the red metal frame of Castries Market on the other side of the road, already bustling with vendors and shoppers. The road came to a T-junction as we entered the town with the port on the right. It was almost eight o'clock in the morning when I first entered the main M&C store building from the small rear car park. The concrete clad building was on three floors, the first two levels for sales departments and the top floor housing service departments and the Company's offices, and it was to that level we headed, mounting four flights of stairs in the process.

I took in the large open plan office with management offices on three sides. There were high level louvre windows above and behind all but one of the side walls, which, together with the ceiling fans allowed air movement to ease the mean heat and humidity. Each desk carried heavy paperweights ranging from rocks to cricket balls to prevent the office turning into a confetti factory. Curious looks and smiles greeted my presence as I crossed diagonally to Rodney's corner office, soon to be mine when he returned to London.

It is fair to say that I had had a full briefing on the Company's structure and operations when I was at Bookers offices in London's John Adam Street and had the additional benefit of Maurice's commentary last night, but I was ill prepared for the mysteries of what I came to call a wonderful disorganisation. In fact, that was to be problem number one, namely that here I was to work, fresh from having been party to building a modern, indeed sophisticated business in Zambia, to find myself stepping back in time tasked with rescuing a business from chaos. As Maurice had warned me, the conservative forces resisting change were stacked up like a defensive fortress in the form of the previous owners and their favoured staff.

Essential reading for anyone attempting to take on business in the small islands of the Caribbean is a book titled *"Don't stop the carnival"* by the American author Herman Wouk. The writer records the trials and tribulations of an advertising executive from Madison Avenue who decides to collect his savings and up sticks from the safety of the Big Apple to open a restaurant in a fictitious island. I had read the book and was thus well armed for the tasks ahead. Indeed, Wouk's island could well have been the one I was standing on.

Mike Hearder, Bookers' Overseas Division Chairman, had arrived in St Lucia two years before me with his sidekick Thomas Moerry[30] (pronounced Murray), a scholarly intellectual who had emigrated from Eastern Europe after the war. I found it hard to understand how his scholarship fitted into Caribbean trade, I must have missed something. Bookers did love their Fabian heritage it must be said, so why not give an academic such commercial responsibility?

Seeking to expand the Group's business base in the Caribbean the two had met the owners of M&C. Later, as I got to know the Devaux family, I learned that some of their ancestors had arrived from the west of France in the eighteenth century and had managed to avoid the travelling guillotines and kangaroo courts which arrived unannounced off commandeered war ships, sent out from France during *La Terreur* which followed the French Revolution.

The deal had been completed with the cousins Joe and Fred for the outright purchase of their businesses in St Lucia,

---

30. Thomas Moerry is not the character's real name, to protect his incompetence

which left their family with a substantial sum in cash and a bundle of shares in Booker McConnell Limited. Whether it was a good or bad decision would only be revealed in time, but the decision to retain the family management team indefinitely following the takeover was surely not a clever idea, flying in the face of conventional wisdom about such things. Could Humpty Dumpty repair his own broken shell? After all, the first of the King's men, Maurice, had been prevented from doing so and had given up. Step up Derrick, no better equipped than Maurice, but at least with an appointment to join the Board. Mike Hearder's deal gave Bookers the largest piece of the commercial action in St Lucia, whose Edwardian practices had to be advanced by seventy years of commercial development if it were ever to become a competitor in the contemporary world.

M&C employed just over one thousand people. It was the island's largest employer outside the banana plantations and the public sector. It comprised many parts, each had been managed by a family member or a trusted appointee, who kept their own books. There were general stores in Vieux Fort and Soufriere, a large department store in Castries, a drugstore and pharmacy, catering and food businesses, three hotel boutiques, liquor wholesale and retail operations, all to be my responsibility, and services in travel, Lloyds underwriting, builders' merchants, a fruit drinks plant, shipping and airline agencies, and an agency distribution business all under the control of Fred Devaux, younger of the two cousins. Finally, there was M&C Motors, a servicing facility with new and used car sales which was the responsibility of David Devaux, the son of Joe and his wife Joan.

Bookers had brought in a bright qualified accountant called James Hill as Finance Director. James had worked hard to combine the accounts of each department and introduce retail accounting. The results of his labours and the clever sleuthing of his chief accountant, Patrick Leow, began to show shrinkage rates in the retail parts of the Company of as much as six percent of sales. The whole Company was bleeding, the losses had to stop.

All this became clear as the morning progressed when I met James ahead of Donald Macdonald, who I was down to meet in the late afternoon. The latter had just replaced Edgar Redwin, the first man sent by Bookers to be local chairman. Donald had served many years with Bookers in Malawi, although I had never met him in Africa. Donald's predecessor Edgar Redwin had willingly transferred to see out the two years before he retired, having overseen the nationalisation of the sugar estates in Guyana.

At midday we set off on a walking tour of the various parts of the business, meeting my many new local colleagues in the process. We started by crossing Bridge Street at the front of the department store to see the "Canteen" known locally as a *snacket*, which served low cost meals and beverages to the public. It was closed. It opened in the morning and in the afternoon but in keeping with Herman Wouk's dictum, it closed in the middle of the day so that the staff could go to lunch.

Next came the liquor store which sold local and imported alcoholic drinks at retail, wholesale and *"demi-gros"*, a common practice in francophone countries I learned, being a discounted price for three of more bottles of the same item. Sure, a patois was spoken in St Lucia, but English was the official language, not French. It must have been a relic from earlier days. Looking as if he understood my thoughts the manager, Joseph Antoine, gave me a smile of unconditional welcome and proudly took me through his buildings at the rear of which was a long lean-to shed which accommodated a bottle washing plant, at least it was full of large round ladies teamed together to hand-clean clear glass bottles, which made total sense on an island that had no glass factory. I decried the loss of re-usable glass in England, replaced by plastic, the great polluter. Joseph gave me a bottle brush for use at home and I somehow felt by that gesture I would have an ally in Joseph. He might help me get under the skin of St Lucian culture and its strange ways. It was blindingly obvious that island life had little in common with my central African experience.

Saying farewell for the moment to Joseph, a short dapper man with a full head of white hair, we took a short stroll up the street to the pharmacy on the same side of the road but on the corner with Micoud Street to the right. Before entering the shop, I glanced further up Bridge Street towards the Castries River and the rising ground of the Morne beyond, high ground overlooking the town from where the river fell and flooded in the rains.

The M&C Drug Store had an adjacent home hardware shop. It was the one retail property belonging to the Company that had air-conditioning, necessary for the type of stock it held. The dispensary was at the far end about ninety feet from the front. My first thought was that the area was far too big for the range of stocks on display, so either the ranges had to be enlarged or the space re-allocated.

After our quick tour of the home hardware shop, stocked entirely from US imports, we walked down Micoud to look at a couple of warehouse storage buildings and to meet a few of the staff. From there we were met by Peter Robinson, a white West Indian who had married into the Devaux family and whose job it was to manage the cold store business. Peter imported butchery, poultry and prepared meats from the US and Ireland. The cold storage buildings were a half mile away beyond the banana boat wharves on the sea front to the right of the road, close to the island's main Victoria Hospital. Beyond was the road up to Tapion point which overlooked one side of the entrance to Castries harbour and across the water to Vigie. By the time we arrived on foot I was sweating like one of the proverbial animals in Peter's largest freezer room, so I decided to join the hanging carcasses for a minute to let the heat ooze out of me. Mercifully, the office had AC. We got a lift back into Bridge Street after twenty minutes with Peter during which time he gave me a thorough account of his functions and ideas for change, he seemed to welcome a listening ear. I felt I had another potential ally here. Taking us back into town by car, Peter told me he was sorry the firm had lost Maurice and was surprised that I had known him in Zambia.

We crossed Bridge Street dodging potholes on the way to look at the store's display windows. The mannequins looked a tad tired, but the display work seemed good. It was mid-afternoon by then, and time to meet Donald. Why is it that chaps called Macdonald are all called Donald, like the Campbell male is invariably called Colin? I have five friends called David Taylor and another five called Peter Smith. Donald's wife Nan, a gracious lady turning grey and without make-up, was introduced to me as she left her husband to get back to matters of business. Nan insisted I visit her with my family that coming Sunday for lunch at the house the Company had recently rented for them overlooking Rodney Bay in the north of the island. Meanwhile she asked if she could visit Tory at the Malabar two days hence.

Donald's welcome was as warm as Nan's had been, he

seemed pleased, even relieved, dare I say, to see me. Many years in Malawi had little effect upon Donald's Scottish burr, he was clearly from the western side of Caledonia in contrast to the softer Midlothian tones of his wife. Something reassuring about the Scots *awa' fem heim*, they can never deny their origins, just like a host of people who had been part of my life since leaving home, witness my house sharing chum Peter Brawley, our neighbours John and Dilly MacEwan, late of Ceylon, The Swan and the Black Isle, then Zambia's Norrie Greig, Alex Riddle, Roy Ritson, Jimmy Crawford, Martin Haliiday-Brown and Chick Beveridge all of ZCBC, Maurice Renwick of the Ndola Lions and Barclays DCO, Jock Lumsden now with Margaret in South Africa all of whom, without exception, had spent most of their years far from the land of their birth.

There were some papers for me to sign when James Hill joined us with more forms for my signature. There was to be a Board Meeting the next day to confirm my appointment, in the meantime I was in Rodney's hands to complete my introduction and get my office set up. James took me across the main office to his own perch to meet Pat Leow, who came with Mr Redwin from Georgetown. Time was getting on, it was close to four O'clock when, Maurice had warned me, work would stop abruptly. By two minutes past four all was quiet, we had the office to ourselves, hard to imagine only a few minutes earlier it had been bustling with fifty or more souls at work, such was the speed of the end of day escape. Pat suggested we try a tot of vintage Guyanese rum, which we did, then we called it a day. What a day, I thought.

Back at the Malabar I had to take a sea bath, local parlance for a dip in the briny. Tory was full of beans having been given a tour in the north of the island by James's sparkling wife

Beverly. That had been thoughtful of her. I told her about Nan Macdonald coming to visit her the day after tomorrow. The kids had slept long in the morning before Beverly's tour, which took in place names we would very soon be wholly familiar with such as East Winds, Choc, Pigeon Island, the Cap Estate and Gros Islet. On the way back Beverly took Tory to see the house we were to move into at Choc, up a twisty steep road, the house overlooking the Halcyon Beach Club hotel and Rat Island beyond. The Hills had yet to move out to take over the large house occupied by the departed Redwins with views across Rodney Bay, which was the property being presently decorated which delayed our moving. Pecking order at M&C was clearly determined by length of local service. I chose to act the new boy and bank the brownie points, realising that the relatively small house we were inheriting had the virtue of proximity to the town and the office. Tory and the children would enjoy a longer stay at the Malabar.

Between the hotel bar and the beach was a plate glass window to keep any bad weather at bay. From where I was sitting at the bar next to Maurice, who had called by for a debrief on my first day, we could see the setting sun falling to the horizon. "It's green flash time" said my pal as he recharged my rum punch, "tradition dictates you must have had two drinks at least to see the flash" he added with an earnest expression as he peered through his convex spectacle lenses. I was about to witness the set sun popping back up from the horizon in a flash of green light before slumping over the edge once again as it went to bed, only seen through glass by a trick of refraction. Maurice explained his plans to set up a business in St Kitts where he had been earlier in the month before our arrival. He wanted to know what plans our old mate Brendan McShane had for the country club he and Dominic Eedle were looking to buy in partnership with their accumulated savings. I was able to tell Maurice that the country club project had gone belly up and the boys had bought a pub in Bath on the rebound called the *Rose and Crown*. Dominic would run the pub as landlord and be a lot closer to his mother who lived alone in Bath.

I had seen Brendan two weeks before leaving the UK. Tory's sister Katy and her husband had invited us to babysit Longmoor Lodge whilst she and Richard took their three children on holiday, giving us the chance to invite friends from far and wide to make our big farewell as we prepared for a new life in the West Indies, so not surprisingly Brendan and Dominic came up from Bath to our temporary home in Berkshire.

"So, what will McShane do?" asked Maurice. I was unsure, but no doubt we would hear soon enough, I suggested, and in the meantime, I was sure he would be attending to the social wellbeing of the locals working both sides of the pub bar. Maurice could see I was dog tired and left us soon after for an early bedtime, not before suggesting we all have dinner together at a restaurant the following evening., arranging to collect us at six and to bring a babysitter to keep our two angels safe.

In the morning I was given the keys to a low mileage second hand green Singer estate car which had been delivered by David Devaux. Given the pristine state of the bodywork I suspected the car had been in an accident before attending the bodywork shop. I resumed my tour of the department store whilst Rodney arranged interviews for a secretary for me at mid-morning. It was soon clear that most of the sales floor staff knew who I was through the chatter line, so I got out my notebook and wrote down the names of all the ones who introduced themselves, listening very carefully to the musical language tones of Saint Lucians. I found a staircase which led up to another part of the top floor where I found the display department and the all-important tailoring and seamstress sections managed by a wonderful lady dressed as if stepping from an Edwardian film set, respectfully known as Mistress Montoute. In the islands the title Mistress was widely used to address married women. I could not help myself from thinking how interesting it was that the old forms of our language are retained in English speaking countries far away over the seas but had fallen into disuse at home. I hoped there and then that Mistress Montoute would take kindly to me and become a source of information and background knowledge, a hope that was to be happily rewarded in the months ahead.

The interviews did not take long, for me Miss Winifred Richardson was the only one candidate. *Winnie* was a cheerful beauty in her early twenties who had been working in one of the service departments and whose conversation suggested she had ambition and vitality. She was engaged to be married in six months. Lucky fellow, thought I.

The store and offices closed at midday so all staff could partake of lunch, the doors re-opening at one O'clock. I took the opportunity to brave the heat and walk down Bridge Street to the port. There was a cruise ship tied up. It dwarfed the nearby stall holders and hustlers seeking to profit from the visiting passengers. Today it was the turn of the Cunard Countess to visit us. I turned right, keeping the harbour on my left, and strolled towards the red market building I had spotted the day before, turning right again to make a circular walk back to the office. I was now on Laborie Street, ahead of me I spied a large church which I decided to go into to find some respite from the hot sun. Its name board declared the building to be the Cathedral of the Immaculate Conception, clearly in the Roman tradition of Christianity. I resolved to find out where the Protestants worshipped, that is, if indeed there were any in the Catholic Archdiocese of St Lucia. Stepping out of the Cathedral I turned to my left where a square opened out with fine trees spreading shade over the grassy open space beneath. A sign said Columbus Square; the Cathedral took up one whole side.

On each of the other three sides were wooden frame houses painted in various colours, three and sometimes four stories high, all looking onto the square across narrow roadways and storm gutters separating the properties from the open space which someone had dedicated to the navigator of 1594. The finest of all those buildings was one with bright white walls and emerald green paintwork picking out the struts, the doorway and window frames. I walked beyond the square, then turned to my right back on to Bridge Street to find the store once more, open to welcome customers for the second session of the day. I remembered I had a Board Meeting to attend.

I headed back to my office and bumped into Donald who was having a heated conversation with three white men, two much older than the third but all similarly dressed in shirt jacks, not dissimilar to the bush jackets I had once worn in Zambia, only more ornate. My presence seemed to bring an immediate hush before I was hastily introduced to Joe Devaux, his companion Fox Dulieu, and his younger cousin Fred. "So", I thought, "I confront the family at last". To me they seemed a pleasant enough bunch. I left Donald to it.

The new Board composition was finally resolved when the meeting started at two O'clock promptly without David, who arrived in St Lucian time ten minutes later. Fox, Joe's old chum resigned, and David was stood down, it mattered little to him it seemed, provided he could keep his motor business.

New boy that I was, after one and a half days in the business, I decided to make my statement in front of *l'ancien regime* of Joe and Fred. I made it clear that I had not been appointed for any reason other than to bring the business to profit and that I intended to do that, even if there would have to be some unpleasant decisions ahead, but as retail was a people business, my first task was to assess every one of the thousand or so employees and managers and the systems they worked with. I would report back to the Board on a monthly timetable with my plans openly exposed to get their unequivocal support and understanding of the actions we would then take. Heads nodded and Donald smiled as the meeting closed, a good start I thought.

I drove back to the Malabar in my green shooting brake and took Tory on a test drive around the airport road and Vigie, with Andy and C-A bundled happily in the boot area. Tory would need the car more than I would, I guessed. Maurice arrived as we parked the car back at the hotel with a pretty girl to babysit our children, the sister of a friend he explained, and after the young ones were settled, we drove into town, parking at the roadside in Columbus Square. The white and green painted chattel house I had admired at lunchtime turned out to be *Rain Restaurant*, carefully decorated inside to the theme of Ernest Hemingway's book *"Cat in the rain"*. Our host Al Hayman was the proprietor, a retired New York advertising executive, late of J. Walter Thompson of Madison Avenue. The food was great, crab backs and a West Indian fish pot; I could not help myself wondering whether Wouk had inspired Al, or was it the other way around? Certainly, the after-dinner conversations we had with Al suggested his experiences in setting up *Rain* deviated little from the story line of *"Don't stop the carnival"*.

16

HMS Tiger and the South Atlantic squadron

(Year turn 1976/77)

A month after enjoying crab backs at *Rain* I bumped into Al again on the tree lined William Peter Boulevard at the side of our main store. I had been to *Valmont's* bookshop on Laborie Street and was standing outside *Y de Lima*, one of our competitors for better end goods. We arranged to take coffee together at *Rain* a few days later, something about wanting my advice.

Rodney had returned to London as planned. Alan Lang, a bright local man in his late twenties had just been appointed to be General Manager of the store. Alan shared my ideas for re-organising most of the departments, but first we had to set up a proper personnel structure. By the time a second month had past we had interviewed every member of staff and created proper records for each one of them. We had also analysed everyone's job function enabling us to write up job descriptions, giving our managers the means of assessing the performance of all their staff. It would point the way for training needs. This was all basic stuff, but in St Lucia I was a revolutionary.

Stock levels were all over the place with no visible financial targets, budgets or expense controls, the system, for what it was, worked, I was assured, through the authority of the individual department managers. No more, I told Alan, he and I would in future countersign every order issued to suppliers and M&C would no longer be a soft touch for any itinerant salesman from the States to pick up orders each time they decided to pay us a visit. In fact, we put a stop on all buying whilst a separate buying office was set up. James was called in to help us set up financial stock records once I had drawn up my first budget and full year plan. Alan was relishing his part in the changes. A stock take was to be organised under the procedures I had brought from Zambia which should produce a starting point for the re-organised departments and their managers. The pace of change was fast. I was delighted that Winifred and Alan were keeping up with me, I certainly valued their committed support and sense of right and wrong.

From what I have told you so far you could well imagine that I had committed heresy in the eyes of Joe and his cabal of department heads, a few now the target for my guillotine. Joe was a kind man old enough to be my father and deserving of respect, but he had sold his business and for it to prosper, the new owners had to wrestle it into the modern world. I invited him to work with me, there were no secrets or hidden agendas. He got the message without really wanting to understand it. What aggravated me was that Joe allowed our actions to be moaned about and criticised by those who longed for things to go back to what they were before I came to upset their equilibrium, indeed he seemed to allow himself to act as a sounding board for those I had made discontented or worried about their job security. Maurice had suffered most by Joe's unintentional interference before me. Never a good idea, my friends, far better to face the music and bight the bullet, to use two metaphors in one sentence. I was determined to be not so undermined.

We had made the most of our few days at the Malabar then moved into the house at Choc on the day our cases arrived out of customs and were delivered intact. They contained the remains of our possessions brought from Ndola together with our wedding presents stored these past four years by Tory's Mother. The view from the balcony was stunning, looking out onto the hotel sixty feet below, beyond which was the tiny *Rat Island* standing a hundred yards offshore with the open sea behind. To our left we could see the Vigie promontory but the airport below was hidden from view. We had engaged a maid, Amilta Augustine who had seven children by six men, all cared for by an aunt while she was at work. No husband, no problem she explained with conviction. She lived in a small chattel house in Vide Bouteille on high ground above Castries, accessed with difficulty by car up a winding road with potholes in the middle and wrecked cars abandoned at various points on the side, a journey I became quickly familiar with when taking Amilta home after babysitting sessions. She was glad of the cash and happily looked after our friend's children as well when they were dropped off at our house. Sometimes she would sleep overnight in the room we kept for her next to the carport.

There was hardly a house on the island that was not built on a slope. If the house was arrived at from the rear, as ours was, then the stilts supported the rear. In the open space beneath the house was a water storage tank which took its supply from rainwater flowing into it from the corrugated roof. An electric pump was employed to use the tank's fifteen hundred gallons reserve should the mains supply fail. If the electricity supply failed as well, we could draw water through a tap below the house and lug it round in buckets. These arrangements were the law under building regulations to mitigate the after-effects of tropical storms and hurricanes.

The garden surrounded the house on a steep slope and was stocked with poinsettias and frangipani and even had a small plot for pineapples, banana plants and passion fruit. One day Andy discovered a *chongololo* eating the poinsettia. He had spotted the same type of giant caterpillar that we had in our Zambian garden, the Zambian word *chongololo* is a catch-all for millipedes and other long creepy crawlies. Sure enough, the caterpillar had devoured all the leaf growth on two plants, but he was not alone, there were at least a dozen other hungry members of his army, all over four inches long.

Andy had started at a private nursery school at Tapion and had to be taken each day and collected in the afternoon. The drive between our house and the office took seven minutes. I would *"take a drop"* from Tory in the car on her morning run to the nursery. Most days she would drive in to pick me up for a shower before taking lunch at home.

There were three Banks operating in St Lucia, the Bank of Nova Scotia, the Royal Bank of Canada, and Barclays DCO. I chose to open an account with the Royal, I had met Mr Fernandes, the manager, at a bridge evening during our second week in St Lucia. Oddly enough it was Joe Devaux who had asked me if I played the game, before inviting me to partner him at the Bridge Club, a weekly event on Thursdays at Cap Estate Golf Club. Playing duplicate helped the social aspect of the evening as the players circulated around the six tables in the club bar room. I soon found out that these evenings doubled as an opportunity for the great and the good of island society to meet and exchanged chit-chat and at times, valuable intelligence. Joe's regular partner returned the next time I went with him, so I partnered with an engineer, Peter Parminter and accepted his invitation to be a regular player. The club usually ran a minimum of six tables, sometimes more. It was here that I was able to rub shoulders with people who made the clocks tick on the island, being advocates at law, solicitors, the Premier himself and a couple of other senior politicians, the chief medical officer, a judge, the chief of police and several men and women from the business community. These were invaluable contacts for a new boy like me.

I joined the Golf Club at Cap and began to play irregularly. The Cap course was a nine-hole cross country scramble, still in its early years, and it showed. You could lose a ball or more on the fairways where the cracks in the clay topsoil were wide and deep, showing no mercy to stars and hackers alike.

Tory made several friends through Tapion School to add to our social contact with our neighbours, Helen and Theo Gobat, and others of similar age to ourselves who we had got to know through the Hills and an American seaman's family who lived next door. We had no shortage of invitations to dinner, to beach parties on Sundays or to more formal occasions through my job.

We both joined the St Lucia Yacht Club, grandly named, a dinghy sailing club situated right on Rodney Bay beach. The clubhouse had a balcony on its first floor above rows of assorted small vessels kept on trailers. The club held regular barbecue parties. I soon discovered that the great and the good of the island also patronised the Yacht Club, when one

Sunday afternoon I spotted John Compton in shorts wearing an apron and holding barbecue tongs aloft in animated banter with Julien Hunte, his close colleague, and an attentive mixed group joining in. John clearly knew how to put himself about, like any seasoned politician worth his salt.

We had been made very welcome as a family in a strange and foreign land that nonetheless exuded familiarity through its historic links with Britain. Our house was less than two miles from the centre of Castries, the hub of the island's economy and commercial life which supported two thirds of the population. The Morne was a substantial hill which rose steeply to a dominant position overlooking the town and its harbour, indeed to go anywhere south you had to drive up and through the twisted z-bends of Government House Road before descending to the gentler slopes and valley of *Culde-Sac*. There the way split to give you the option of dodging potholes down the west coast to Soufriere and Vieux Fort beyond, or to cross the interior where bananas grew wherever the terrain allowed and the rain forest prospered on steep mountain slopes. If you chose the latter route you would emerge into Dennery on the east coast then head south through Prasliin and Micoud to meet your alter ego in Vieux Fort who would have arrived a few minutes after you unless held up by a chugging banana lorry, the type which took very seriously Marshal Philippe Petain's famous speech in 1916 before the Battle of Verdun, declaring *"ils ne passeront pas".*

The island's districts or parishes are named after earlier plantations, owned as they were once upon a time by pre-revolution French nabobs. The darker side of history began in the seventeenth century with the replacement of the indigenous Caribs by West Africans sold from the Gulf of Benin by dominant chieftains in places such as Bodagry in

Nigeria to merchants from Europe and America. Such cargo of human misery could be offloaded at St Lucia's second natural harbour, the safe hurricane refuge at Marigot Bay, where at the barracoons of the West Atlantic auctions were held. The captive workers were then made ready for onward despatch to other islands, or to destinations within St Lucia itself, or more probably to the plantations of America.

Whilst all that had started under French occupation and settlement, during the eighteenth century the island's ownership was heavily disputed by the British who took power and lost it back to the French some sixteen times, depending upon whose navy had the biggest warships at anchor. British territorial sovereignty was finally put beyond dispute once Napoleon the First was packed off to St Helena and the slaves were freed. The Caribs disappeared after a thousand years on St Lucia, although some remain in Dominica, two islands up the chain of the Windwards between Martinique and Guadeloupe one hundred miles to the north. Before the Caribs were the Arawak, people believed to have arrived from South America whilst the Romans still enslaved Europe and north Africa. We found evidence of both the earlier inhabitants in rock drawings and engravings at Cas-en-Bas, where there are some monolithic outcrops of rock close to the beach on the east (Atlantic) coast. The emancipation of all the peoples of the island resulted in much mixing in the reproduction process, most evident perhaps in the urban parts.

Marigot Bay was a beauty spot which belied its history. Once it had passed legislation to abolish slavery, the British government of the day applied the new laws to the world at large, allocating scores of fast war ships to the squadrons ordered and charged with the huge task of intercepting slave vessels and privateers which had managed to evade the coastal blockades before crossing the Atlantic Ocean from West Africa. Marigot provided a perfect hiding place and a well-stocked base from where the navy could harass the criminal ships on the final leg of their long voyage to the Carolinas, or other destinations on the American continent. The bay's beauty was recognised much more recently by Richard Fleischer, the director of *Doctor Doolittle*, the film, a box office hit which starred Rex Harrison, Samantha Eggar, Richard Attenborough, and Anthony Newley in 1967. That latter event became an important call-bird for the fledgling tourist industry now being heavily promoted by Mr Compton's island government.

For the most part the pretty chattel houses of St Lucia are colourfully painted and often stand on stilts perched precariously upon hillsides, half hidden by vegetation which might have been planted to plan or just overgrown by nature. Such houses, big and small, are scattered all over the Morne, at the summit of which is a fort built with outbuildings constructed from Plymouth bricks by the early British occupying forces, brought out as ballast in empty sailing ships whose cargo holds would be filled with the fruits of the sugar cane fields and spice plantations on their return journey. The economic style of building the brick casemates next to the older French stone fort is reminiscent of Wellingtonian structures found throughout Britain, for example at Weedon on the Grand Union, and British possessions across the globe such as the British barracks within the Red Fort next to the Yamuna river in Delhi. A stark reminder of the hazards of tropical life in the seventeen hundreds is provided by the graves of three young French naval ensigns, no older than twenty-one years of age, all named as successive Governors of *Ste Lucie* (I guess because they were each in turn the ranking officer at the time) and each death inscribed on gravestones dated the same year. Three young lives lost to yellow fever within months of each other.

Now if on your journey by road south to Vieux Fort you had taken the westerly route at the bottom of the Morne, you would have passed Marigot within twenty-five minutes of leaving Castries, having passed the nearby *Bounty* rum distillery at Roseau. You would then have taken a helter-skelter route which followed the uneven coastline through thick impenetrable scrub for the most part. You might see the odd fruit and spice orchard beside isolated settlements, before finally dropping down to sea level at Soufriere where we had a M&C store at the end of the main street. On the town beach, where many festivals in the African and Catholic traditions are celebrated with much enthusiasm, you will see fishing boats. Behind the town are the towering two Pitons we first sighted from the Dakota on our arrival. The profile of those two mountains is replicated in the design of the Island's flag, yellow and blue with black and white, telling the story of the sun and sea, and the people.

On the left side of the road leading away from the town is the entrance to *La Soufriere*, the bubbling hot sulphur springs within the crater form the world's only drive-in volcano, so it is proudly proclaimed. Below the volcano on the water course of the hot springs the early French military built a bath house. Those brave enough to partake of the baths, I discovered, were not allowed to be submerged for more than fifteen minutes before towelling down, for fear of prompting a heart attack. The after-effects of submersion provide a blissful feeling. Despite the ambient ninety degrees Fahrenheit temperature outside you are left with an enervative sensation, cool by comparison with the assault on your body heat by the hot sulphur-spring waters of the baths. Clever, those ancient Frenchmen, it is worth every penny they charge on entrance.

Once past the Pitons and the drive-in sinus service centre provided by the sulphurous waters, the land begins to flatten out as you pass small fishing villages and arable crop farming before reaching your destination close to the International Airport. The drive will have taken about ninety minutes given fair weather and no Marshall Petain trucks. In Vieux Fort itself we had another M&C store designed in the Hollywood tradition of the wild west, complete with hitching rails.

Modernising the stores at Soufriere and Vieux Fort was the least of my priorities, I would see what stock taking would tell me. Old fashioned they might have been, but they seemed to suit their purpose of supplying the local communities. I realised, as I completed the first three months of my new job, that most of the component parts of the M&C business were functional and suited to the market of the time and that the Devaux family had made their place in St Lucia and the wider Caribbean in the same way as their competitors or peers. They had no shareholder or bank pressures to contend with, and if they were vastly overstocked, as they most certainly were, that was no bad thing, just fat for the figurative forthcoming winter. In other words, life passed by pleasantly enough, they took a semi-patriarchal stance towards their employees and everything was fine. But it wasn't, not really, not now, because a) the business was being robbed blind by their employees and b) they had sold their way of life and assets to a London multinational who did have shareholders to answer to and who did want to see a return on investment.

The most obvious component part of the business which was dysfunctional was the department store. Its size was far too large for its market, and it could not decide what its market was, so it tried to satisfy everyone and every taste and had fallen flat on its face doing so. The next Board Meeting loomed as did a visit by the regional director who would want a progress report from me, for sure.

My second big problem concerning my life in St Lucia was personal. Before my arrival the Government had hiked up income tax by introducing super tax bands. I had no warning of the change. My employment contract included the usual expatriate family benefits of paid airfares to the UK once a year and at end of contract, furnished company accommodation, a non-contributory pension scheme, emergency medical insurance and education costs for boarding schools in the UK from when a child reached seven. We had come to the West Indies with every intention of staying many years, but with the unexpected tax drag on my pay cheque I soon found that to live even modestly required me to import funds from England, hardly the purpose of working abroad, or indeed even at home.

A copy of my first month's payslip had been sent to Mr Moerry in London with my first report and a request that something be done to pay me offshore. Donald had echoed this request, but as nothing further had been heard, I was none too happy. To make sure my feelings were understood, I sent a further letter to my masters in London's John Adam Street by registered mail. Someone would have to sign for the delivery. I received an acknowledgement but no resolution just before my Mother arrived to spend six weeks with us over Christmas

Brother John had moved his family to the USA not long after we had left the UK for the West Indies and was now living in Ellicott City near Baltimore, leaving Mother without any of her four boys in Britain. She had arrived in good spirits, but it was not long before we knew she was masking grief. It would be my eighth Christmas in the tropics and once again we were entertaining not only family but also two of my closest chums. Brendan arrived on Christmas Eve from Georgetown where he had recently taken on a "consultancy" job for Bookers who had offered him good money in return for being dragged out of the Rose and Crown. His task was to sort out insoluble problems under the management contract the firm still had with the Guyanese government.

Helping us to feast on one of Peter Robinson's imported turkeys were Maurice and his latest flame Arlette, an engagingly intelligent lady from the local radio station. Her sister had been our babysitter at the Malabar. Christmas lunch was served by Tory in traditional British style to our large glass top table on the balcony of our house above the *Halcyon Beach Club*, now *Sandals*. We were serenaded with carols played on well-honed oil drums by the hotel's cabaret *"steelers"*. Steeling is at the very heart of West Indian music, just like the calypso and reggae, so how lucky we were to enjoy the live sounds. Before sundown we slipped away to *East Winds*, a beach side bar and eatery three miles away at the end of a dirt track to the left from the half-way bus stop on the road to Cap. There, another band was playing, dressed up as Santa's tropical helpers. A Christmas plunge in the crystal sea beckoned, so in we all went, Grandma in the vanguard.

I had bought a second or third hand speed boat with a fibreglass hull from Patrick Montplaisir, husband of Merle who was one of my newly appointed buyers. The boat was about twenty-four feet long with a forty-horsepower outboard motor. I had put it in the water at *Ganters*, a small commercial mooring tucked in at the end of the Vigie runway, looking out towards Tapion Point on the other side of the Castries harbour entrance from the sea. We soon discovered that weed grows on the bottom of boats in the warm sea water quite regardless of however much anti-fouling paint you apply, as much as a foot in length every month. The small vessel had to be beached to allow for scrubbing else the weed would act as a drag. So it was on the Sunday after Christmas Day that I was able to chug down to Marigot in the boat with the family and Grandma as crew, beach it there, clean up and then go water skiing with Tory at the helm and feeling a lot safer than on the Zambesi, my last skiing adventure.

At work I had at last found a former policeman and detective to head up the expanded security department Alan had been busy re-organising. Patrick Didier put his team in new uniforms, which provided a visible presence on the shop floors. Not long after his appointment, one of Didier's men had apprehended a uniformed policewoman who had been caught shoplifting. To my surprise our new security chief was not in the least surprised. The woman was held securely in one of the cold rooms off the supermarket. I was called in to decide what we should do. Everyone knew the policy, namely we pass the felon over to the police and they decide whether to prosecute. But this case was potential dynamite. George Odlum, the opposition leader, was giving John Compton a lot of grief in the Assembly on the matter of law and order. The Premier on his part was disturbed by the links Odlum appeared to have with emissaries from Castro's Cuba. If the Press got hold of this case the Government would be severely embarrassed. I resolved there and then to call the Premier, refusing to leave a message, thankful that in this small land my name was already known to those in the inner circle enabling me to interrupt the top man. "Give me ten minutes and I will have an unmarked van at the back of your store" were the words down the 'phone in response to my brief report. He went on to say: "please have the officer outside ready to be collected, can you hide the uniform? And (short pause), thank you". Not long after I had put the telephone down a non-descript young woman wearing an oversized white overall left the store on the arm of one of Didier's men in similar dress and was unceremoniously bundled in to the back of a black van along with a shopping bag in which her peaked cap was concealed. The lady later lost her job, I was informed, and that was that, nothing in the local *Voice* newspaper nor in any other organ of local media. No more was ever said.

Another Directors' Meeting followed in the afternoon. Much of what had happened in my world was already evident in that I had converted half the furniture department's floor space into a buying office with glass room dividers all around to allow contact of sight between the new office and the store. I had moved my office away from where I had been to be adjacent to the upper sales areas and with my office staff all in sight of me. I had left Winifred behind in the corner room I had vacated to become Personnel Manager, a job she was eminently capable of holding down and implementing all the changes. She seemed thrilled at the promotion which had come before she sent me an invitation to her wedding at the end of January, insisting that my Mother should come along with us.

Out came a copy of my latest report to London telling about the changes to cash register locations. The new cashing up procedures were bearing fruit in the main store, both in simplicity and security of cash handling. Thirty something staff had been dismissed, ten with prosecutions, all linked to cash or theft. Buyers had been appointed, splitting the business into four areas of financial control, namely food, furniture with furnishings and music, all apparel and finally hardware and gifts. Two ladies from Bookers buying office in London had been and gone. Marion Sipser and Wendy Green, two experienced merchandisers had been seconded to me to help analyse stock before stocktaking in late November. They had stayed for three weeks in the Malabar. There was much more to report in detail, I won't bore you with it all, suffice to say we had by now sorted out all staff changes, some retirements, and had a well understood chain of command, well at least for the most part.

As the long meeting ended, I collared Donald to broach the subject of my returning to London. We needed new suppliers and a visit the Spring Fair at the NEC in Birmingham might move things along faster. I was planning a new tourist gift shop within the hardware and drug store building which would carry souvenirs and an expanded merchandise range that we could also sell in the hotel boutiques. Just as importantly, I wanted to pursue my personal pay problem rather than wait for Tom Moerry's next trip. Donald seemed happy to agree and dates were set, I would be away only seven days.

Winifred got married in the Catholic Cathedral by Columbus Square and became Mistress Blanchard.

We joined the wedding party at a private house off La Pensee Road not far out of town. The place was a traditional timber frame construction, the wooden walls, which were whitewashed inside, reflected the fairy lights which the owner, a middle-aged aunt and surviving sister of Winnie's late mother, had lovingly installed for the big day in her niece's young life. Grandma settled down happily with a group of ladies of similar age, which included Mistress Montoute from the store, all being entertained by Joseph Antoine who no doubt regaled the ladies with one of his lessons on the history of rum. Judging by the rolling eyes of Mistress Antoine, I believed the story had been told before. It was a joy to see her laughing with all those happy West Indians, infected by Winifred's smiles as she did the rounds in her bridal glory. Only a day before, Mum had at last taken the cork out of her grief bottle and cried her eyes out, in a way I had never seen her do before; she was due to fly home in the morning.

It must have been a Sunday. Tory and I had been joined by our children to wave goodbye to their lovely Grandma at Vigie where she took the short flight on a LEAT Fokker Friendship to Bridgetown to join the BA flight to Heathrow. The local airline was not renowned for its reliability but today it left on the dot. I had booked to leave the following Tuesday and hoped to break away from business to spend a night at Mother's flat in Bray. From the airport we called home to pick up our barbecue gear and picnic food, which we bundled into the boot space occupied by Grandma's suitcases a short while before, making our way to *Smugglers' Cove* at Cap. The cove lay around the left headland from the *Steigenberger Cariblue*, a luxury German owned hotel by Cap Estate, a long-term residential development then owned, I believed, by a Venezuelan property firm.

Most of the small number of houses that had already been built in the development were on the western Caribbean side, where the plots were on gentle sloping land. The area included the golf course I have spoken of, itself located closer to the Caribbean than the Atlantic coast on the east, between which lay the estate's fifteen hundred acres of undulating scrub. At the north of the island, Cap enjoyed a low rainfall, in stark contrast to the mountainous island interior to the centre and south where heavy precipitation nurtured the rainforests and agriculture. From a high point at Cap we enjoyed sights of the breath-taking western shoreline of St Lucia all the way to the Pitons and on most days, in clear weather, one could see Martinique, the French island to the immediate north and HMS Diamond Rock just off its coast.

The light stone of the rocky little island shone out like a jewel in the sun, hence its name, the honour to be called HMS stems from the sea wars between Britain and France, when the steep sided small island was captured and occupied by forces under Admiral Hood. A naval officer from Hood's flagship The Centaur called James Maurice was transferred to "captain" the rock, which by then had been given the status of a naval warship by Hood and named HMS Diamond. A year later in 1805 the French recaptured the rocky fortress, looting its supplies and medical facilities. The crew of the French man-of-war then promptly abandoned the rock to run back to France after news reached them that Admiral Lord Nelson was on their tail. I guessed that was in the early part of that historical year since the great Horatio was otherwise occupied in October at Trafalgar.

The path and rough drive on the left of the tarred road to Cariblue was overgrown and hard to spot, but we had been there before and parked the car in front of the thick woodland which covered the steep cliffs down which a pathway had been made to access the Smugglers' beach. That day we met a group of friends, including the parents of Katie Durkin, who was a classmate of Andy and clearly his new-found best friend.

Sundays were my time out of the madhouse, my newfound pleasure to commune with the fish, swimming with snorkel and flippers and at peace in a silent sea world. Before eating I took a long swim out to the reefs and coral outcrops along the right-side promontory, spotting small fish which darted in and out of the branches of coral, just like butterflies on shrubs. A few large *jack fish* ventured closer to me meaning no menace, the sea urchins were the things to avoid. Apart from the black spiky urchins like those which had given me grief in Mombasa, I was able to dive down to collect different sizes of several round and flat skeletal remains of another type of urchin known as a *sand dollar*. I added a few that day to my collection.

It must have been half-way through the afternoon, after a filling barbecue, when I was standing up to my waist in the sea, looking back towards the crowd on the beach, not more than ten yards out, when the waters suddenly receded to ankle level; I had no time to react to the shouts from the shore when a wave crashed over me from behind, casting me like a piece of driftwood onto the beach, head first and down. I scrambled up in acute pain in the sure knowledge I had dislocated a collarbone.

Someone gave me a lift to the Victoria Hospital eight miles away on the far side of Castries where Owen King was on duty. I knew Doctor King through playing cards, he was in general practice but did duty at the main hospital, lucky for me as that day he was there to wrench my shoulder back into shape and detail a nurse to wrap me up in a figure of eight bandage. He prescribed some hefty painkillers, then sent me home to Tory who had somehow managed to decamp from the cove with all our gear. Owen cleared me for the flight to London.

It was on that flight, two hours or so out from Hewanorra that I got up from my aisle seat, always my preferred option on an aeroplane, to walk the short distance for a comfort break at the back, but fainted into the open arms of a passing BA hostess. The next thing I knew, I was sniffing smelling salts and gazing into a pair of blue eyes set in the anxious, if not angelic face looming above me. I felt sheepish, muzzy, and cold, and even more in need of that comfort break. This time the perambulation down the 'plane's walkway had a successful conclusion, still under the watchful eye of the crew, my caring hostess being joined by the head steward. They needed an explanation, as all incidents in flight get reported for whatever reason, probably for the purpose of insurance liability, so I explained the details of yesterday's accident on the shore and my subsequent treatment by Doctor King. We agreed the painkillers, combined with changed air pressure were the likely causes of low blood pressure shown on their portable machine rigged up to my arm. I felt fine and slept fitfully for the most part of the journey, knowing that Tory had probably been right in asking me not to be pig-headed and to postpone the trip.

The trip to England had gone largely to plan, although my ideas on tourist merchandise had been greeted with scant enthusiasm. I had made no progress on the salary front, Mr Moerry was away in Trinidad and Mike Hearder was not prepared to handle the matter behind his back. I had enjoyed a splendid meal with Bernard Windsor, a graduate of Bookers cadet scheme in Guyana or Trinidad some years before, now working with David Taylor in Personnel, his main job seemed to be entertaining visitors from abroad, a task to which he was undoubtedly well suited. You just had to like Bernard, a real Mr Nice-Guy. Bernard took me to *Inigo Jones*, a fine dining venue in Covent Garden where I ate his suggestion of hare fillet cooked rare. I have never had it since, never even seen it on a menu, but do not ever turn it down if you get the chance. Bernard's other favourite watering hole was *Pomegranates* in a Thames-front basement behind Dolphin Square in Pimlico where he lived, a restaurant I often frequented in later London life.

Back in St Lucia a week or so later I found an envelope under my car's wiper blade. I then remembered we had six guests coming for dinner so put the envelope on the dashboard and drove home to help prepare for our visitors by mixing two jugs of rum punch to the Bajan recipe of "one of sour, two of sweet, three of strong and four of weak", the sour being freshly squeezed limes, the sweet is home-made sugar syrup, the strong is white island rum or cane spirit, at least 50% proof and the weak a selection of whatever fruit juices you have in the 'fridge. I added my signature two shakes of Angostura bitters, a splash of grenadine syrup and a pinch of ground nutmeg. Hey presto, ready to roll. Taking a sample slurp of punch, I set up the record player with a new LP by Linda Ronstadt, which our Record Department manager Julian Joseph had urged me to buy.

Regardless that It was now February, Tory had prepared the traditional St Lucian Christmas dish of a tarred ham, which Amilta had helped her get ready all week. The salted hams, which arrived from Ireland into Peter's cold store, were completely coated in solid tar made from wood pitch. The tar had to be peeled away, and the ham inside immersed in fresh cold water for at least five days, changing the water twice daily to leach out the salt. The combination of the brine treatment and subsequent tarring preserved the hams for indefinite periods, a technique which fed folk on the high seas or in those wagon trains across the prairies in centuries past. The ham was delicious, served with the remains of our one and only pineapple from the garden.

Waving goodbye to our guests I remembered the envelope left in the car but did not open it until the morning. It read something like this: *"Mister Derrick, you have two white haired children and you have stopped my job I will have no mercy"*. My mind was cast back four years to Kitwe.

If you do not have the answer to a problem, the best thing to do is to share it with someone, which I did when I got the office and called for Didier, showed him the note and said we should see Donald. My security chief wanted to handle the matter himself, but I had to inform Donald so that if anything happened the Company had prior notice. Donald agreed that Didier should go ahead quietly to sort it out, not before recounting one of his many tales about Malawi, an encouraging story about a security guard being decapitated with a machete, as I recall.

Tory had given me a drop that morning. On our way past the cruise terminal I had noticed that, quite unusually, there were no ships or other working vessels tied up on the quays at the end of Bridge Street. After leaving Donald I got on with a load of paperwork in the office between seeing various buyers wanting this and that signed off. A telephone rang on my desk, as it did from time to time. Angel Roberts, my new secretary put a sheet of paper in front of me with the letters BGR scribbled in bold text, raising her eyebrows as I simultaneously picked up the receiver. "Swain is that you?" came the clipped tones of the new British Government Representative whose acronym I had the good sense to recognise from Angel's note. Now up until that day I had never met the man, which was a bit odd as there were still very few Brits in residence on the island permanently, no more than fifty I believed, which I put down to me being in trade, still considered by some in the Foreign Office to be a bit beyond the Pale, however it seemed he needed my compliance as he went on: "Two Navy men tonight, hope you can do dinner and look after them, HMS Jupiter in port, pick 'em up at seven tonight". More a command than a request, just like the public school prefect I suspected he had been, vague and painful memories flitting back in my mind. Well, what could I say? Certainly not "Sorry, old man, busy playing bridge" which is what I had originally planned for that evening.

To those of my countrymen who had served longer in St Lucia, the BGR's curt order would come as no surprise. The South Atlantic or 7th Frigate Squadron of the Royal Navy paid regular visits to the Commonwealth island nations of the Caribbean, calling into St Lucia at least once a year as the flotilla ploughed the oceans down to Tierra del Fuego and the Falkland Islands, criss-crossing from Africa to South America patrolling the high seas in warships fitted with sophisticated radar, armed with some heavy duty missiles with nuclear warheads (so I was told). It was the custom to entertain the officers whereas the warrant officers and ratings who had no watch took shore leave on their own if they were lucky. The duty of providing entertainment for the officers was delegated to us British residents. To be fair, the BGR did call back with the names of the two Lieutenants allocated to my household, at the same time inviting us to The Residence tomorrow for a luncheon reception for the Governor and others of importance in the St Lucian establishment, to meet the naval commander and his staff.

What the BGR did not tell me was that Her Majesty's Royal Navy's officers have an enviable capacity to compete in the booze stakes with any tropical expatriate I have ever come across. A quick call to the house alerted Tory to the impending invasion of our dinner table. The result was a veritable feast prepared entirely from local ingredients, so confident had my wife become in keeping pace with her friends and their culinary hints.

I had time before collecting our guests to add another couple of jugs of punch to the one left over from the previous night and believed my armoury to be well stocked, but at midnight I found myself mixing pina coladas. On the altar of hospitality, I had to sacrifice the one remaining bottle of Guyanese vintage rum left behind by Brendan at Christmas.

The clock chimed two in the morning when the chaps had finally cleaned us out of rum. I got the night porter at the *Halcyon Beach Club* below to send up a taxi to carry the men back to port, taking me with them for a "night-cap" on board. At the port I was whisked past the gate sentries inside the perimeter fence and piped aboard with my hosts up the gangway and onto the ship. Earlier I had been given a tour of the *Jupiter* when I first met the men before driving them home to Choc, so this time we went directly to the wardroom where a smartly dressed steward attended the bar. I asked him to mix me a glass of water. A cup of black coffee followed, then another one. The music system suddenly came to life with a loud rendition of the fourth movement from Holst's *The Planets*, I should have known it was Jupiter, the Bringer of Jollity. My dinner companions were now acting out as would-be conductors, waving imaginary batons in a convincing parody of *Flash Harry*. More water and good conversation saw us through to the unseen dawn when I was delivered of a fine English breakfast, after which I bade my new friends goodbye to walk the short distance up Bridge Street and start a new day's work.

17

Jubilee

(1977)

I have been and am still fascinated by plants wherever I have travelled, particularly those bearing fruit or spices. The tree on the lawn at The Residency of the BGR was a cashew, a noticeably big cashew over forty feet high and in full fruit. The plant's fruit resembled small red apples when fully ripe with funny green pods protruding from the base. The cashew nut is hidden inside the pod, one nut for every fruit, yet one rarely hears about anyone eating the fruit, which I am told should best be taken when dried, they are otherwise a tad acidic. There were hundreds of red cashew apples all over this tree whose spreading foliage reached almost to the ground. All this I learned from a diminutive lady in a floral dress who was, she told me, on the personal staff of the island's Governor, His Excellency Sir Allen Montgomery Lewis GCMG GCVO KStJ, who was at that moment talking to Tory and Donald closer to the BGR's house at the top of the sloping lawn. I wished to learn more from this bespectacled lady, but we were called to listen to speeches

By the time the formalities were over, we had moved closer to the other guests and were stood by the drinks table alongside my two rum quaffers from last night, now resplendent in white tropical uniforms. Those two fine specimens of British fighting men were with three other officers from the *Jupiter*, receiving the admiration of three St Lucian ladies, the wives of local dignitaries. Their husbands, on the other hand, appeared to be in earnest conversation with each other nearby, clothed in shirts of bright colours and armed with drinks from the bar. We took our leave after Sir Allen had departed in his chauffeur driven limo.

Although being invited to the reception was an honour and a special experience, business was inescapable for me. Just before going back to the office I had spoken briefly to the BGR who had been in conversation with two senior Naval Officers and who said he would call at my office sometime but, sadly, he never did. When I did get there, I discovered that Didier had solved the mystery of the threatening note. It had been posted to my car by a casual worker employed by the food warehouse manager. The warehouse itself had been leaking stock like a sieve, indeed Alan and I had our sights on it, suspecting a crooked conspiracy. The young man had been sacked for stealing, caught in the act in the supermarket loading bay. It turned out he was a brother of our lady police shoplifter, suggesting kleptomania might run in the family. I had no further cause to worry, or so I was assured with a knowing smile by Henry, Didier's oversized assistant. Funny that, all twenty men and one woman in the security department used only their first names to identify themselves, maybe it was a legacy from their police service?

Those days living overseas the mail was a lifeline for us. Telephone calls abroad were expensive and used only when necessary. Brother John sent me a card from Maryland to say his new job in the States was better than he had expected and had decided to buy a house outside Ellicott City between Baltimore and Washington DC. He wanted to know when we would be visiting, forgetting I had already invited his family to the West Indies. At the same time Tory had a long letter from her friend Jenny Blackburne who had stayed on in Zambia. It was good to hear news of our friends, although the main purpose of the letter was to let us know that Mike Owen, Jenny's younger brother, his wife Cilla and baby Tanya were moving to St Lucia. Mike was a doctor and would be taking up the post of Deputy to the Chief Medical Officer of St Lucia, a man from Yugoslavia and well-known extrovert called Sasha Popovic. I knew Sasha well from bridge and golf. Jenny's letter had taken a couple of weeks to reach us, its arrival only a day ahead of a 'phone call from Mike who was already on the island and had taken up residence in a house on the harbour side of Vigie. We quickly became friends. The couple arrived just in time to enjoy the Carnival, the Mardi Gras, which was the biggest event in the island's calendar.

For our part we joined the throngs of revellers following the floats, all dancing to the music of loud bands, some just steelers and others whose volume was fortified through ghetto blasters powered by car batteries. The costumes were imaginative and richly endowed in colourful abundance, every village and organisation represented in their intricately designed stage settings atop trailers pulled by tractors or just transported on flat top lorries. The whole island people seemed to be involved, the heaving crowds determined to make the best of the day before the denials of Lent. Since anything goes in the carnival they call *"mas"*, revellers formed themselves into spontaneous conga dance lines causing mayhem when they broke up. For the many no alcohol was needed to be intoxicated by the exciting atmosphere all around. People kissed and embraced each other, be they friends or strangers, all were welcome on this special day. It was hot enough by courtesy of Mother Nature, but it got more red-blooded and virile as the girls showed off their assets in their gorgeous but scanty costumes. The procession snaked slowly through the streets of Castries for two hours before breaking up into serious party mood wherever there was space in the crowded town. None of our group felt threatened in any way, why should anyone care when we all wanted was to make *"mas"*.

Director Tom Moerry arrived from Trinidad after spending two weeks in Port of Spain. I had heard from my pal Brendan that he had called in to check up on his activities in Georgetown, but whatever transpired was lost to me when the telephone connection with Guyana broke, as it often did. I spent the rest of that Friday morning with Roger Sutherland at Bryden's, our agency division, Roger and Fred had signed up a distributorship with Gallo Wines of California and wanted me to promote *"Night Train Express"*, a wine-based booze line which had been launched in the States with spectacular success in the Afro-American markets. That was the fun side of retailing, *stack 'em high and sell 'em long*, tried and tested by Jack Cohen, the Tesco founder. The less funny side was to come in the afternoon, our monthly Board Meeting, after which I gave our visitor from London the full tour which included meeting my management team before I hit him with my personal concerns. Frankly, I expected Thomas to raise the matter before I did - he had plenty of warning - and whilst I fully understood I was a small cog in the corporate machine, locally here in St Lucia I had put in train a programme of reforming the business and wanted to see it through.

"How did it go with Mr. Tom?" asked James as the two of us strolled along the narrow beach at East Winds the next afternoon. We were with our families at a lunch gathering organised in our visitor's honour by Donald. James and I had foregone a game of golf to join the happy throng but had left Tom Moerry in the company of Fred and Joe for a private chat. "Absolutely bloody nowhere", I replied," just the usual verbal diarrhoea......." and at that moment, the diatribe I was about to embark upon was nipped in the bud as I sensed the presence of someone right behind me on the soft sand. Having caught us up, Thomas tapped me gently on the shoulder seemingly to join us on our beach walk. He gave no indication he had heard my last remark, but I suspected he had. Well, what the heck, nothing to lose I mused, before I went for a cooling swim to renew my friendship with the fish.

Nothing was resolved, I was given a small raise in our local currency, the East Caribbean Dollar, almost all of which was eaten up by John Compton's tax man. I did get a timely call from Thomas once he returned to London to confirm that he wanted me to meet Brendan in Port of Spain and carry out a review of the *Stephens* department store recently added to the Bookers business portfolio. I had a bundle of work on my plate in St Lucia, but here was an opportunity to get off the island for a few days, meet my old chum from Africa, and perhaps do something useful for the Group with a chance to meet some new colleagues, particularly the local boss Danny de Verteuil. Danny had come to our Group from *Ross Drugs*, a chain of pharmacy stores based in Trinidad's second city San Fernando, which Bookers had also acquired as they sought to expand in the region. I had to leave almost immediately on the new mission, leaving poor Alan to take charge of the extraordinary stocktaking organised for the month end.

The journey to Port of Spain entailed a transit in Bridgetown with a four hour wait between flights, time to let my mind wander. Why, I asked myself, was a diverse business like Bookers, with interests in shipping, packaging, sugar, rum, tea, irrigation and farming technology, two department stores in England, food cash and carry, health food retailing, grocery stores and publishing, why had they invested in retail service industries with additional management contracts in far flung places in the Caribbean, Africa, Canada and Malaysia? The answer was, I concluded, that the London buying office set up by them to serve their overseas businesses had become the prime focus for earnings.

If my purpose was to work up profitable business for the London buying office whenever supply sources in Europe could be preferred, then what we had achieved in setting up well-disciplined buying controls would certainly help our parent company, but only in small part. St Lucia on its own was a small market. It was easy to conclude that the tail was wagging a chihuahua not a bull mastiff. Until the likes of Bookers Guyana and CBC in Zambia had been nationalised, the income which those big operations provided was more than enough to support the buying office in London, but as the years went by and those businesses were taken away from Bookers, through legalised robbery some would say although others call it nationalisation, business volume had to be developed from other sources. It would be interesting to see what Trinidad had to offer.

Perhaps I could share some of these thoughts with my old mate when I got to Trinidad, because if my career was to flourish with Bookers I needed to be convinced I had a purpose beyond being a sticking plaster covering the wounded limbs of the M&C investment. We could, of course, lick them into shape, but it would almost certainly regress without adequate skilled management in the long term, and as things stood between me and Tom Moerry my future in St Lucia was not likely to be a long one. If management had to be brought in from outside the Eastern Caribbean region, then a far better incentive and reward structure had to be put in place, quite regardless of whether I would last the course. But I had my doubts that the creepy beach boy Tom would twig it.

I met up with Brendan at the Hilton Hotel next to the Queen's Park Savannah. Queen's Park is like nowhere else, it is extraordinary, a huge park containing a Test Cricket ground on its south side and surrounded by glorious trees with colourful blooms and deep green foliage. Behind and half hidden by the trees were many large one-time residential properties, indeed they were architectural follies. Built over the last century, the prestige from winning the annual prize for architecture spurred on the designers to out-style previous winning entries each year in their grandeur and originality. The latest recipient of the architectural *victor ludorum* was a Trinidadian of Chinese descent, chosen by the judges for constructing an amazing cantilevered house which protruded two thirds of its footprint from a cliff top directly overlooking the Savannah. The Hilton itself was built on an adjacent cliff top and was known as the *"the upside-down Hilton"* because the guest rooms were all on floors below the reception level.

Cecil Gomes, a small but lively man whose lineage would keep a DNA machine unusually busy, met me at the airport and was the one to tell me about the architects. Cecil was General Manager at *Stephens*, a purpose-built department store in the image of, say, the *Bonne Marche* in Paris. It was a busy week in which we immersed ourselves in the rhythm of Trinidad's most exciting city. As we took a thorough audit of the business, we made time to enjoy the scrumptious Caribbean food on offer and meet some wonderful people in the process. Our new-found colleagues Danny and Cecil were open and helpful, making it easier for us to compile a report which was uncritical of the management but suggested some radical changes to the internal systems and merchandise offers at the *Stephens* store. The *Ross Drug* operation was, in our view, a brand that could be exported around the region with success. We did propose some staff changes involving early retirement for a half dozen long-serving heads of departments.

In our time together Brendan recounted his recent experiences in Guyana. By boating up the Demerara River and covering distances atop a motor bike through the sugar plantations and the jungle beyond, which stretched all the way to the border with Brazil, he had tried hard to better his wild bush experiences in Zambia. Rather like the people of Trinidad, the folk in Guyana had evolved from their roots in Africa and India, Britain, France, Portugal, and China. What had struck him particularly was the high standards of education and literacy amongst both the men and women; the romantic appeal of the latter, so he claimed, was world class. He confided that he would be sorry to leave when his contract period of three months finished in April, he would miss the interesting friendships he had forged in Georgetown. We had some free time to ourselves at the Hilton and found ourselves grateful for the room minibars. Whilst we emptied them in both rooms the two of us continued with some competitive card games, as if it were our duty to maintain the tradition established on the Copperbelt in memory of Westy, Peter, Steve Smith, and others. This time our school consisted of just two players causing the imperative to invent a new version of brag.

We settled on a variant of the four-card game, playing high and low or both as declaring options from any combination of three cards out of the four. The game was never patented but was added to our list of achievements in the oil rich Caribbean island just off the Venezuelan coastline

Back in Castries the stock taking results showed some general improvement, but we still had major leakages, particularly in the food warehouse and drugstore. It was obvious we had a serious situation with dishonest staff or management, most likely involving outside collusion, so an action plan was hatched with Alan and Didier, the latter now convinced that Edwards[31], the pharmacist was up to no good.

Before the day was out, I had a visit from Peter Robinson who voiced serious concern for his latest consignment of frozen New Zealand lamb which had been transhipped by container in the port of New York. The *reefer* container had arrived with the original seal intact. The contents were fine despite the transit time of ten weeks. What caused alarm was the paperwork, which bore a US Customs veterinary declaration that it had been condemned as being unfit for human consumption. Peter reckoned that the meat had not been inspected by a vet or by any other authority in New York as the original seal on the container had not been tampered with. Here was the probable scam: the all-powerful Longshoreman's Union in the pay of the Mob (or vice versa) could have leant on the forwarding agent in New York (through whom our payment was routed), pending its onward shipment through the feeder service to the Windward Islands. Having accepted the condemnation report and certificate, a full insurance claim would have been made by the agent. The proceeds of that

---

31. Edwards is a pseudonym for the drug store pharmacist

claim would be added to our payment for the goods and the resultant booty would then be split by some crooked formula to pay off the Union, the Customs agent, the forwarding agent and no doubt their buddy, the veterinarian. Corruption in the Big Apple's docklands was almost par for the course in the '70s.

Why should we bother, you might ask, we had the goods we paid for, in perfect condition which we could sell into the market, to the public, to the hotels and the restaurants, all starved of lovely lamb? There might be a new President in the White House in 1977, but he was unlikely to have much impact on organised crime and its links with the Unions and supine politicians in pocket to the Longshoremen. Legally we were in receipt of condemned food, although we knew it was completely healthy, and legally it was our duty to point out that the St Lucian Customs had missed a trick, although in their defence the condemnation certificate came to us with the papers, not with the ship. It was the forwarders who had slipped up by sending us copies to prove the felony.

Peter was nervous because his name was on the documentation. I suspected that he had little stomach to report the Mob whose arms stretched all along the Windward and Leeward Islands. I confess I felt the same way. There was only one way to handle the matter, we had to make our own insurance claim and share the problem with the underwriters, which we did. It was then up to the insurance people to take ownership of the meat and to report the matter to the FBI: at least we were no longer to be part players in the drama. Our local port vet passed the goods and sales of mint sauce boomed for a couple of days.

A relieved Peter organised a brilliant Sunday barbecue party at Plantation Beach. I had driven from our home in

Choc to the village of Gros-Islet. The road wound through lush tropical rain forest and coastal growth, past isolated commercial buildings and the island's only comprehensive secondary school, through a rising escarpment, where these days the road to the cricket ground branches off to the right, then down the hill in view of Pigeon Island on the seaward side of the bay named after the Admiral Lord Rodney. Just past the new yacht marina a dirt road to the right took us a tortuous two miles of a sump scratching drive through scrub bush to Cas-en Bas. There the furious Atlantic thrashed through the rocky reefs before its waves swept up the waiting sands to break on the east coast's only moderately safe beach, in total contrast to the benign, sheltered west, tsunamis at Smugglers' Cove notwithstanding, recalling my accident with a collarbone. We found Peter hard at work cooking. He showed me the wonders of an American Weber kettle barbecue and how to use it to slow-cook joints of beef, collecting the juices in in a drip tray you suspend with wires under the joint.

The undertow and lively waves kept us on careful watch over our youngsters who frolicked naked on the otherwise deserted beach, the only stretch of sand to be enjoyed on the whole length of St Lucia's east coast. It was a good party that day, both Alan and Peter brought their families, which pleased me because these two St Lucian nationals with their family origins in Britain had told me that because they feared that contract people like Mike Owen and me could come and go, they generally kept themselves socially apart, less they suffer the loss of friendships when we left. I tried to explain that as St Lucia had the population of one small English city, so the same fears would apply to us if we were in England, given that we no longer stayed in one locality all our lives. It was not long after that we threw a return party one evening at home for some thirty guests, all people we had become friends with since arriving in the West Indies.

Our party had gone on until the small hours, so Amilta, who had done a stint of overtime to help us with the catering, had to be taken home in the morning, which is why I found myself driving through the winding streets on the hilly outskirts of the town. Having dropped my passenger at her house, I was navigating my way past colourful chattel houses and broken vehicles when I had to put the brakes on as the road ahead was blocked by a small flat truck whose driver had started up a conversation with a couple of pedestrians he had spotted. The narrow way left no room to pass. I waited patiently for two minutes expecting the animated discussion ahead of me to finish, but it did not. I made the mistake of announcing my presence to the driver ahead with a gentle beep on the horn, only to receive glares from all three chatterboxes, one of whom shouted "Hey, man, don't you know, you are on a small island now!" They meant no hostility, just to tell me that here, time had little meaning. To pass the time pleasurably was far more important than meeting deadlines or subordinating oneself to a timetable, which was what I was doing right there and then in my need to arrive "on time" at the office. They had a point, not that their declared philosophy could work alongside a modern economy, but "look man...", they might have said "....making a float for the carnival, now that was truly important work, and if you needed a few dollars to buy food, or even a few beers, hey man, you could get a job on the docks for half a day and night, and hey presto, let's go to the snacket". Eventually the men did make way for me, doffing their hats in a sweeping gesture as I passed by.

Maurice had kept his rented house a couple of miles up the road to Cap on top of a dangerously steep slope, his disaster-prone life chalked up two more events that week, the first being a puncture to his recently acquired water bed. He would not say if he was on the bed the moment it burst, he was certainly not alone in the house to witness the waters cascading down the steep metalled driveway. The other calamity was also water related.

We had enjoyed an impromptu picnic at Cas-en Bas at that part of the beach where we could leave the cars without having to walk far. It must have been a full moon although in bright daylight the cheesy disc was not visible, but the higher tide was. We realised all too late that the rising sea water had been flowing behind us through a sandy gut. Large pools quickly formed in the undulating coastal sandy soil, almost entirely hidden by a thick undergrowth of succulent greenery. It seemed the sensible thing to beat a retreat from the beach. What happened next had to be seen to be believed.

I drove our green wagon out first, with the family aboard, taking a guess that the course I took was firm below the cover of water and greenery. Once we were on dry ground, I looked back to check that Maurice and Arlette were following me. I gasped. The mini had missed the pathway that we had driven along and was already afloat in deep water up to the top of the wheels but sinking fast. Through the mini's windscreen I saw two shocked faces reminiscent of a comic strip scene, a hand poking through the open sunroof. The car sunk before our eyes, up to and over the top, but two bodies emerged through the open roof, Arlette first, making it to safety but not before a second emersion as the two slid off the roof of the car into the murky warm water surrounding the vehicle with our live audience applauding the amazing feat of escapology that had been so cleverly staged for us. The kids made room for the soaking new passengers for the bumpy drive home.

Amazingly, Maurice's car was rescued the next day and dried out by the village garage at Gros Islet. The engine was restored to full working order despite its twelve long hours in salt water, which says a lot for the skill and ingenuity of the St Lucian mechanics. Maurice sold the car two days later, *caveat emptor* my only comment.

Maurice left for St Kitts before the much-awaited opening of our tourist shop *"Calypso Corner"* on the intersection of Micoud and Bridge Streets. Our music department manager Joseph had arranged for a local singing star and the eight-piece band he managed, called *Magic Circle Express*, to take *"Calypso Corner"* as the title of their latest album. We arranged for a photo-shoot outside the store early one Sunday morning, the idea being to feature the Band posed with their instruments at the front entrance of the new shop. I was given the photography proofs to select and approve a couple of days later so that the sleeve for the long play record could be printed. The shots were excellent except for one thing, the door of the store was in locked up mode showing roller shutters, not the bright and cheerful interior as I had intended. Joseph explained that the security man with the second door key had overslept and the band could not wait because they were taking a 'plane to St Vincent. Joseph had given the go-ahead to the photographer. Well, what the heck, thought I, we can't afford a re-take, so let's get the group to call one of their tracks "roller" or "shutter" or "closed" or whatever, and on that basis I passed a proof for production. They never changed the song titles.

Joseph and his boys were not the only ones flying to Saint Vincent, the island immediately south of St Lucia. The Golf Club at Cap had received a challenge from the only golf club in St Vincent for an inter-island trophy put up by a well-meaning sporting philanthropist. Volunteers to join a team were called to put their names down and, as I had never had cause to visit Kingstown or St Vincent, I decided to try my luck. And as luck would have it, I was selected to join the other fifteen players, possibly on the strength of last Saturday's low score when, for once, I missed the water hazard on the seventh. Our party of international golfers and their WAGS just about filled the St Lucia Airways flag carrier, in fact their only carrier, the faithful Dakota, for the thirty-five minutes hop to Kingstown from Vigie.

Our match was played on nine holes with eighteen tees set in a long extinct volcanic valley surrounded by tree covered hills. There was no clubhouse as I recall, but every hole was well stocked with coconut palms attended by young men armed with well-honed machetes who climbed up the palms to dislodge the large green fruit which they opened with deadly strokes of their razor sharp blades. The ready refreshment cost one dollar (EC), the smile of the vendor was free. It was hot and humid in the valley with little air movement due to the surrounding high ground. Our team lost shamefully but made it back to St Lucia at the end of the day, not before we had met the press at a reception given by our hosts at the airport bar. For the record, I was partnered by Lindell Moon, wife of the Club's captain George, ladies' champion of St Lucia whose sense of humour matched the indelible smile on her face, a smile which no doubt hypnotised our Vincentian opponents, as it did me. We won our match with holes to spare, how could I possibly disgrace myself in front of the lovely Lindell?

A national holiday was declared by the Governor on 7th June to celebrate Queen Elizabeth's Silver Jubilee, with the St Lucians responding in typical style given their propensity to party. A notice had been placed in the local newspaper, *The Voice*, announcing a big time *jump up* at the fishing village of Gros Islet. Looking out to sea early that morning, Andy spotted a big ship, which later turned out to be HMS Tiger, flag ship of the south Atlantic squadron we had hosted months before. That day we had two parties to attend, the first with James and Beverly at their home, then on to the Yacht Club for the Premier's reception, a barbecue beach party with a twist. A long naval surf boat came into view around the southern tip of Pigeon Island three hundred yards across the clear blue waters of Rodney Bay. Coming closer to shore we realised it was heading straight for our beach and the rowers were Royal navy sailors dressed for the eighteenth century, the Admiral standing rigid in his frock coat and white breeches at the bow. The boat closed to the shoreline, not missing a beat as it rode the final breaking wave to land on dry sand in front of us, allowing the Admiral to step off without getting his shiny buckled shoes wet. In what must surely have been a finely choreographed performance, Mr Compton received the Admiral who handed him a scroll tied with red ribbon containing Her Majesty's greetings to the Premier and to his island nation. How wonderful it was for us to celebrate such a landmark occasion on a remote Commonwealth seaside, under a sunlit and cloudless blue hemisphere.

18

Monty Python

(Mid-year 1977)

We had made a pleasant enough home for ourselves and had come fully to terms with local life. We now knew most of the expat families on the island and had made some special friends, but additionally and happily, we had been made welcome by many locals seeing people for what they were, not what their colour might be, and counting them amongst our closest friends in St Lucia. Indeed, there were several people amongst the expatriates whose ancestry was not entirely European. We were quite a mixed bunch. I think it was easier for us to get alongside West Indian culture than for us to have taken on a Zambian way of life, notwithstanding the strong human relationships that we had shared in Africa. I sometimes felt that whereas our Zambian staff, at all levels, saw work as a means of life support and betterment, for many St Lucians work got in the way of living and was a necessary, but unwelcome burden on their time. When I discussed that with James he laughed and commented that he knew a lot of folk in the UK who would fall into both camps. I had to admit that I counted myself closer to the Zambian work ethic and closer to the St Lucian ethos when it came to culture and human relationships.

It was not only the progression of our work at M&C which brought me closer to James Hill, rather we needed to sound off our mutual concerns for our employer and our future. Together we began to develop strategies for job hunting, no easy task being four thousand miles from London. We listened with amused attention to the tapes I had acquired about how to get interviews produced by a fictitious but down to earth personnel consultant called Percy Carew and his equally fictitious targeted employer Mr Snodgrass. It was Percy who advised that if you, as an interviewee, were offered a plate of biscuits containing only one chocolate covered cookie, you should choose the chocolate, demonstrating your independent and forceful characteristics, someone who knows his mind. I have never forgotten the wisdom of Mister Carew, nor, do I suspect has James. Percy also told us that only after you had secured the interview and got the job offer should you decide if you wanted it or could do it. He determined my future belief that I could tackle anything in general management regardless of a company's function or industry type, that it was of much more significance whether you liked and respected your future employer, and that your employer has every reason to hold you in good esteem.

About that time Anne and Mike Foster, friends from our days in Kitwe, came to stay for a week. They followed our advice to book an inclusive flight and hotel package, the cheapest they could find, seeing that the deals made great savings over standard air fares. On arrival I would contact the bed and breakfast they were due to patronise and cancel their booking, which in any event had been prepaid, so no worries for the owners.

The Fosters were followed by Maurice's parents, Arch and Lena Widdowson who came to visit their son, now in his mid-thirties. Maurice, ably assisted by Arlette, entertained them royally after sundown. During the daytime Tory enjoyed the company of the elderly couple and I think they enjoyed fussing around Chrisrty-Anne and Andy, when he came back from school, spoiling them both equally as if they were the grandchildren they were yet to have. Maurice's sister Jennifer had a husband she had met in the States called Richard. Both had led busy lives in California without time to raise a family, much to Lena's chagrin. The lovely grandmother-in-waiting seemed unimpressed by her daughter's lack of enthusiasm to bring forth a new generation. We soon had time to judge for ourselves when the happy couple from Los Angeles came to stay in St Lucia, overlapping with Lena and Arch for a few days. Watching Jennifer play with the children I took the view that it was probably Richard who feared the patter of tiny feet disturbing the pattern of his predictable existence.

Whilst Tory was entertaining Maurice's family as her own, I was called to the offices of a prominent firm of solicitors where I joined Donald and, to my surprise, the Premier Mr Compton. The message inviting me to join Donald had appeared a bit cloak and dagger, it had come in the form of a hand written note on the solicitor's notepaper delivered to me in the office by a messenger, asking me to come straight away. I had not far to go, my destination being two doors down from Antoine's liquor store. On arrival I became committed to the verbal equivalent of signing the official secrets act in the form of giving my assurance that nothing said would go beyond those present within the four walls of the solicitor's chambers. I knew the lawyer from bridge. Having got my assurance, the Premier left us.

It transpired that the local law firm had been engaged by Leon Hess, head of the Amerada Hess Corporation of New York, refiners and distributors of oil and petroleum in the USA. Whilst Richard Nixon had released many elements of what was known as *"The American Stockpile"*, it remained the policy of Washington to subsidise oil imports so that OPEC oil could compete with the domestic market prices prevailing in the States, the reasoning being at that time that by using imported oil, principally from the Gulf or Nigeria, the oil reserves on-shore USA would be preserved, at least to an extent. Hess had established offshore oil storage capacity known as *"tank farms"* in St Croix, an island of the US Virgins, because US Longshoremen would not handle any ship at any US port whose crew were not paid wages equivalent to those agreed with the US Marine unions; by off-loading giant tankers crewed by lower paid "third world" seamen, such as Koreans or Filipinos, for storage outside continental USA , the massive cargo could be fed in smaller lots by coastal vessels crewed by American seamen to the US, a practice acceptable to the all-powerful Unions. The value of the subsidy was considerable. Hess was working at full storage capacity in St Croix and was looking for additional land to build tank farms.

The St Lucian government had been approached and had been asked about a site at Culde Sac. Mr Compton's people were keenly interested in the additional employment any such development might offer as well as tax revenues. But to make the land asset viable would require removing a small mountain and transferring its aggregate into the steeply shelving sea to form a mole long enough to accommodate quarter mile long tankers arriving from Saudi Arabia or wherever. The removal of a small mountain could have hidden political booby traps, moreover Hess had given the Premier its undertaking not to negotiate with other possible hosts in the Caribbean whilst the Compton government was considering the matter. There was a time scale of four weeks for a decision to be agreed. The lawyer indicated that apart from Donald and me, only one other person on our island was aware of the negotiations other than John Compton himself, and that was Mr Hunte, the Minister. Why, I asked, were we being told all this?

The answer came as a bit of a shock, but understandable, I supposed. The Premier needed to have an independent assessment of the economic and social impacts the existing store units at the St Croix tank farm had brought about, both during its construction stage and as a functioning operation now. He could not afford any leak. Donald had to be let in on the secret, as only he could give permission for me to do the job. They wanted me, because I was not a St Lucian and could be considered apolitical, because they thought I could do the job well for them, because I would have no vested interest, and because if the secret got out they would know it had to have been Donald or me who had let the cat out of the bag, and we were both on the island with work permits which could be withdrawn without notice. Ugh!

As luck would have it, I had already received an American visa from the Consulate in Barbados in anticipation of the trip we planned to see John on our annual leave. On the pretext of attending an urgent meeting abroad I left the island two days later, with the names and addresses of contacts on St Croix who would meet me and look after all arrangements during my stay. The flight to Frederiksted routed me via

Puerto Pico. The 'plane taking us to our final destination filled up with islanders, mainly female, returning to St Croix (pronounced "Kroi"), who all carried shopping booty into the cabin which ranged from baskets full of fruit and vegetables, ghetto blasters, TV sets, dogs and live chickens. The sounds around me were happy ones. The US Virgin Islands are the closest thing the Americans have to a colony, they call it an "unincorporated territory". St Croix derived its name from the Spanish *Santa Cruz*, or Holy Cross, via the French, who sold the island to the Danes in 1733 for three quarters of a million French Livres. The Danes re-named it Sankt Croix. In 1917 Denmark sold the three islands of St Croix, St Thomas and St John to the Americans for twenty-five million US Dollars in gold bullion, but the colonial names persist, the other town on the island is called Christiansted, after another monarch of the House of Glucksberg. Walking through the capital I spotted two little sentry boxes, replicas of the ones I had seen occupied by soldiers with bearskin headgear in Copenhagen.

The Hess people were forthcoming and generous with their hospitality. I first enjoyed the sheer delight of eating freshly grilled conch at a waterside spot in Frederiksted. I wandered around speaking to tradesmen. I got a lift with a taximan around the island for half a day. The Hess people gave me a conducted tour of the tank farm and I met the few employees who worked there. I also met Mr Cyril King, the Governor, a local man elected to the post, who happened to be in town. In two days on St Croix I had learned enough to make a positive report when I got back, deciding to do it in person so that no typing by a third party was needed. I did warn that the employment opportunities would be largely confined to the construction stages, the tank farm itself would need few employees in the long term. I could see little spin off to the commercial community, such as M&C, but tourism would not have any downside since the site chosen was at the remote shore end of a large banana plantation, although the arrival and embarkation of shipping would be a consideration for the Marine Police Unit to monitor.

A few months later work started, the dynamite blasts became part of the scene at Culde Sac, the massive civil engineering project initiated by John Compton at the Buckeye Terminal became an operational reality a few years on. I regret the passing of the mountain, my small part in its demise only becoming public knowledge as you read this narrative. My life in St Lucia was certainly shaped by people I had met playing bridge, in this case Mr Compton and his lawyer.

Joe Devaux, who introduced me to the bridge players in the first instance, had a friendly business rivalry in his old acquaintance and neighbour Peter Bergasse, another bridge player. The rivalry between the two men spilled over into the world of diplomacy, for Peter, the younger and more adept of the two competitors, had secured the honour of representing the French Republic as its Consul in St Lucia, whereas Joe, hugely proud of his French ancestry, had to settle as honorary Consul for the Royal House of Orange-Nassau. Joe always displayed a miniature flag of The Netherlands on his desk at M&C. Joe was essentially a kindly man, who struggled with his sense of family responsibility and, I sensed, for ever seeking to live up to his wife's expectations.

Whilst Joe seemed perpetually worried, Peter always carried an air of confidence about him, characteristics which made it hard to read their minds when bidding a hand on a Thursday evening. The francophone island of Martinique is not only a close neighbour to what they call Ste Lucie, it is administered as part of metropolitan France and thus part of the European Union today. Each year on Bastille Day a French dignitary would arrive by a special Air France flight, to be greeted at the airport by the agent for the French flag carrier, which was our firm M&C, represented by Mr Devaux! The dignitary would proceed under escort to the centre of Castries where a ceremony took place in his honour, attended by the massed ranks of local nabobs and politicians and, wait for it, the Diplomatic Corps, led by Peter Bergasse. Singing *La Marseillaise* at the top of his voice, Peter called lustily to *Les enfants de la Patrie* to announce that "*Le jour de gloire est arrivé*". It was, after all, his own day of glory, which he carried off in style and briefly putting dear Joe in the shade.

Without a work permit Tory could not take a paid job. Her busy life included voluntary work and full-time home making. It was the same for her expatriate friends such as Cilla and Beverly. Christy-Anne was almost three and was proving to be a handful, more so for she had proved herself accident prone with two visits already to the Victoria Hospital, on both occasions after using our bed as a trampoline. Once she had broken a shoulder bone, on another occasion she needed urgent stitches after gashing her face on the corner of our bedstead; she bears a faint reminder of her early gymnastics to this very day.

There was no television service in St Lucia. The main source of international news came to us through the BBC World Service radio, many of their news bulletins were relayed to us through Radio St Lucia, our local channel. The local radio station performed a commendable public service, for example storm and adverse weather warnings and tips on preparing for them. My friend Mike Owen felt that the island should be better prepared for a direct hurricane hit than it was and set about putting together an action plan for government approval. His work later proved a life saver. But lives were lost every day as the human life cycle went around. Each morning before breakfast the radio announced the passing of local inhabitants with brief obituaries and sombre background music. I felt the service added to the dignity of the dead and their families and reflected human concern for them. Being a small nation, the daily programme added something good to the sense of community.

The main platform for reporting events and local debate was *The Voice* newspaper. Compton's adversary George Odlum made clever use of the paper but his vocal support for Castro's Cuba and revolution spurred on only a small minority, the majority of island folk just wanted a peaceful life under the sun and hope of better things to come.

I had hopes of better things to come as I made one last effort to get a change to my terms of contract so that I could begin to save some money, at the same time perusing the situations vacant columns of the London Times and the Daily Telegraph which we received two days after the publishing dates. Armed with Percy's advice on how best to present letters of application, synchronising my experience to the demands of the advertised post, I began to get interview appointments for my UK leave in early September. Before going on leave James had arranged a surprise party at his house to celebrate the thirtieth birthdays of Beverly and Tory, all guests to be clad in clothes of mourning. There were some inventive costumes as you would expect from the Carnival madness around us, but the party itself went off in great abandon, in quite the opposite fashion to any funeral intended to mark the passing of the girls' twenties. As sunrise sent hints of its arrival the few remaining revellers drove the two miles to Cap, following a winding dirt road up to the lookout point, where some kind soul had built a thatched open sided shelter with wooden benches. From that vantage point HMS Diamond Rock was shining in the low reflected light of the early morning sunshine in the eastern sky. In high spirits we followed the magic moment of dawn with a swim and breakfast at Rodney Bay, watching the fishermen casting nets beyond the light surf. It was truly a time for Harry Belafonte to serenade us with his songs of banana boats, a yellow bird, and his island in the sun.

Our entry point into the United States was Miami. I had left my work behind and now it was time for a holiday. Passing through immigration I got stopped by the man at the passport desk. He said: "Hey, you British?" I confirmed that I was indeed from the sceptered isle. "You know Monty Python?" he asked. Now he did not want to know if I had met Dick Whittington, or The Queen or even Alice in Wonderland, he wanted to know about Monty Python, who, incidentally, I knew nothing of having not seen UK television for eight or nine years. "A great friend of my father" I replied. "Hey Carl", he said to the man in the next booth, "This guy's paw knows Monty Python".

My new-found celebrity status did not last beyond the airport's immigration hall, but I had much enjoyed the humour of our first moments in the land of the free and looked forward to the week ahead with happy anticipation.

19

Gold Cufflinks

(August-December 1977)

An airport coach service took us to our hotel in the centre of Miami which had a rooftop swimming pool with a diving board, from where Andy could jump into the water and view the city at the same moment. The little boy would have happily stayed put in this branch of the Holiday Inn empire for the entire week, but at first light the next day we were up and out to catch the Gray Line coach to Orlando. I had pre-booked an overnight excursion to Walt Disney World. Six hours each way on the coach was tiresome and challenging for the children, but it was worth it.

At Disney World, the good manners and well-groomed appearance of the student staffers, their consideration for their visitors and the all-round cleanliness of the new resort, then only in its sixth year are the memories of that trip I cherish. As many parents would agree after such a visit, I think we adults enjoyed the experience in Orlando much more so than did our children. There was not a peep out of any of us on the return journey to Miami, we slept through most of it. Tory and I had ended up pushing both our young ones around Disney World in hired buggies. We were tired.

Brother John met us at Dulles Airport in their Ford shooting break. I guess we had a half hour drive to the new house he and Wanda had bought in Ellicott City, Maryland. It was set in woodlands on a gentle slope, a fine setting. I was pleased for them. John's enthusiasm for life in his newly adopted country knew no bounds, and as we were thirsty for our first experience of America, we had four happy days before the time came to fly on to London.

This period of home leave was going to be quite different given my job-hunting plans. Mother generously loaned me the use of her car, which I made use of to take Tory and the babes to Exeter where she could catch up with her mother. I set up my HQ at Mother's flat and attended three interviews in the first four days, one involving a day in Manchester. I contacted past friends from business, including Miles Pitts-Tucker at Courtaulds who had often urged me to keep in touch. He had a couple of jobs he thought I could be interested in. I made an appointment to see Mike Hearder and Tom Moerry in London two days before I was due to return to Castries. Moments after the call, Bernard Windsor was on the line to invite me to lunch when I came up to Town.

During the first two weeks of our leave I had managed to secure nine interviews and six job offers and one request for a second meeting. You might think it was going well, and it was, but nothing really grabbed me, so I arranged to look up my old friend from Zambia, Mike Foster, who was then working for the same company he had been with in Zambia, Morison Son and Jones Ltd. (MSJ), the major subsidiary of Arthur

Guinness, based in Basingstoke. Mike and Anne had bought a house on their return to England, which was in the market town of Wokingham, close to where Tory's sister lived and where we had partied a year before. By this time Tory and the youngsters had re-joined me in Bray.

We arranged to meet for dinner, Tory was looking forward to seeing Anne again and I had much to tell Mike, which included getting a dispassionate view on my next move. It was late afternoon the following day when Mike called me before he left his office in Basingstoke for home, to tell me that he had been at a meeting that day and heard from his MD, Peter Hoare, that because of the rapid expansion of Morison's business in Nigeria and in Malaysia/Singapore in particular, the company needed to recruit a marketing manager to develop more commercial opportunities in consumer goods distribution.

Morisons had subsidiary or associate companies in fourteen countries throughout Asia and Africa. A job based in the UK, but focussed overseas, was right up my street, I mused, and Tory agreed. I knew by now how much she wanted to return "home", and we both had concerns for our children's education, not wanting to send them away to boarding school, the fate of most children of expatriates working abroad. Mike confessed he had mentioned our discussion of the previous evening to Mr Hoare, who said he would like to meet me. This was Tuesday. We were due to leave for St Lucia on Sunday.

By ten O'clock on Wednesday I had arranged to meet Peter Hoare at two that afternoon. I had explained how short my time was and he was sympathetic, a good start. An hour into our meeting Peter took me to meet his colleague Wyndham Freyer, who worked with Michael Ogle, the Chairman, who appears earlier in this narrative in connection with Jeremy Thorpe's visit to Lusaka. I must have passed muster, for when I returned to the MD's office, Mr Freyer had had time to call Mr Hoare on the internal telephone to give me the nod. I declared my interest in joining MSJ. Peter Hoare proposed sending me an offer overnight so that I would receive it on Thursday morning. I had promised to reply by telephone.

Our breakfast was interrupted by a call from Courtaulds pressing me for a reply to their offer letter for the Managing Director's job in the north of England. It was the only one I was seriously considering, but with the arrival of the morning post I felt much more comfortable about the opportunity with MSJ. Having made the call to Peter Hoare to confirm my acceptance of his offer, a start date for early January was agreed. I then penned a letter of resignation to Mike Hearder, giving the three months' notice I was contracted to, consciously bypassing Tom Moerry, but sending a copy by airmail to Donald. I suppose I did that for the sake of good form, the letter would most likely arrive in St Lucia later than Sunday afternoon, when we were due to land once again at Hewanorra.

For once I was not kept waiting when I arrived on time at The Adelphi for the meeting with Mike and Thomas. When you work abroad for a company the relationship between you and your ultimate employer seems more like that of a nephew with his uncle, you are part of the family and the uncle has duty of care. My resignation should have come as no surprise, but Mike seemed genuinely taken aback, leaving me with the impression that our Mr Moerry had not even discussed my case with his boss. The letter I had written yesterday to the man who now sat before me had been short and to the point, assuming he had knowledge of my disenchantment with the terms I was working under, so I held nothing back when asked to explain why I was leaving, and remained coy about what I was going to do. I was interested to see if the Company valued me sufficiently to make amends for doing nothing for a full year to repair the terms of my contract. At midday I was asked if I could come back to see Tom after lunch, so I gathered my belongings and sought out Bernard who was doubtless waiting to enjoy another tax-deductible lunch on the Company with me, a client from abroad.

Bernard had whisked me across the West End to *Le petit Montmartre* in Marylebone High Street by taxi, where his impeccable taste pointed me in the direction of some *goujons du brochet* and a bottle of Chablis. My host gave no indication of being in the know about my earlier conversations, which I took at face value as he returned me to his director at two o'clock. I said farewell to my gourmet guide whose company I had much enjoyed that day.

Thomas announced that he had "persuaded Mike to set aside five thousand pounds a year in Canada which he would back date to the start of my time at M&C." As I could not imagine our divisional chairman allowing himself to be persuaded on any count, I took our Mr Tom to be telling a porky. He had had his knuckles rapped, and that was good enough for me. "Thomas", I said "why has it taken a year for you to sort this out? Why have I had to resign to get this outstanding matter resolved? My resignation stands because I know that in a year's time we will have got no further with our ambitions for the Caribbean, and because I have lost confidence in you and probably the Company as well". I went on to say that I would work out my notice and finish everything I had started. I valued a tidy back garden. I went back to the family at Bray with the news that we would soon be finished with life overseas, sad to contemplate but happy to have new purpose.

The fat lady was yet to sing, we had three months before our time in the West Indies would be over.

During the four weeks we had been away *Mabotee* had been growing weed at its Ganters Yard mooring. The underside of the fibreglass hull had a dark green beard and needed scrubbing down, such a job had to done in shallow water. It had been a busy week since returning from England. James was pleased for me and shared some news about his own job hunting. His assistant Pat Leow would be well able to take on his job. I had wanted Alan Lang to be my successor although he felt himself not yet ready for the responsibility, and he was right.

Alan and Peter Robinson reminded me of what they had said at the time of Peter's beach barbecue party, that they just get to know us and then we are gone. I felt bad about that, but what could I have done differently? To make some amends I arranged a return party on the small beach at the far end of the causeway which connected Pigeon Island to the main island, just to the north of Gros Islet village. The causeway was sixty yards wide; its construction had been completed two years previously and was intended in the long term to be built upon. I had heard there were plans for a hotel and beach club. The tidal flows from north to south along the coast had been interrupted by the new causeway barrier, bringing about changes to the coastal currents and causing some beaches to recede and others to grow. The effect was felt six miles to the south on the beaches at the Halcyon Beach Club below our house, and the one at the Malabar Hotel where we had our first dip, both losing twenty feet of sand above the water.

The barbecue kit, food and drinks were bundled into *Mabotee* at Ganters, where we left the car for a slow trawl up the coast from Castries Harbour to Rodney Bay and the causeway. Forty minutes later we anchored the boat in close to the sandy beach and off-loaded our cargo. At beach barbecues the guests seem to know what is expected of them, it was not long before a group set about preparing the food. Mike Owen, Alan, and Peter helped me clean up the bottom of the boat's hull, a job which took twenty minutes of splashing around in the warm sea water. We packed up late afternoon after a happy time in good company and with just over an hour until sundown. I set off back to Castries with Mike accompanying me. Cilla took Tory and all the children in her car back to the Owens' house on Vigie to await our return in the boat. Not unusually a fresh breeze blew off the land on our portside roughing up the waves.

We had reached a point not much less than a mile distant from the Vigie headland and the entrance to Castries Harbour beyond when the outboard stuttered, choked, stuttered once more, then stopped. I made a few adjustments to the motor's settings, checked the fuel flow from the tank and tried to re-start the engine but without success. Now we were only a hundred yards or so off the shoreline when we took stock of our predicament. We had one oar, no power, we were drifting away from the shore, the daylight was dimming, there was no coast guard and being a Sunday there was no-one at Ganters who recorded our morning departure let alone our destination or planned time of return. We still had two bananas, but no other food or water to drink. The girls had the remains of the party in Cilla's car. Mike could not swim so I could not abandon him on the boat. The Venezuelan coast lay five hundred miles away to the south west. We were well and truly up the Suwannee.

A few minutes passed as the seas rose in the strong offshore wind during which we donned our life jackets and ate the bananas. We could hardly see the shore, by now a quarter of a mile away. I put a yellow life jacket on the end of the oar and waved it in big sweeps, in the vain hope that someone might see us from the shore, but no one did. Five precious minutes of the dying day light passed when Mike yelled out. He had spotted a fisherman returning late from his work in the ocean, it was one of those long "dug-outs" with extended outboard at the stern, operated by the loan seafarer standing upright on his feet to have a view of the pitching bow some thirty feet in front of him.

He saw us and brought his vessel around to close into our lee, beckoning me to throw him our line. Whatever he shouted in his patois I could not understand, but sign language sufficed. The line was grabbed on my second attempt and secured to his stern. As we got under weigh a large wave cause the rope to slacken then pull so tight it snapped. I should have thanked the Akela of the 21st Ealing Cubs for his instructions of 1951 on nautical knots which enabled me to make good the two ends of the broken line, my bowline holding fast for the next nerve-wracking thirty minutes as our deliverer fought his way in darkness towards the calm of the harbour. A few lights twinkled on the hill sides, but the lights of Castries were not yet in sight, hidden as they were by the slopes of Vigie. Quite suddenly the line between the two vessels broke once more, this time leaving us only three or four yards of usable rope, just enough for one last knot. Our trailing boat was by now a dead weight, the bow almost touching the one in front.

Our rescuer dropped us at the entrance to Ganters but would not accept all the cash in my back pocket which I held out to him. I know it was a wholly inadequate token of thanks, but I had nothing else to offer. The man just waved his hand in the gloom, saying something like *"la tradition de la mer."* How we wanted to thank him, he surely saved our lives, yet he left us without even knowing his name. What a wonderful human being. Mike and I had a shared experience that evening we would never forget, but back at the Owen residence our two wives were blissfully unaware of the drama played out on *Mabotee*, rolling pins figuratively at the ready. The two lovelies were waiting to chastise us for visiting the Coal Pot bar, little did they know the real reason for our late arrival, and in any event, the bar was closed on a Sunday.

Didier had asked to see me with Alan, a meeting set up for Monday morning. Alan had told me at yesterday's beach party that he thought the security men had some good news for us, I suspected he knew more but was not going to talk shop and eat barbecued fish at the same time. He had put the finger on Edwards, the pharmacist who we had long suspected of running some kind of racket, but we needed proof as the man had been with the firm since Joe had first employed him twenty years before after college in Trinidad. Two years ago, long before my time at M&C, Edwards had set up a small pharmacy shop in another family name. No-one knew of the connection until one day one of Didier's staff, a lady security officer, had by chance noticed an item on sale in the pharmacy shop with one of our bright fluorescent orange M&C price tickets on it. She bought the toiletry item with the petty cash she carried for comparative shopping, insisting that the assistant give her a receipt. All the evidence was there, it only remained for us to have a few words with the said Mr Edwards. By late afternoon I had the pharmacist's resignation in writing, my preferred method of dealing with the matter rather than a time-consuming prosecution, in any event, the loss of his job and pension would suffice as a just punishment. He would now need to pay for the stock in his store.

I still had one last serious problem to solve in the food warehouse, but in the main, most of the holes had been plugged, and shrinkage levels were down. We had a stock taking in October, the results showed that the Company was on break-even for the first time since its acquisition by Bookers.

Whoever would come after me would inherit a business in a different shape to what it was before. I became preoccupied with the tasks of setting plans for the year ahead so that Alan and the management team were set fair. When I asked Donald if he had any advice about my succession he declined knowledge, but with two weeks to go before our departure for England he put his head around the glass door of my office with the words "You'll never guess who they are sending to replace you, Derrick". I waited with raised eyebrows for him to continue "None other than Bernard Windsor!"

Now I had clear evidence that Tom Moerry was never up to his job, he was sending out the urbane Bernard, a man who had once spent a year or so in the Caribbean as a young Bookers' cadet and who retained some romantic impressions of life in the tropics with tiffin and punkahs. "They will eat him alive" was my sad reply, what a lousy thing to do to such a gentle man. It made me even more determined to seal up the twelve months plan I would leave behind.

Whilst Tory and Amilta were overseeing packing up our possessions for the shippers I sat on the balcony with a lunchtime sandwich in my hand, looking out to sea and imagining the grey skies which awaited me back in England. In a few days the people from the Geest Line would collect everything, just before our departure. Tory planned that we would spend our final night at home, so that Amilta could clean up when we left and inherit the bedlinen, towels, kitchen utensils and a lot more she could make good use of.

The familiar sound of a Dakota, making its daily run from Vigie to Bridgetown, made me look to my left to spot my favourite aircraft, which this time gave the impression it was on a bombing raid because things were splashing into the sea as it passed my line of vision. The bombs I had spotted were thankfully not explosives launched from a bomb bay but rather a succession of suitcases dropping out of the 'plane's hold into the calm blue sea three hundred feet below, right in front of our house. One just missed making a direct hit on Rat Island. I rushed to the telephone inside to ring the airport, too late to do much about it since the veteran aircraft was already beyond radio contact. I heard later that by the time the flight reached Barbados there was no luggage left for any of the passengers to collect. I thought that even Herman Wouk could not have thought that one up. It turned out that the freight handlers had forgotten to shut the hold door. I was going to miss the West Indies where there seemed never to be a dull moment.

Our two kittens, Ant and Bee, had grown into cats. We found them a new home on the Morne with the family of the Barclays Bank manager, whose wife I had met playing bridge. I asked them to keep an eye out for Bernard. Waiting for Bernard's arrival only two days ahead of our departure we had enjoyed a lot of Caribbean farewell parties, not least one at the office where I was presented with a pair of gold cufflinks in the shape of our island, St Lucia, by the very lovely Merle Montplaisir on behalf of those she had collected from, and a card with over eighty goodwill signatures. Those links have secured the French cuffs of successive dress shirts ever since, and remain a useful talking point when conversation fails, but better still, they are a lasting reminder of those days of many surprises.

On the final morning I played out my final act. Alan had arranged our transport to Hewanorra for the evening flight, so we had plenty of time. I placed Bernard on a chair at the back of the small office he would inherit and sat in my chair, I was still the boss, after all. Gregory[32], the Food Warehouse manager arrived with Alan and Didier and I introduced him to Bernard. I bade the food man to take a seat and then confronted him by saying that I wanted his resignation, that I had irrefutable evidence of his criminality through the theft of stock.

When he challenged my evidence, I replied that the evidence would be given only to the police who would be collecting him from the office in fifteen minutes, unless he gave me his resignation in which case the matter would end, my final gift. It was up to him, life for a few years behind bars, or walk out a free man. Bernard was shocked but remained quiet, I had told him of my plan after the office party the day before. "But you don't have any evidence" he mumbled, but I quickly and forcefully replied "I don't need any, I just know". It was a bluff, but as Gregory knew that I knew, or at least he bought into that notion, he took the prepared letter that Angel Roberts had typed that morning for me and signed it. We shook hands, and he was gone. One less problem for Bernard, I told him, and added that had Gregory been innocent he would have had nothing to lose by refusing to sign the letter, but as it was, he could not risk prison.

If we are on this earth with the gift of life it must surely be to help others and make a good account of ourselves. As we drove to the airport at Vieux Fort, I thought about that time I

32. Gregory is another pseudonym allowing for his notoriety as a felon to be spared.

had ignored the dangers of taking my boat out without cover, putting Mike's life at risk quite apart from my own. What would the family have done if I had perished? My Creator had spared me through a nameless local fisherman. He had taught me a lesson that no matter their perceived societal status or occupation, each person had a value and gift to offer to someone else. I remembered all the people we had come across and our experiences from living in Africa and the West Indies, such as I have tried to recount in the preceding chapters, and felt glad that I would be returning to my homeland better equipped to take on whatever came my way. I had the certainty of a wonderful marriage to back me up, and a few shillings in the bank. Hopefully I would be a little wiser than I was when I had first stepped on that 'plane at Heathrow to take my seat next to Sam Kelly.

Epilogue

It would hardly be fair to leave this book with the lives of the main characters hanging in the air, so what happened to them after Christmas 1977 when our family moved back to England? Many stayed overseas, unlike us, but in doing so they remained points of company and hospitality in my travels. Not just the Scots diaspora, rather my own diaspora. It was inevitable that I should lose touch with some. If I do not mention them again on these final few pages you will know I have no further news of them.

Not so long after I departed Bookers in St Lucia, the Devaux family bought M&C back and did well by selling the department store and its retail offshoots to local buyers whilst retaining other viable constituent parts. The shares they had acquired in Bookers from Mike Hearder as part of the acquisition costs had increased greatly in value, so I hope they disposed of them well. Bookers in the form I knew it is no more. I was able to visit the island in the '80s and met Joe then. He had appointed Winnifred Blanchard (nee Richardson) his PA. Alan Lang moved to Canada, then returned to take the job of MD at St Lucia Distilleries, makers of Bounty Rum near Culde-Sac. Roger Sutherland made a success of the Agency business Bryden and Partners, which Fred had retained, before moving to Canada.

After a short time back in England, James and Beverly Hill settled near Auckland in New Zealand to live a happy and successful life and be blessed with another son. Beverly provides us with regular news of people with whom we shared time in St Lucia.

Mike and Cilla Owen stayed on in St Lucia for a few years, Mike made a success of his job and took the leading role in the island's health care. Cilla had two more boys after Tanya. They went on to take jobs in Swaziland and Monserrat, where Mike became Chief Medical Officer. David Taylor of Bookers was co-opted to take over from Rex Hunt as Governor of The Falkland Islands immediately after the Argentine war, then moved to Monserrat as Governor. David moved to Canada in retirement, but had contacted me when still in Stanley when I was MD at Portman in the '80s, he sought a London confirming house for the Falkland Islands Company which supplied the colony's inhabitants with consumer goods and other supplies.

Mike' Owen's sister Jenny and her husband John Blackburne sold Mfubu Ranch in Zambia and moved to Norfolk where he took on a pig farm. Their East Anglian small-holding measures fourteen acres; the money John received from the sale of the fourteen thousand acres of bush pasture and citrus orchards at Mfubu along the Kafue river was of little help, blocked in the same foreign exchange queue as the balance of our own funds, now worth a box of matches due to hyper-inflation.

Mike Delaney worked for Edgars in South Africa for a few years, then took on a senior job with Meyers in Melbourne. Lorraine gave him another daughter, Patricia. The family moved to Emerald, close to the Dandenong Range in Victoria, where Mike started a book business. I caught up with the family on four occasions whilst on business for Portman and they visited us in London six months before Mike died with cancer in 1998.

Westy got a job in Johannesburg in '76 but quickly started his own company Westcor, distributing sun- glasses and fashion accessories throughout South Africa. He visited me in London in the '80s after getting news of me through Al Chuah, a Malaysian customer of Morisons, who he met by chance at a trade fair in Rhode Island, USA. I next saw Westy in Jo'burg in '95 when on a visit to the office I had set up in that city for my firm Possibilities. Malcolm has done well in business and now lives with his second and long-standing wife Liza on the waterfront in Cape Town. He has two sons.

Margaret and Jock Lumsden worked in Durban, where they eventually retired and lived happily into their nineties. Their daughter Marlene had two boys with Richard Hesketh, became a banker and later moved to California where she remarried. Trudi, a cheeky schoolgirl and precocious teenager became a mother of two after marrying a mine engineer called Phil Piper at a service in Pinetown, Natal, which my wife and I flew out to attend. How could we miss the wonderful event hosted by Marlene and Richard? In Johannesburg we stayed with Mike and Gay Johnstone, enjoyed Mike's cooked carrots in gin, then drove 400 miles via Ladysmith to the wedding. Trudi helped me set up an office for Possibilities at her home in Emarentia where she still lives. Both Trudi and Phil started successful companies.

My tennis partner Bunny Mackintosh married Jim Sanford, a businessman from Kitwe. They moved to the UK to open a bookshop in Wallingford. Before she died in '99 she came to dinner at our house in SW12, the other guest was (Dean) David Elliot, then Rector of St Paul's, Covent Garden. One of David's converts was Gwen Powell, one-time fashion buyer at ZCBC, who found herself in David's first Parish of Elstree on moving to England. Gwen was a guest at the home of Chris and Denise Chapman on one of my many visits to stay with them when Chris worked for Pernas in Kuala Lumpur and later for Robinson's in Singapore. David died six months after we had hosted him with Bunny, his memorial service was conducted by the Bishop of London at "The Actor's Church ", which became a venue for an annual reunion of many Ndola parishioners of our day, including Maurice Renwick, who had recruited me into The Lions; for years Tory provided lunch in the vestry for forty after the service we held in support of Ndola's Cathedral of the Holy Nativity.

Stephen Pedley returned to England after his ministry in Kitwe and later became Bishop of Lancaster, a position occupied by one of Tory's relatives, Anthony Hoskyns-Abrahall, for twenty years from 1955.

Jack Gibbs was ninety and in fine form when I next saw him by chance on a visit to the Lumsdens at Umgeni Park, Durban where they all lived in late retirement. Jack had managed to stay on in Zambia at ZCBC until giving up work in the mid-eighties.

Peter McManus set up his own business consulting office in the UK, taking on a long-term contract which took him for many years to Venezuela. Something involving oil. His brave wife Sue had another boy. Peter lost his wife to illness and now manages life on his own in Warwickshire.

David Seaman of Mobil Oil acquired and ran a protea farm in the Eastern Highlands of Zimbabwe, he was another I caught up with on a later trip to Johannesburg. He married Memory Hughes and now lives in California, keeping a bolt hole in Edinburgh for occasional trips back to his homeland.

Penny Sutton, our neighbour at Nyimba Crescent moved back to Surrey to set up her two boys at school, her husband Tony died of cerebral malaria before he could join her. Penny now lives in Essex. Our names have been on the same page in three telephone directories, Zambia, the Guildford Area and London, is that a world record?

Mike and Anne Ball-Foster were the closest of friends when I worked for Morison's (Guinness). Mike and I often travelled together in Nigeria and along the west coast of Africa. On retirement they moved to Bournemouth whence they originated; Mike died when on holiday in Cape Town, on a golf course.

Maurice Widdowson lives in St Kitt's with his wife Debbie who he met in London. They have two children. Not only did Maurice make a success of Caribelle Batik at Romney Manor but also took on Wingfield Plantation, at both venues he has created beautiful gardens and tourist destinations.

Maurice has travelled widely with me and our mutual chum Brendan, we were all able to do business together over the years I was at Portman and Possibilities. Brendon moved to St Lucia not long after we had left the island where he established a separate Caribelle workshop and tourist destination on The Morne above Castries. Sea Island Cotton Shops became his next venture along with a clothing factory he ran jointly with Dominic Eedle after the pub in Bath was sold. Brendan has three children. He met his wife Claudette locally in the '90s, they have run restaurants and a tropical plant centre together.

Dominic returned to Britain after a fire closed the factory to buy a franchise business in Manchester and enjoyed a deserved success. He retired to a house in southwest France where, in the summer of 2016 he organised a reunion over several days attended by Westy, Brendan, Maurice, himself and me, with our respective ladies. This was the first time we had all been together in forty years.

Tory and I lived in Old Basing, Hants for fifteen years where we made many good friends and were blessed with a baby girl, Naomi, a sister for Andy and Christy-Anne. After my business start up the family moved to southwest London, and finally to Faversham in Kent in 2002, where I served four years as a Town Councillor. We will have been in Kent twenty years when we celebrate our Golden Wedding.

~

Dear Reader, I hope you've enjoyed reading this book.
It would be lovely to read your review which you can do so here
www.talesofexpat.co.uk

Acknowledgements

I am grateful to Dr Patricia Reid, my Editor, for her guidance and instruction. Her encouragement and critical appraisal made the time spent in the preparation of "Gold Cufflinks" an enjoyable challenge and taught me a great deal.

The pages of my book will introduce the reader to many of the characters I met half a century ago, and they are all real people. I thank them all for sharing a piece of their own lives with me. The source of my story is my memory. If I recall detail in a way different to that my characters might remember, it matters little, the substance of the narrative and its outcome is what matters most. There are many people not mentioned in the book but who remain part of the story. I would love to hear news of them.

I thank my son Andy and his wife Pauline for their design of the book's cover, the photographic work and the maps, the latter an aid to the readers' orientation of those far flung places they might be unfamiliar with.

The book would not have happened had David Price not encouraged me in the first place, I thank him and his friends in Ireland. I would also like to thank Michael Reidy, an author from Massachusetts but writing in the UK, for his advice freely given. My thanks also to the poet, Fiona Clark Echlin, for her introduction to both David and Michael, and Roger Marsh for introducing me to Fiona.

I must thank Merle Montplaisir, wherever she is now, for her choice of the gift which gave me the idea for the book's title.

The several central characters gave me carte blanche to write them into my story, I am grateful for their trust and I hope, above all, that I have been fair to them. My thanks, therefore, to Brendan McShane, Maurice Widdowson, Malcolm Westmore, Peter McManus and James Hill, all former colleagues at work and lifelong friends.

The image of me, aged 27 as seen on the front cover, was taken on the Morne Brabant beach in Mauritius in 1970 by one of my companions.

Finally, to my wife Victoria (Tory) my everlasting love and appreciation of her selfless support, and my gratitude to her for giving birth to Andy, then Christy-Anne and Naomi, his two beautiful sisters.

goldcufflinks@uwclub.net

www.talesofexpat.co.uk

About the Author

Derrick Swain was born in London in 1943, the second of four brothers. His work has taken him to many places and he has lived for extensive periods abroad. *Gold Cufflinks* is his first book, which tells us something about his early life experiences and the extraordinary times he spent in Africa and the Caribbean in the immediate post-colonial years. He believes the Commonwealth today is a force for good in the world and that it offers a massive opportunity for the harmonious advancement of humanity. Derrick's interests include studying history and politics, listening to classical music and modern jazz, and the promotion of common sense. He now lives with his wife Victoria in a historic market town in north Kent.